Victoria falls

# SOCIOLOGISTS AND RELIGION

THEMES AND ISSUES IN MODERN
SOCIOLOGY

# Sociologists and Religion

## SUSAN BUDD

*Lecturer in Sociology,*
*London School of Economics and Political Science,*
*England*

COLLIER-MACMILLAN PUBLISHERS
A DIVISION OF CROWELL COLLIER
AND MACMILLAN PUBLISHERS LIMITED
LONDON

Collier-Macmillan Publishers
Blue Star House
Highgate Hill
London N19 5NY

The Macmillan Company
Collier-Macmillan Canada Ltd, Toronto

Library of Congress Catalogue Card Number: 72-86502

ISBN 0 02 972450 3 (paper)
     0 02 972460 0 (cased)

First printing 1973

Printed in Great Britain by
The Camelot Press Ltd, London and Southampton

# CONTENTS

CHAPTER I   Introduction—The Study of Religion        I

1 The Definition of Religion
2 The "Truth" of Religion
3 Religion as Rational or Irrational
4 Conclusion

CHAPTER II   Religion as Single Entity—Evolutionary    19
         and Anthropological Theories

1 Social Evolutionary Theories
2 Psychological Theories
3 Religion and Uncertainty
4 Durkheim on Religion
5 Functionalism, Anthropologists and Religion
6 Religion Redefined
7 Religion as Functional

CHAPTER III   Max Weber and Religion as Meaning    53

1 Karl Marx
2 Max Weber
3 The Protestant Ethic
4 Religion and Social Groups
5 Relative Deprivation
6 Millenarianism and Syncretism
7 Religious Organizations—Church and Sect
8 Conclusion—Religion as Meaning

CHAPTER IV   Religion—Some Evidence        82

CHAPTER V   Religious Beliefs        86

1 What do they believe?
2 Exceptions and Variations
3 Religion as Social Label

CHAPTER VI   Religion and Social Group            104

   1 Sectarianism and Success
   2 Protestants and Catholics
   3 Religious Expectations and Social Experience
   4 Cults of Success
   5 Class and Congregation


CHAPTER VII   Religion and Secularization         119

   1 The Definition of "Secularization"
   2 Britain—Disengagement
   3 Secularization, Socialism and Social Control
   4 Christian Socialism and the Social Gospel
   5 The Role of the Clergy
   6 The Secularization of Knowledge


CHAPTER VIII   Conclusion                         147

   1 Reality and Myth
   2 Strange Gods
   3 The Loss of Control


Annotated Bibliography                            157
Index                                             193

# PREFACE

The form taken by this book has been dictated in part by the purpose of the *Themes and Issues* series, which is to provide the student or teacher with a guide to, as well as a personal assessment of, a particular field of study. Many introductions to the sociology of religion exist, some of them excellent; if I have ventured to provide another, it is because my interest in the subject is in some of its less orthodox, but, I believe, important and neglected, aspects. This book reflects an eclectic and critical judgment rather than one based on part of the more organized traditions of research. I have almost entirely neglected the research on religious organizations, partly because it is adequately covered elsewhere, and partly because, although it is successful and growing, it seems to offer us little purchase on the central question: what is the role of religion in our society? My own belief, in common with some other sociologists, is that the answer is to be found in that layer of fragmentary, unrealized, emotionally charged symbols and beliefs which structure reality for us and make common understanding possible. But what relationship does religion bear to these in a secular society? Yet on the other hand, I believe that we must go beyond this answer, to avoid the phenomenologists' tendency to merely state the role of religion in structuring reality and to provide a few illuminating examples. This can only be done by returning to the classical tradition of sociology; that is, by trying to quantify beliefs and symbols, to relate them to groups, to relate them to historical experience, to trace how they have changed, and to find out why.

This answer aggregates the sociology of religion to the sociology of knowledge, and I hope that this will enable us to attack the greatest weaknesses of each. The sociology of religion will no longer take religious beliefs and symbols as if they were separate from other beliefs and did not interact with them, and the sociology of knowledge can learn from some of the work done on religion that it is possible to show how general ideas are embedded in contexts, how they are changed and simplified and re-amalgamated once they pass outside the intellectual élite and are transmitted throughout society and used in specific contexts.

My chief debt is due, as so often in sociology, to the work of Weber and Durkheim; our homage to them is not barren if it forces us to re-open our minds to broader questions and comparative analyses. In addition, I am also grateful to the painstaking help of my editors, Mrs Jean Floud and John Goldthorpe, to J. H. Smith, and to Bryan Wilson, who showed me how to relate the analysis of religious institutions to society as a whole. And finally, my thanks are due to my husband, who made the time in a busy life to give me the time to write this book.

# CHAPTER I

# Introduction—
# The Study of Religion

The study of religion has an uncertain status among other branches of sociology. It can be unkindly characterized as a field of behaviour which is still in search of a successful theory and method. After an initial series of brilliant and suggestive theoretical works, mainly concerned with religion in simple societies, interest in the subject waned during the twentieth century, and has only recently been revived. Although the new interest has produced some excellent studies, there has been as yet no generally accepted theoretical statement which could provide a setting for the new information and the partial analyses. Without this future researchers cannot proceed with a common definition of the important problems and the ways in which they might be approached. But the revival of interest seems to stem from a general conviction that there is something crucially important about the field for the study of society in general, and that its failure to develop may be symptomatic of general distortions or biases which are hindering the progress of sociology as a whole. Part of this conviction undoubtedly stems from the growing anxiety in industrial society about increasingly intolerable rates of disorganized and anti-social behaviour and whether they are not in some way connected with the declining saliency and power of religious thought and institutions; part is due to an attempt to widen the scope of sociology to the study of knowledge, ideas, and subjective meaning, which had become neglected.

There are many reasons for the decline of the subject and the lack of interest in ideas and subjective meaning until fairly recently. The nineteenth-century theorists of religion, like their Enlightenment predecessors, for the most part had either no or very liberal religious views. They viewed conventional religious belief as an intellectual error, which the progress of science and rationality would ultimately weaken to the point of disappearance, except possibly among an unenlightened minority. Religion was consequently something which was rapidly becoming of only historical interest, and was peripheral to modern society. Because religion was generally identified as a set of *beliefs* which it was generally assumed would be corrected by science, scientists in general, and social scientists in particular, became largely agnostic. Those interested in the sociology of religion on a theoretical level have for the most part remained so. Thus the sociology of religion has largely been studied by a professional group which tended to the view that religion was in some sense untrue or irrational, in modern societies at least.

Many recent writers in the field, influenced by a cultural taboo which prevents repeated probing of deeply held metaphysical beliefs, have adopted the view that religion can be discussed, analysed and explained without questioning the truth or falsity of the beliefs on which it is based. This view is tactically desirable, given that much of the audience for the sociological study of religion is to be found among religious functionaries and liberal theologians, despite the views of some theologians, who consider that "true" religion consists in belief, which sociology cannot describe, rather than in institutions and practices. The study has thus proceeded rapidly in areas where beliefs, and the behaviour associated with them, are not the focus of explanation. Much successful research has been completed in areas where positivist[1] conceptions and research-methods have been most useful, for example, in

---

[1] "Positivist" will be referred to extensively in this book. Like all terms with strong emotional penumbras, its meaning varies considerably, but it is used here in the general sense of "scientism": i.e. the approach to knowledge which is based on views such as that:

i. only that which is directly observable can be studied, which shades over into the implication that

ii. what is *not* directly observable—motives, feelings, ideas generally— is not important, or even misleading;

iii. general explanations of human behaviour which are not based on detached observations of events are inferior to scientific ones, and,

iv. the observer can and should be detached from what he observes, and the information which he loses because of his detachment is misleading anyway.

studying the relationship between levels of church attendance in various cities and their overall socio-economic and demographic characteristics (Boulard, 1960). Another major field that avoids touching on the validity or otherwise of religious belief is the study of church organization, and the structure of parishes in terms of the attendance patterns of their congregations.

Research of this kind has shed little further light on the wider problem of the role religion plays in society, but it has illuminated many features of religious institutions. It has enabled the techniques and theories which have been so successful in other areas of sociology to be applied to the study of religious behaviour, and grounded a discipline which has suffered from heated and uncontrolled speculation on a basis of fact. Until the adoption of statistical analysis and a systematic approach to evidence, the sociology of religion was prone to the general weakness of the history of ideas: generalizations from the experiences and views of the articulate were used to explain the behaviour of the rest of society. Apart from its biased nature, a major disadvantage of this approach was that, viewed from the standpoint of a largely secular intellectual élite, religion was unimportant and could offer little justification to those who wished to study it. In modern industrial societies, religious behaviour of an easily measurable kind is both diminishing and largely restricted to women, the old or the unskilled working class. These people seem relatively unimportant in shaping society, since they are peripheral and subsidiary members of the worlds of work, power and politics (D. A. Martin, 1969). In addition, religion is revealed by many surveys to be relatively ineffectual in modern societies as a determinant of attitudes, opinions or behaviour concerned with, for example, politics, economic life or morality. (This has only recently become apparent, for religious membership as a crude index does correlate with other patterns of behaviour, for example, fewer American Catholics become businessmen or go on to further education. But closer inspection has usually revealed another variable as the true determinant—much can be explained about the behaviour of American Catholics in terms of their regional distribution and class and status position.) Thus the study of religion in formal and exterior terms has little interest for the student of modern society.

Religion was defined in terms of belief, but this was abandoned because beliefs were avoided as causal forces in explaining human action. Then it was defined in terms of institutions
and measurable behaviour, but this made it seem peripheral
and unimportant in modern society. Recently, the long-delayed
impact of existentialist philosophy on Anglo-Saxon thought
has brought subjective experience and belief to the centre of the
sociological stage. Viewed in this light, the recent rapid growth
of research (undertaken primarily for the Protestant churches
in America and the Catholic church in Europe) is essentially
market research whose conceptual framework was set by the
interests of employers rather than by intellectual criteria,
resulting in a concentration on church-oriented religiosity
studied by narrowly sociographic techniques. In a recent
influential work, Berger and Luckmann (1963) contrast such an
approach with that of Weber, Durkheim and Pareto, whereby
religious ideas are studied as forces active in every area of life,
shaping all men's experience and behaviour. They believe that
this is still so despite the fact that in modern industrial society
church-affiliated religiosity has become a minor and minority
activity. The positivist pressure on sociology, these authors
believe, is leading to a fatal neglect of the realm of subjective
social reality. It is the subjective reality of our existence in
society which creates our experience, defines our choices, is
made objective to us mainly through language and, despite its
immense importance in human action, is only very partially
institutionalized. In short, they believe all men must accept a
socially structured and socially created view of an ordered
reality to shore themselves up against the underlying chaos and
despair. The acceptance of this socially constructed reality is
never complete, but religion occupies a decisive role in con-
structing and maintaining it. At crisis points sacred formulas
must be reiterated to ensure that our world does not get out of
control. This view subsumes the sociology of religion under the
sociology of knowledge, and takes the subject matter of both to
be all the legitimating intellectual and moral structures of
society, including scientific, psychological and political ones.

If this argument is accepted, it undoubtedly restores the study
of religion or quasi-religion to a central place in the study of
society, since sociology is redefined as the study of the nature of
subjective reality, or of the way in which man's world appears

to him, and the conclusions for action which he draws from it. Two otherwise contrasting groups of thinkers, structuralists and phenomenologists, have such an approach, and both are increasing in influence. In addition, much of the most fruitful research of a more conventional kind in other areas of sociology —for example, into voting decisions—is increasingly taking the subjective world-view into account. Whilst this may restore our confidence in the importance of the sociological study of religion, it does not remove the problems. Rather, it creates three problems, which are irrelevant if religion is studied as institution and behaviour. How is religion to be defined? Are explanations of behaviour in terms of the supernatural beliefs of actors to be treated as "true", or must they be due to other social facts? Can sociology explain behaviour such as spirit-possession, which is non-rational not only to the observer, but often to members of the same society?

The first question is problematic once we take subjective meaning as our central concern, because then we see that definitions of religion vary widely between and within societies, and we can no longer impose a "correct" one. We formerly dealt with this by dividing actors' explanations of their behaviour into accounts based on scientific, or "true" and metaphysical, "untrue" beliefs, but again, in a subjectivist world it makes no difference to the explanation of action if the observer classifies a belief as true or untrue. But then why do beliefs change? Here again, we used to define beliefs as rational or non-rational in terms of criteria available to the actors, and explain why the beliefs were held in a different way in the two cases. There are both philosophical and practical difficulties in trying to maintain these distinctions in the sociological study of religion. They are discussed in the remainder of this chapter in order to demonstrate why it is that the sociology of religion has remained so problematic, and why the account of the research which follows starts off from so many different points in defining what is to be studied, how and why.

## 1 THE DEFINITION OF RELIGION

All works on the sociology of religion devote an initial chapter or section to an analysis of how the term has previously been defined, and then proceed to establish the author's definition. The definition is crucial to the author's intentions, because it implies what will be included and excluded, and how it is to be analysed. For example, perhaps the most famous definition is that of Emile Durkheim (1947), who saw religion as "a unified system of beliefs and practices related to sacred things, that is to say, things set apart and forbidden—beliefs and practices which unite into one single moral community called a church, all those who adhere to them". From this definition flowed certain characteristics of Durkheim's analysis. He did not wish to distinguish, as many anthropologists had, between belief in supernatural beings and belief in other non-empirical entities; he believed that little could be learnt from the specific entities or objects which were sacred, since they were symbols of something else. And he was concerned with religion in so far as it had a social expression, rather than with sporadic or private religious experience.

It is difficult to use this definition of religion in modern societies, because most of them combine high rates of religious belief with low rates of religious activity, and have several different sets of religious beliefs and practices within each social group. If we continue to think in terms of the conventional churches, such societies cannot be united into a single moral community by means of collective religious acts. In late industrial societies—apart from exceptions such as Holland, Belgium, and Northern Ireland, where religious divisions parallel and reinforce economic and political ones—men do not seem to be as strongly concerned with religious groups as they are with many other groups and concerns. Because of this, sociologists have broadened Durkheim's definition of religion to include all beliefs and practices concerned with questions of "ultimate meaning". In this sense, even the most secular societies possess a national set of myths, symbols and beliefs, some of which are collectively reaffirmed on remembrance days, and some of which are attached to the installation of unifying figures such as monarchs and presidents. Can these myths be clearly identified, and do they indeed have an integrative function?

Other definitions of religion imply quite different perspectives. Wach's (1944) "religion is the experience of the Holy" assumes that men will naturally have religious experiences, some of which will become socially recognized and connected with the orthodox religious practices of their society. Such definitions, in contrast to functionalist ones, are acceptable to conservative theologians, for they confine religion to what members of each society would themselves define as religion, and imply that it is not merely *learnt* beliefs and behaviour but has a "real" existence, based on non-social feelings and experiences. In this respect, such definitions are like those of Freud, William James, and other psychologists, who also view religious impulses as springing from non-social roots, and then being partially absorbed into conventional religious beliefs and practices. Explanations of this kind of religion are causal and historical.

A basic distinction can be made between Durkheimian and many other functionalist analyses, and historical and causal analyses of religion. Functionalists do not restrict their definition of religion to what members of each society identify as religion, and assume that some of the effects of men's religious behaviour are unknown to them. In their weak form, such explanations assert that religious beliefs and behaviour have further functions than their ostensible ones. It is usually asserted that they serve to unify men in some way or justify behaviour and beliefs which might otherwise be weakened. (For example Geertz's (1966) statement that "sacred symbols function to synthesize a people's ethos and their world-view".) In their strong form, such explanations assume that every society has a value system common to all of its members which legitimates activities contributing to the maintenance of the society. The creation and protection of these ultimate and unifying values is the function of religion. To adopt either form of the functionalist definition raises some problems and begs many questions.

One obvious difficulty is the assertion that the "real" meaning of religious beliefs and behaviour is not what its participants have assumed it to be. Theologians, and sociologists concerned with the ethical effects of the discipline, have been concerned about this assumption. The conflict between a subjective and an "exterior" explanation is sharper here than in other areas of sociology precisely because the "exterior", and often positivist, explanation is so limited and hard to achieve. It is hard to assemble accurate data, and the relevance of religious behaviour to structural concepts such as "social cohesion" is extremely problematic. Often, the hypothesis about the way in which a particular religious belief or organization is functioning for its members is suggested to the observer by his sympathetic identification with the participants, but he is forced to extrapolate from his own very different reactions as a non-believer.

The issue is further complicated by the large extent to which most people are capable of deliberately playing roles in which they do not entirely believe, but recognize to be socially necessary or desirable, or which they may undertake so as not to disappoint the expectations of others. Goffman has convincingly described the operation of such partial cynicism in the performance of occupational roles, and it seems likely that much religious behaviour in all societies is carried on in a similar state of suspended disbelief. Glock and Stark (1969) have documented the widespread practice in the United States of regular church attendance combined with a lack of belief in the major tenets of Christianity, and Parker *et al.* (1955) found a similar disjunction between belief and behaviour in New Haven. They found a difference between the social classes, in that lower-class church-members were likely to have religious beliefs, but not to attend church and to feel guilty about it, whereas the most educated group were in some cases regular church-attenders but lacked orthodox religious beliefs, and so condemned themselves as hypocritical. Churchgoing in Britain is similarly sometimes defensively justified as mollifying to women or as setting an example to children, and B. R. Wilson (1967) found that the Exclusive Brethren, whilst fully accepting a transcendent belief-system as true, were also perfectly aware of its latent functions for the unity of the group. To identify one of a set of partial motives, of which the individual may well be aware, and to assert that it is the "true" function or purpose of religious behaviour is to oversimplify as badly as Frazer (1890) or Radin (1937) did when they assumed that the priests and magicians of primitive societies, who may manipulate oracles and signs to get plausible answers from the gods, were therefore knaves.

A more important objection to the functional analysis of religion is that the definition must exclude many interesting questions concerned with the relationship between religion and society. The functionalist generally defines religion in an essentialist way; that is, he asserts that religion corresponds to, or can be identified with, one social or psychological function such as social solidarity or ultimate meaning. But in some societies or social groups these variables appear to correspond with beliefs which are not conventionally described as religious —for example, humanism, communism, or a belief in science or psychoanalysis. If the sociologist then defines these as substitute religions, he obscures the question of whether modern society is influenced decreasingly by conventional religion, and whether it can survive with no religious beliefs of the conventional kind. In particular, it remains to be seen whether those who are more strongly attached to conventional religious beliefs, such as women and some sections of the poor, will find alternative beliefs as satisfying as they apparently are for educated men, or whether the different exigencies of their lives do not require very different solutions. It cannot be taken as given that members of a society do possess a set of shared values, feelings of solidarity, and so on, whether or not they are conventionally religious. The conservative argument that modern societies offer their members a decreasingly stable and meaningful existence because of the attenuation of religious belief and shared values cannot be simply defined away.

Research is needed on a wide range of difficult points before the effects on the individual of religion, as opposed to other kinds of belief, can be assessed. In particular, little is known about the moral and metaphysical beliefs and values of the agnostic and the non-churchgoer, nor about his behaviour during the type of stress which is usually supposed to lead men to religion. Several studies of the effects of death on the survivors (Gorer, 1965; Bowman, 1959) as well as much suggestive material in Argyle (1959) on varying frequencies of religious belief, suggest testable hypotheses. Other interesting, but unexplored, areas would include the nature of the popular image of science and its future possibilities, and the extent of superstitious behaviour. Jahoda (1969) lists the very few studies dealing with superstition in modern urban areas. It should also be possible to separate out the kinds of issues and exigencies which prompt references to religion on the part of secular institutions and movements; Gusfield's study of the American temperance movement (1966) and Parkin's of the British Campaign for Nuclear Disarmament (1968) provide good examples of the symbolic structure of very general movements for social change. Here religion is seen as generally justifying an area of concern, rather than providing specific beliefs or arguments. It is important to distinguish between churches applying

B

direct pressure on political and legal institutions, and the very undefined set of beliefs among the general public which classify certain areas or arguments as the province of religion.

In support of the functional definition of religion, it can be convincingly argued that when states do adopt legitimating but secular belief systems, they are rapidly altered and institutionalized in a manner very reminiscent of religion, with political martyrs and messiahs, holy books and ritual celebrations of the birth of the nation, etcetera (Apter, 1963). The parallels are too close to overlook; though this may be because they have been deliberately instituted. Nonetheless, it may be that such secular ideologies differ systematically from religions. Apter, for example, argues that individuals need transcendental beliefs for three purposes; the acceptance of death, to establish individual personality, and to identify objectives. Political religions in the new African and Asian states satisfy these beliefs differently, by transposing personal immortality to the future of the state and problems of identity to citizenship, and claiming the new society as the source of purpose and morality. But, unlike conventional religion, such political creeds are weakened by their limitation to members of the state, the possibility that ultimate ends and material ends, such as a high growth rate, may diverge, and the erosion of the meaning of the revolution by the passage of time.

These questions imply not only research but the need for agreement on how we should define religion, and here, because of the general attack on functional theory and the more specific objections to the functionalist view of religion, some anthropologists and sociologists have recently argued that we should return to looking at religion in intellectualist terms, as consisting essentially of a belief in superhuman beings, and men's socially patterned relationships to them (Spiro, 1966b). (This position also involves a shift in the analysis of ritual, from a searching for its function and social symbolism to the study of the ideas which it embodies about man's relationship to deities.) Another reason for starting from what each society considers to be religious beliefs is the impossibility of finding universal categories for religion, since many primitive cultures do not distinguish between supernatural and empirical knowledge, and attempts to define religion as a feeling have not been successful (Goody, 1961). Such a definition avoids the difficulties of "exterior" explanation, since religion is viewed from the standpoint of the believer, just as Max Weber deliberately avoided the definition of religion by confining the field of study to "the conditions and effects of a certain type of social behaviour ... from the viewpoint of the subjective experiences, ideas and purposes of the individuals concerned" (Weber, 1965, p. 1).

For Weber, the social behaviour in question was concerned with man's attempts to find ultimate meaning through the range of beliefs and practices called religious. Because Weber assumed that ideas and religious impulses were important causal forces which could originate independently of changes in the social structure, he was able to discuss very well the intellectual differences between religions which formed the basis of moral and social thinking and the kind of impact which various kinds of belief had on society. However, he could not always offer a very convincing explanation of why men came to hold particular kinds of religious belief. *The Protestant Ethic* sketched vividly the discomforts of believing in Calvin's doctrines, but offered no explanation of why some men came to believe in them.

## 2 THE "TRUTH" OF RELIGION

Definitions of religion contain implications as to its truth. For the functionalist, it is as "true" as its effects; for the Marxist and the Freudian, it is based on a false diagnosis. The question of whether religious beliefs refer to real but other-worldly entities, or whether these entities are symbols for aspects of worldly reality, cannot be determined any more than a "true" definition of religion can. But sociological analyses of religion cannot ignore the question, because the answer to it determines the acceptable level of explanation. Explanations can be seen as moving back from the event or phenomenon until the inquirer reaches a level of meaning which he accepts, and the point at which curiosity is satisfied lies at different levels for the believer and the non-believer. Thus, for Fr Ronald Knox, S.J. (1950), evangelistic and prophetic groups arise because of the intellectual error of separating religious truth from individual experience; movements such as Wesleyanism and Jansenism are products of certain kinds of error which true religion is perpetually likely to engender. For Knox, the belief of the majority in "true" religion requires no more explanation than the belief that there has been technical progress in Western society.

Other observers assume that some religious beliefs need more explanation than others. Those which are seen as especially problematic are beliefs which appear to flout common-sense observations of reality, or which are at odds with those of the social majority. These are commonly seen as needing special defences and boundary-maintaining mechanisms to separate believers from non-believers (Yinger, 1960; Heberle, 1949). This has meant that sociologists of religion explain the beliefs of sectarians in a more "materialist" way than the beliefs of members of churches or secular intellectuals, and the consequent difficulty of explaining the latter means that there has been very little attempt to do so.

The degree and kind of reductionism varies between functionalists, psychologists, and Marxists. Functional explanations attribute religion to a biological or a social need and, consequently, it is as "real" as other social institutions. Functionalist explanations are usually employed in conjunction with psychological explanations. (In fact, psychological explanations are often used in an *ad hoc* way to explain the *minutiae* of religious belief and behaviour, when the general explanation is quite different.) Observers who explain religion as a response to psychological needs vary in what they identify as the need that is being satisfied—oceanic feelings, search for security, projection of authority, etc.—and in how universal and strong they say the need is. Some authors assume all men need a religion, though some may live without it, whereas others see it as necessary only to those with weaker personalities or intellects, or the victims of misfortune. The theories of religion as a response to relative deprivation implicitly assume the latter view. Above all, such theories differ in the directness with which psychological need is thought to have determined the structure of religious beliefs and practices; many of the nineteenth-century theorists saw a very close connection between religious beliefs and the fears and confusions which caused them.

Marxist explanations of religion ultimately push the explanation back to the level of social and economic factors. Religion is produced by the efforts of men to come to terms with their experience of the social or economic situation. General changes in theological beliefs are a response to the changing social and economic conditions of certain groups. With the Marxist, in contrast to other explanations, the problem is the presence of religion, not its decline. Religion is frequently interpreted as a forerunner of more effective modes of action, and this view has been applied very successfully to explaining the birth of new religious movements among the colonized and suppressed. Since the religious beliefs themselves are assumed to be false, most attention is devoted to the social changes which explain their presence.

## 3 RELIGION AS RATIONAL OR IRRATIONAL

Whether religion is true or not is related to the issue of whether it is rational or not, and this in turn hinges on how we are to interpret the behaviour of people whose assumptions are not our own or those of Western logic or science. This issue has been the subject of a complex debate between anthropologists and philosophers, who have usually taken alien religious beliefs as examples of behaviour whose explanation is problematic. The main points can be quickly summarized.

Evans-Pritchard (1937, 1965) is the foremost of many anthropologists who have emphasized the difficulty of understanding the religious beliefs of another culture. This is due in part to the absence of a common terminology, and in part to the lack of a common logic. For example, in his study of the Nuer people (1956) he found that the translation of the Nuer term *kwoth* as "spirit" failed to convey the complexity of the idea, which is not paralleled in any of our categories. "Spirit" is a creator and a high god, but is socially refracted also into many separate spiritual forms. Totems and nature sprites represent or manifest "spirit", and the different degrees of religious perception are "spirit" manifested on different social levels. Rain, storms and so on are not symbolic of god, but they are him and revelations of him; nonetheless he is not them. "Spirit" is fused with its material representation. These ambiguities could be partially resolved by the observer if he considered these ideas in relation to the social order, since the relativity of the conception of god was paralleled by that of the Nuer conception of lineages, which at some levels were divided and opposed, and at higher levels were one. There was no confusion for Evans-Pritchard in these terms when he lived with the Nuer; the perplexities were those of analysis and not of experience.

The view that alien beliefs are only comprehensible to those who identify imaginatively with an alien world was familiar to Weber and the German historical tradition, and has been forcefully argued by Winch (1964). His arguments for a complete relativism in the understanding of human behaviour are received sympathetically partly because of the increasing doubt among contemporary moralists about the nature or existence of rationality. Evans-Pritchard had distinguished between the scientific and reality-based world-view of some members of Western civilization, and the logical, but magical, world of primitive peoples. Winch suggests that both were coherent universes with internal concepts of "reality" which cannot be used to criticize each other, but that religious views are partially shaped by human life itself and are consequently important to an understanding of it. (A general feature of the debate has been the difficulty of providing *logical* grounds for regarding magical or religious understandings of the world as inferior to scientific ones; see Horton, 1960.)

It is difficult to analyse the operation of religious beliefs in society since they may not only express reality, but conceal it (Gellner, 1962). Gellner argues that Winch is mistaken in claiming that to understand the concepts of a society is to understand the society. Because part of the function of concepts can be to mask reality, their *operation* must be studied. This entails studying how they are reformulated before being put into use. For example, in relating Protestant beliefs to capitalist activities, should Weber have taken the relevant theological texts as evidence of Protestant beliefs, when they bore no relationship to capitalism, or was he justified in suggesting the interpretations that the holders of such theological beliefs must have made of them? The latter can be plausibly said to be those which actually influenced their behaviour, but then the explanation is circular. (Weber's critics and defenders typically diverge on this point; Samuelsson [1961] argues that the causal force of the explanation is lost if theological beliefs can be reinterpreted by their holders, whereas Tawney [1927] distinguished between the logic of theological concepts and their meaning to their adherents.) All beliefs are explicable if interpreted sufficiently in context; in our own society, we know how far it is legitimate to introduce context, and when beliefs are generally held to be false. In an alien society, in our efforts to avoid ethnocentrism we may be unduly "charitable" to beliefs by interpreting them as sensible interpretations of reality, rather than as false or crazy.

Frazer and Tylor, by discussing magic and witchcraft simply as sets of beliefs, could condemn them as false and insufficient; but to reinterpret witchcraft as reducing anxieties, or maintaining social boundaries, tends to check our inquiry into men's sensibleness in holding such beliefs, since their social functions are made to seem so comprehensible. For example, Leach (1964) interpreted the complex and confusing concepts of the Kachin of Highland Burma as allowing them to juggle with two political systems, a feudal and a village-based, so as to extract the maximum advantage from each, rather than as serving an explanatory function. A religious belief in the sinfulness of the poor is obviously personally useful to entrepreneurs, as well as having the useful social function of preventing the dispersal of capital.

Lukes (1967) summarizes the various positions which have been adopted by anthropologists in attempting to explain apparently irrational magical and religious beliefs. They can be seen as symbolic of something else; the underlying reality must therefore be explained. Or it can be asserted that such beliefs are essentially irrational and incomprehensible to outsiders. A more charitable view explains them as merely different— logical and real by mystical standards. Or they may be seen as attempted rational explanations of events, which use at least some rational procedures of thought. The most charitable position is to assume that all beliefs have an interior rationality which is given by the culture.

Spiro (1964) is inclined to discard the issue of the rationality of religious belief, or to restrict it to a definition in terms of internal logicality. He describes religious beliefs as false, but not therefore irrational. They solve both emotional and cognitive needs, and it is not irrational to hold them unless superior explanations of reality exist within the culture, any more than it was irrational of scientists to hold scientific beliefs which have since been revised. Consequently, religious beliefs are only irrational in modern Western societies, where the contradictory scientific world-view is also culturally available; only in such societies have religious beliefs become detached from the general world-view, and judged by different criteria of truth and logic.

The persistence of religious beliefs in cultures where science has become a dominant perspective must consequently be explained as being due to the fact that they are functional *alternatives* to scientific explanations, but not functional *equivalents*. Like many authors, Spiro emphasizes that only religious beliefs can offer satisfactory explanations for some aspects of reality, primarily those to do with suffering. The fact that many religious systems pay scant attention to what appear to be major problems of meaning, or even frustrate rather than satisfy emotional needs, Spiro holds to be because beliefs correspond to deep-seated preconceptions which we acquire as children concerning the behaviour of powerful figures and the difficulty that we have in relating their behaviour to our actions. To a large extent, religious beliefs are insulated from rationality because we acquire them as part of our culture and, like other culturally central beliefs, they are "confirmed" by empirical experience.

It may be added here that not only religious beliefs are confirmed by culture; *we* acquire culturally a general receptivity to the prestige and success of scientific explanations. A study (Budd, 1973) of a small number of English people who adopted a scientific belief-system in place of a religious one shows that for the most part, they were influenced by reading works of interpretation which argued that science was superior to religion, rather than by experiencing a crucial test of either set of beliefs. Science has replaced religion less because its explanations are superior than because it has greater prestige in our society. The efforts of modern theologians to accommodate religion to science only intensify this process.

The empirical basis for scientific beliefs in all societies may be very much stronger than that for religious ones but, except in a secular society, the motivation to believe in them is much weaker. Spiro (1966b) believes that religious beliefs are to be explained both causally and functionally, but that with the above considerations in mind, this can be done without imputing irrational behaviour to the religious individual.

Spiro's solution seems the most satisfactory in that it offers *sociological* explanations of why beliefs are rational in some contexts and not in others. He also tries to incorporate the fact that, although religion is widely assumed to provide an answer to suffering, many religious beliefs create suffering *via* guilt, and other religions are silent on topics which we assume concern all men. But there are still considerable difficulties in his position. He imputes certain "needs" to individuals, and although this accounts for continuing to believe within an existing tradition, it cannot explain the rise of new religious beliefs, especially in societies where "superior" explanations exist. The functional alternative/functional equivalent distinction commits him to a weak defence of functionalism, since presumably in modern societies both scientists and the religious must have some emotional or cognitive needs left forever unsatisfied. He attempts to explain religious beliefs which *create* anxiety by reference to psychoanalytic theory, but the psychoanalytic theory of the origins of belief in, say, a threatening father-figure as a god, is itself a complete explanation which coexists uneasily with a social functionalism. Perhaps the problem can be reformulated if "needs" are seen as general and cognitive. It matters less to me if I believe in a God who will punish what I will almost inevitably do than it would matter if I believed that there was no order in the universe at all, that my actions are neither good nor bad, that suffering is random. What is important about religious beliefs, as Durkheim said, is not their specific content or whether they are rational or not, but that they establish categories—good/bad, fellow-believer/outsider, sacred/profane, reward/punishment.

## 4 CONCLUSION

Many of the issues touched on will be taken up again in the context of a more detailed discussion of theories and evidence, but it is worth repeating that the problem for the sociologist of religion is that the analysis of religious beliefs and behaviour, and their relations to other parts of society, is peculiarly unsuited to the methods used so successfully elsewhere in sociology. It is quite plausible to assume that religion has outlived its functional or epistemological usefulness, and that its existence in modern society can only be explained as a residue. The difficulty of tracing any concrete effects which are due to religious beliefs *per se*, rather than to membership of communities which, amongst other things, have a religion in common, increases the conviction that it may be unimportant. The fact that its impact tends to be greatest among groups which are marginal to the obviously important political and economic aspects of modern society—women, the old, the very poor, the distressed and stigmatized—does not enhance the professional prestige of the sociologist of religion. It is often implied that these groups will ultimately find satisfaction or solutions in "secular" activities and remedies, just as discrepancies in individual world-views are commonly treated as something which will fairly rapidly disappear. (For an examination of their extent and importance, see Converse, 1964.) There is, however, no reason why the world-view of the healthy, well-educated and successful should be regarded as either more normal or more "real".

It is such a viewpoint, the dismissal of religion as unimportant both to members of modern societies and to their operation, that is more and more often condemned as a symptom of the artificial restriction of what we know of and can find out about human behaviour to a "rational man", or "homo sociologus" mould. Lévi-Strauss came to see categories such as rational and irrational, intellectual and affective, logical and pre-logical, as meaningless for explaining human behaviour. "In the first place, there existed beyond the rational a category at once more important and more valid: that of the meaningful . . . those actions which seem most purely affective, those results which seem least logical, and those demonstrations which we call pre-logical, are in point of fact precisely those which are meaningful in the highest degree" (Lévi-Strauss, 1961, p. 59).

Although this view is gaining currency and doing much to restore the study of religion and knowledge to a more central place in sociology, the problems of definition and method it entails seem far from being solved.

In the next two chapters, the development of two broad traditions in the sociological study of religion are described. The first is anthropological; its greatest exemplar is Durkheim. Because it originated in the study of small primitive societies, it sees religion as a single entity defined and described by the purposes which it serves for society and for men. The second is historical; its themes were set by Marx and Weber. Because it is concerned with changes in religion and its influence in complex societies, it offers no definition of religion, but takes it as it is defined in the social group itself.

# CHAPTER II

# Religion as Single Entity— Evolutionary and Anthropological Theories

To define the operation of religion in society, we need to be able to imagine a society without it. The sociological analysis of religion requires a secular milieu. The Enlightenment provided the basis for this, as for so many other branches of the social sciences. The *philosophes*, in discussing the role of religion, tended to divide it into two kinds; all primitive religions and medieval Christianity, which were morbid, superstitious, and deleterious in their effects on men and society, and, on the other hand, contemporary deism and the religions of classical antiquity, which at least in part fostered knowledge, liberal morality, and devotion to the public good. Many of them thought of religion, as well as societies, as oscillating between the poles of barbarism and progress, but this oscillation gave way in the nineteenth century to progressive and evolutionary schemes. David Hume's *Natural History of Religion* (1757) contains both sorts of movement, as well as many interesting observations about the relationship between the perceptions of men and how they conceive of the supernatural.

For Hume, since religion was an intellectual error, the main problem to be explained was the origin of the religious sentiments. They, and their form, were determined both by the emotional needs of men, and by their intellectual mistakes as they attempted to comprehend the world. Hume thought that all primitive peoples were amazed by the natural order because they could not understand its causation, and so their incessant hope and anxiety about it led them to create gods who could control it. The savagery and wastefulness of nature argued for a pantheon of contradictory and quarrelling gods. The tendency for one god to become preeminent as society advanced might be because he was the heavenly reflection of a now-supreme earthly ruler, or because the more intelligent savages, like eighteenth-century *savants*, perceived that the absolute regularity of natural events must be ruled by a single supreme intelligence. But the impetus toward theism was constantly reversed by the minor gods and protective powers—saints, mariolatry, graven images, relics—that appealed to the needs of the ignorant.

The psychologistic explanation of religious concepts as the solutions to certain emotional needs was to become a popular one. The question of why what were presumably universal human needs should produce such a variety of concepts was never adequately answered. The evolutionists could claim that man's emotional needs systematically evolved—and so did the reflexive concepts. But the explanation is fundamentally erroneous, in that it assumes that "needs" are translated into "beliefs" without both being structured by a societal matrix.

A century later, knowledge of simple societies had greatly increased. In particular, there were now accounts available of the beliefs of the tribal peoples from Africa, America and Oceania. Theories of the origins of religion in terms of primitive explanations of nature, previously based on evidence from the Indo-Germanic religions, were inadequate to explain fetish-worship, ancestor-worship, and totemism (Schmidt, 1931). To the Victorian scholars who studied them the most striking feature of these newly revealed societies was their superstition. A large proportion of their beliefs were false and magical. It was evident to them that their own civilizations had previously been like these, for remnants of similar superstitious and magical beliefs were being reported by folklorists from among the ignorant and country-dwellers. The similarities between contemporary superstition and primitive magic, and the dominance of evolutionary frameworks in the study of history and the natural sciences, provided a fatally easy structure for explaining religions. Societies began to be ordered in terms of the rationality and purity of their religious beliefs, from those which were the most primitive and had a high component of magic and ritual activity, worshipped natural forces rather than deities, and had little ethical content, to those societies like the authors'

own, which had the most advanced religions—the mono-
theistic, universal, ethical religions "of the book".

The sociological study of religion had proved and still proves
to be highly sensitive to changes in the general intellectual
climate. Ambiguities about just what was being studied and
what effects it had, made the field a natural battleground
between evolutionists and historicists in the nineteenth century,
and positivists and existentialists in the twentieth. The initial
focus on explaining primitive rather than advanced religion was
socially convenient in that questions of intellectual and moral
relativism, the historicity of myth, and the reflection of society
in the nature of the deities, which would have been threatening
had they been applied to contemporary Christianity, could
safely be argued in the context of primitive religions (Geertz,
1968). (Though Robertson Smith was dismissed from his post
for writing about early Semitic religions in such terms—the
parallels with primitive Christianity were too close to be over-
looked.)

Evolutionists and historicists disputed over whether the very
simplest societies had any religious beliefs at all. Max Müller
and others argued that some contemporary primitive super-
stitions were degraded anthropomorphic forms of a previous
higher and more abstract religion. (In retrospect, Müller was at
least aware, as many evolutionists seem not to have been, that
contemporary "savages" had a history at least as long as that of
civilized society, and that there was no reason to suppose that
their societies had not changed a great deal.) Müller's views
were supported by a group of Jesuit ethnologists, who could
thus argue that God had revealed himself directly to the
earliest men, giving them a natural moral law and mono-
theistic religion, from which many tribes had lapsed by the
time of Christ and the second revelation. These men formed the
basis of the German historical school, which at least took primitive beliefs on their own terms, rather than seeing them as the
product of simple minds on the lowest stages of the evolutionary
slope.

Most English and American authors at that time agreed on
an evolutionary ordering of religions, and it was generally
accepted that the growth of larger political and economic units
produced a need for fewer gods with more far-reaching powers
and less identification with particular localities, groups and

problems. Religion was interesting not only because it seemed so important a part of the sum-total of beliefs in simple societies, but also because it was assumed that religious beliefs were often residues or survivals from an even earlier stage of culture, so that from them the original forms of social organization could be reconstructed. Bachofen and Briffaut argued, for example, that since many early religions had powerful female deities, matriarchy must have been an early stage of social organization.

## 1 SOCIAL EVOLUTIONARY THEORIES

The anthropologists and sociologists who established the study of religion as a part of social structure, such as Tylor, Comte and Spencer, were also evolutionists. Their work is still remarkable for its thoroughgoing effort to relate religious institutions to other social institutions and not merely to human need. Both Tylor and Spencer considered that primitive man was essentially reasonable. "Our postulate must be that primitive ideas are natural, and under the conditions in which they occur, rational. . . . Given the data known to him, the primitive man's inference is the reasonable inference" (Spencer, 1898). By divorcing social evolution from human evolution, they were able to produce sophisticated and interesting accounts of how myths and beliefs structure and are structured by social experience. After a period when the ritual and institutional structures of religion within particular societies were the main subjects of study, myth as the key to the intellectual structure of experience has been taken up again in the last twenty years, and the early anthropologists still have much to teach us.

Tylor, usually acknowledged as the first anthropologist, devoted the majority of his first great work on primitive society (1871) to religion. He put forward a modified evolutionism: all human societies were essentially very similar, because all mankind was "homogeneous in nature". Previous stages of development were encapsulated in each society in surviving superstitious beliefs, which could be reactivated by deteriorating social conditions. For example, the belief in witchcraft could readily be reactivated in Europe by religious persecution. The anthropologist should use myths as a guide to how, in particular societies, men experience nature and life. It has always been obvious that events are best explained in natural and causal terms, but in every society men divide events into those which could have been caused naturally, and those which are miraculous, and so must be explained by other means. The crucial difference between ourselves and savages lies only in the larger realm of what we consider to be natural. Thus, for Tylor, the concept of the miraculous or non-natural is an important one in identifying and analysing religious beliefs. For example, the Christian doctrine of miracles was strongly emphasized in the Middle Ages and miracles grew in number and in social importance; they were the bridge by which the old pagan mythologies of miraculous grottoes, trees, etc., could travel from a lower to a higher religion; the same structures became attached to new personages. (An examination of what men in secular cultures call "miraculous" would be illuminating, and might provide a useful way of identifying areas of explanation which are still felt to be beyond science.)

Tylor defined religion in intellectualist terms; the essential minimum was a belief in spiritual beings. The origin and development of animism he derived very plausibly by arguing that the concepts of the soul and immortality would have been produced by early men to explain such natural events as death, sleep and dreams. Each cognitive puzzle that man faced had a number of possible intellectual solutions. Once one solution had been adopted by a tribe, it would tend to imply other solutions to other problems. A belief in an after-life for individual souls, for example, would be likely to entail a transcendent deity who allocates them to heaven or hell; whereas an ancestor-cult would be likely to be linked with a belief in transmigration or the obliteration of the soul at death. (Tylor was mistaken in thinking that a plausible account of why we hold a belief is an explanation of its *origin*, but the idea of a limited set of possible schema, where parts of a cosmology will strongly entail other elements, is one which has recently been revived in the study of mythology.)

The early anthropologists were mainly interested in the beliefs of primitive societies, and devoted much of their theoretical efforts to distinguishing between religion, magic and science. The reasons for this were mainly diplomatic—it was necessary to assert that ludicrous and superstitious beliefs (magic) had always been independent of true religion and/or morality, and that the latter would persist in an ever-purer form, whereas science would cause magic to wither away. Tylor, his pupil Frazer, and other evolutionists were pre-occupied with the view that the difference could be found in the beliefs themselves—religion was ethical, science true, and magic a vulgar but understandable error. (One reason for the subsequent rejection of the whole enterprise was that it had to assume a criterion for measuring and categorizing beliefs that existed outside primitive societies, but which could be applied to all societies.)

Frazer, especially, in branding specific *beliefs* as being essentially religious, magical, etc., and by comparing them with similar beliefs wrenched from quite different cultural contexts, did much to discredit evolutionism. *The Golden Bough* had a remarkably wide influence among the general public and non-anthropologists, but even at the time that the final version was being published, Malinowski had convinced anthropology of the necessity of looking at beliefs only in the context of a very detailed account of a whole culture to examine what role they played. (He had been led to anthropology by reading the original version.)

Spencer's social evolutionism was rather different. Social change occurred not through intellectual progress, but through population pressure and structural differentiation. Since social retrogression was quite possible, contemporary primitive men were not identical with the earliest stages of all mankind. Spencer thought that men had no innate tendency to form religious ideas. The experiences which Tylor thought must have resulted in the belief in souls and gods, seemed to Spencer only to have resulted in a belief in ghosts. These "puerile assumptions and monstrous inferences" were made because of a very limited abstract vocabulary. The origins of religion itself lay in the worship of ancestors. The propitiation of the dreaded dead developed into religious ritual, and the ghosts of the ancestors into gods.

In all cultures, religion was an essential part of social order; political power was founded on a fear of the living, and religious control was founded on a fear of the dead. Consequently the interests of both political and religious rulers lay in close collaboration. As societies moved up from the patriarchal stage, where the father both ruled the group and propitiated the dead, the spheres, functionaries and laws of religion and politics became more distinct, and more elaborate social hierarchies resulted in more clearly differentiated and specialized deities. Religious institutions always acted to "maintain and strengthen social bonds, and so conserve the social aggregate". Spencer's account of how religion did this was partly conventional—it strengthened the past traditions of the society and made the "unregulated explosive savage" cooperative through fear—but some parts of his explanation foreshadowed the psychological functionalism of Malinowski. For example, he argued that mourning was important for social cohesion, as the act itself aroused a set of common sentiments and enforced collective action, and this would result in the muting of animosities and the structuring and strengthening of the social group (Spencer, 1898, Part 4). But with the rise of more than one religion in society, religion would no longer be able to exert such a powerful hold and social control would become more internal. (Like other writers from a Nonconformist background, Spencer attached a good deal of moral value to religious pluralism.)

Such evolutionary theories were increasingly attacked by anthropologists before the issue was finally abandoned. The diffusionist school argued that new beliefs were borrowed more often than they were arrived at by a process of internal development, and a group of American anthropologists argued forcefully that there was little progression of religious belief anyway— primitive religions contained "civilized" elements, and vice versa (Boas, 1911; Lowie, 1924; Radin, 1937). The discoveries at the end of the nineteenth century of Babylonian, Egyptian and Assyrian writings of great antiquity which showed systems of nature-myths and star-myths, and the similarities between the great sky-gods of Indo-European "advanced" religions and those of many very primitive African peoples added factual ammunition to the growing intellectual attack on evolutionary theory.

The logic of the evolutionary approach has been cogently attacked by Evans-Pritchard (1965). Because the evolutionists discussed religious ideas extracted from many societies, they deprived them of their meaning, which consists only in their relationship to other social facts in each society. Ancestor-worship, for example, is not to be understood if we treat it as a set of beliefs comparable with similar beliefs from elsewhere; it is part of a set of family and kin relationships, transitions which the individual makes between stages of his life, means of representing how different lineages are bound together by co-operation and antagonism. Its meaning varies greatly between societies. Nor should religion be taken to be what any society's intellectuals say that it is; the anthropologist must guard against using those with an interest in religion as his sole informants. Their accounts describe what they wish was the case, rather than the indifference and disinterest which many members of simple cultures display toward metaphysical ideas. The anthropologist knows this about his own society; his belief that primitive societies are "more" religious may be due to his informant. For example, accounts of *mana* given by people in the same society vary between that of a priest, who explains it as the generalized essence of deity residing in things, and that of a layman, interested only in its effects, who views it as a source of magical power (Radin, 1937).

Cultures, according to Evans-Pritchard, can only be understood by total immersion. Trying to argue by analogy from an imaginary model of a man and how he might react—the "if I were a horse" argument—is likely to lead us astray. The difficulties of his position were discussed in the introduction; it is arguable that even though we have abandoned the idea of "primitive mentality", we can never know that we so wholly comprehend other men that we are not treating them sometimes as if they were horses—Houyhnhnms, perhaps, if we reverse the moral stance. On the other hand, members of a society may be quite mistaken about it in ways which only detached observation can reveal. (For example, Marwick [1965] found that the Cewa think that sorcerers are women. But those accused of sorcery are mainly men.) But it cannot be denied that the evolutionists frequently went wrong because they did not take the worlds of primitive peoples as comprehensive wholes. Because they treated religion as a set of beliefs which were essentially illusory, their accounts of the reasons for the beliefs were facile and intellectualist. Their hypotheses about what primitive man thought about his world—for example, the naturalist theories that the origins of religions lay in primitive man's feelings of awe at mountains, rocks and waterfalls—tell us more about the emotions of the worried Victorian agnostics who found solace in mountain-climbing and were exalted by wild landscapes than they tell us about primitive peoples, who usually find such non-utilitarian objects unimpressive.

Whether or not particular objects are treated as sacred because they have some practical significance to the people concerned is hard to determine. Durkheim tried to refute the naturalism of Müller by arguing that the totemic objects of the Australian aborigine were such a bizarre collection of the useful and the useless that they were not of value in themselves, nor could they be a source of awe; they gained their power from another source: society. Worsley considers that Durkheim misunderstood the vital importance, in the barren environment of the aborigine, of what seemed to him to be insignificant plants and animals (Worsley, 1956). Moreover, an object may become sacred not only because it is useful or awe-inspiring in itself, but because it may have qualities which are homologues for something else which is important, the relationships between men and women, for example (Douglas, 1970; Lévi-Strauss, 1968; Turner, 1967). Beliefs treated in this way cannot be treated as part of an intellectual progression or evolution.

Recently, there have been a number of attempts to construct more modest evolutionary schema for religious development. Some aspects of societies do appear to change systematically as they develop: their size increases, social hierarchies lengthen and then shorten, social relations become more specialized, and in some spheres more impersonal, and so on. It follows that, if the functionalist view that religion changes as society does is correct, religious development should also show some overall similarities. Swanson (1960), in a large-scale comparative analysis, found some support for the theory of a transition to monotheism with the growth of more elaborate forms of political organization, and Wallace (1966) and Bellah (1964) have put forward new schema for stages of evolution.

Bellah's evolutionary theory is essentially that of the increasing complexity and differentiation of religious symbolism, religious collectivities and the religious self. He argues that religions occur in five stages, in which the last resembles the first in many ways, for example in the acceptance of the world. Primitive religion, the first stage, is marked by an identity between the real and the mythical world, so that men are *identified* by ritual with particular mythical beings, rather than related to them. There can be no priests and no spectators at such rituals—church and society are one. For religion at this stage, Durkheim's analysis is excellent. Later, a distinct cult may emerge, with priests and routines of worship and sacrifice, by which men communicate with the gods and hope to influence their actions on earth. The historical world-religions, the next stage, are all marked by the emergence of the idea of transcendence—for a period of about two thousand years, a wave of world rejection (the reasons for which are unexplained) led all the major theologies to concentrate on life in another world which was controlled by a single god capable of saving all mankind. The dualism of this world and the next, of the flesh and of the true self, resulted in the growth of separate religious institutions set over against a secular society. The fourth stage was reached in Christianity at the Reformation: all men may be saved by faith, so religious hierarchies become less important than the division between the sacred and the unredeemed. A variety of social institutions become entirely secular. Bellah follows Weber and Parsons in optimistically identifying this phase with the process of democratization and the incorporation of agencies for criticism and change into society, which he assumes is inevitable for all modernizing societies. The final evolutionary stage comes with the rejection of the "other world" of religious reference by theologians and by believers, and religion is grounded in "the human situation"; that is, as only one of a number of alternative ethical possibilities, since man's increasing self-knowledge enables him to assume responsibility for his own fate. Such a religion deserts orthodox doctrine and rituals for the freedom and flexibility of modern society.

Bellah, like previous evolutionary theorists, assumes that religion in societies is moving toward the most liberal variety of Protestantism. But as the diffusionists argue, because of culture-contact we cannot assume that religion, or any other social institution, will go through a sequence serially, even if the sequence was followed by the earliest societies to modernize. Societies at any point on the line will now "buy" the secular values of Western or Soviet society along with their technology. Indeed, liberal missionaries have often found themselves rapidly outstripped in the radicalism of their theology by those whom they were trying to convert; for example, the Unitarians in India, whose Hindu converts left them almost at once to found an even more universal, rational and syncretic religion, the Brahmo Somaj.

Wallace escapes many of the difficulties of Bellah's typology —its intellectualism and linearity—by taking religious organization as the basis for an evolutionary scheme. His "individualistic cults" approximate to Bellah's primitive religion, but no society has these alone. Shamanism, which involves approaches to a spirit by an expert, comes next, and then "communal cults", i.e. social groups who approach by ritual a set of deities with different and specialized functions. In time, they acquire specialized practitioners, who approach a powerful god or gods on behalf of a lay and largely passive following. Wallace argues that societies contain within themselves myths, rituals and organizational forms which come from several stages of development; for example, modern American society contains both shared superstitious and magical beliefs, commemorative religio-political gatherings for the entire society, and a series of churches with priests. This confusion of levels is to be expected, in that each stage of development contains within itself the earlier forms of religious and other institutions, still used by its members at some points. There is a shift in characteristic religious goals, from manipulating human and natural objects to the explanation of the natural world by a metaphysic and then to solving problems of individual and social pain. Progress here is determined by the development of technology, and so it is roughly parallel with the changes in religious organization which are related to increasing social complexity.

These new evolutionary accounts are based on far more data than the old, but they have not been adopted. Evolutionary theory was rejected partly because it lost ground as a form of explanation in favour of looking at the way social arrangements operate in context, and partly because it was either too unspecific to be useful, or there were too many exceptions. The recent more sophisticated sequences still cannot overcome these basic objections. Evolutionists also assume a "leading sector" theory of social change in which general belief moves more slowly than, but along the same track as, the beliefs of the "advanced". But effective explanations of beliefs reject this for the view that beliefs are explained by contexts of experience—underdogs are always (relative) underdogs; and "primitive" beliefs, such as those in magic and sorcerers, are related to social tensions, and increase when tension increases.

## 2 PSYCHOLOGICAL THEORIES

The evolutionary theorists had been able to assume that rationality increased as societies advanced; by the end of the nineteenth century, a widespread cultural pessimism led to the view that although man might well be abandoning religion, along with the other bonds of the old communal life, he was not thereby becoming more rational, but rather more anomic, uncertain, and unrestrained. Writers as dissimilar as Pareto and Bergson argued that religion was part of something vital, non-rational and non-logical which was entailed by man's nature, and so would always be important in society. The explanation of religion in terms of the eternal needs of the psyche was revived as new models of human personality were developed which were less mechanistic, and which tried to root human behaviour in more than the "black box" theory of the mind. Attempts were made to relate different types of personality to the religious experience of the individual; William James's classic work, *The Varieties of Religious Experience* (1902), initiated a series of studies of the phenomenon of religious conversion. But the most influential psychological theories were those of Freud.

The psychology of religion lies outside the scope of this book, but when discussing human action, sociologists must necessarily adopt a model of the human personality. The model we use is largely a Freudian one, and so Freud's views on the relationship between religion and neurosis have (often implicitly) been assumed in many studies in sociology and anthropology. Freud's studies of totemism and the origins of the social group (*Totemism and Taboo; Moses and Monotheism*), despite much that is interesting, can be dismissed as speculative evolutionary theorizing at its most extreme. But *Civilization and its Discontents* (1930) and *The Future of an Illusion* (1934) both raise problems of great importance in the relationship between personality and culture. Freud claimed that civilization is built on men's renunciation of the satisfaction of their instinctual drives. The view of the world held by those who are not civilized—savages, neurotics and children—attributes infinite power and hostility either to the individual himself or to the world which confronts him. But this omnipotence or utter helplessness is easier to bear than the reality of man's existence, for the realist must learn to accept the limitations of his body, the hostility and weakness of his fellows, and the indifference of the cosmos.

Religion, to Freud as to Marx, was primarily a narcotic, something which gave a spurious meaning to a "heartless world". To believe in gods who could control an overpowering and indifferent natural order, and could in turn be influenced or propitiated by men to some extent, made the cruelties of nature and of fate explicable, and justified the demands made by culture on men for renunciation. The obsessions, dreams and fantasies of collective life came from the same sources in the psyche as those of isolated maladjusted individuals. As the understanding and control of nature increased, the gods could be expected to become increasingly transcendent, inscrutable or powerless. Nature might be controlled, but the relationships between human beings remained problematic, and so the gods would coalesce into a single deity, and the relationship to him would become increasingly connected with the relationship to the parent. By sanctioning cultural laws as divine, and justifying the demands of culture, religion acted to consolidate authority and society.

Freud did not consider the persistence of religion in the face of apparently superior scientific explanations surprising. The strength of religious ideas was due to their connection with the most interesting and important areas of man's inner life, and in their ability to satisfy man's wishes to make the world resemble what he wished it to be. At the same time, they were a yoke on his desires; without them, only a few would tolerate the burden of culture. Religious beliefs are illusions, but the fact that they are learnt from society, and held in common with other men, protects the believer from individual neurosis at the cost of mass neurosis for the culture.

Several authors have asked whether Freud's social theory, as well as his psychological theory, is not culture-bound. (See Rieff [1959] for general discussion.) Roheim (1950) and Malinowski both argued that the Oedipal conflict was not universal, so that personality needs must also vary between societies. Many studies of religion have been based on the Freudian view of personality development. Bettelheim (1954) discussed puberty rites as part of the effort to establish sexual identity; and Kluckholm (1944) related psychological factors to the social and cultural aspects of Navaho religion. But the aspect of Freud's theory of religion which has been most widely discussed has been his comparison of the nature of religious belief with the private fantasies of infantile neurosis. Freud took religion to be at root an expression of the search for authority; it was a feeling—strongest in infants, neurotics and savages—in which man's lonely ego yearned to be reunited with the world. From the universality of the feeling, with its biological roots, came the whole intellectual superstructure of religion and the institutions which embodied it.

On the factual level, many authors working in the psycho-analytic tradition have indeed found an association between strong religious belief and an authoritarian, neurotic, or other-wise ailing personality. (Some of the studies are summarized in Argyle, 1959.) For example, the series of studies which have tried to distinguish between the "open", creative or liberal mind and the "closed", rigid or authoritarian one have found that those who have conventional religious views are more likely to be antisemitic, authoritarian and prejudiced, despite the fact that the contents of the religious beliefs might have been hoped to represent a charitable outlook. This has led some researchers to try to distinguish between a "true" and a "con-ventional" religiosity (Adorno *et al.*, 1950; Allport, 1954, 1966; Allen and Spilka, 1967; Stark and Glock, 1968). They found that although the majority of religious believers hold conven-tional, and consequently rather prejudiced, views, a small number with an unusually strong commitment to religious values are led to radical disagreement with conventional beliefs. But the research is based on the implicit judgment that the value-system which is relatively liberal and challenges the *status quo* is the "true" one which corresponds to "true" religion. The connection between religious belief and personality cannot be so direct, but must be mediated by the general meaning that belief in religion has within the culture, since it is this which determines who is religious and how.

The explanation of religious beliefs and behaviour in terms of psychological needs is not a complete one. Why should the same needs produce different beliefs? And why should we assume that the infinitely complex varieties of religious experience in a society answer the same need? Like Malinowski, Freud was working with a biological model of man that assumed strong and constant drives which must find their goal or be deflected. Truth apart, psychological explanations of culture which are of this type are over-determined. If we explain a persistent myth about cruel mothers by claiming that it symbolizes reality, that mothers in this society are indeed cruel, and it is objected that in fact they are kind and loving beyond the average, then the hypothesis can easily be rescued by the argument that the lack of aggression in the actual mothers is due to its being channelled and dissipated by the presence of the myth (Lévi-Strauss, 1968). Similarly, when la Barre (1969) explains the snake-handling cults of the American South as due to the desire of the socially impotent to achieve a magical potency by these means, the explanation cannot specify why this remedy and not another was chosen, nor who, out of a large number of the under-privileged, will join such a cult. Most men do not choose whether they want to adopt religious beliefs of a certain kind which correspond to their personal needs or not, since they are born into a context where certain beliefs and behaviour are required of them, and, very often, where other social roles and categories of thought are contingent upon religious ones. Thus if religion answers to personality needs, it answers to those which are general among a group, and sociologists and anthropologists have been inclined to emphasize the extent to which different social contexts produce different personality needs, so that the personality has become only the channel between culture and religious belief. Only those who change their religious allegiances can be said to choose between beliefs in order to find those which are emotionally satisfying. In a society like our own, where religion is an optional solution to personal malaise, it may indeed be an alternative to the Freudian explanation itself. Lofland (1966) found that potential converts to a Californian sect were prone to consider religious, revolutionary political, and psychiatric solutions as alternatives, and to consult in turn the practitioners of each.

Although the explanation of religion solely in terms of psychological need is inadequate, the basis of sociological explanations of religion is either that it is necessary to man in some sense—it performs an emotional or intellectual function for him—or that it results from his reflections on his experience, or embodies social relations for him in some way. In each case, religion must therefore be related to personality, even if it is structured by social experience. Various "feelings"—of awe, or fear, or power—have been suggested as the connection between social experience and the religious response. Perhaps the most fruitful attitude to explore is that of religion as the response to uncertainty.

## 3 RELIGION AND UNCERTAINTY

Freud and Malinowski considered that religious explanations and rituals were used when the outcome of events was unknown or uncertain, but where it was of such importance that this was too difficult for the individual to accept. One of the advantages of this view is that it is susceptible to being tested. Various studies have shown that religious beliefs are indeed generally stronger among those people and at those times when an important outcome is uncertain and cannot be affected by the individual. Vogt and Hyman (1959) showed that water-divining was resorted to by farmers in an arid area of New Mexico, when they were unable to determine where to dig for wells by scientific methods. The effect of divining was to encourage them to dig for longer in one place, and so be more likely to find water. Lewis and Lopreato (1962) found that the mothers of sick children were more likely to resort to the "irrational" acts of prayer and magical routines if they lacked confidence in the power of medical science, or if the disease was such that prognosis was uncertain. Slater (1966) found that interaction in small groups progressed from an initial stage of uncertainty, when a leader tended to emerge and have quasi-magical powers attributed to him by the rest of the group, to one where as the group aged and uncertainty declined, relations between members grew more "secular". Jahoda (1969) attributes superstition in modern societies to anxiety-creating situations and, despite the decline in formal religious beliefs, high rates of superstitious practice are still reported amongst fishermen, miners, steel-workers and members of other dangerous and uncertain occupations.

If these results are taken to confirm the general hypothesis, then the growth of secularization in our society can be attributed to our increasing technical control of many aspects of our lives, which, by reducing uncertainty, has reduced the likelihood of the religious response. (See T. Parsons [1963b] for a similar theory of our treatment of death.) The statistics of religious attendance suggest that those whose lives are relatively uncertain, risky, or uncontrollable are often more religious. The greater religiosity of women can be explained more satisfactorily in this way than by the tautology of attributing it to something in their nature, or by invoking a psychic division of labour in which it is they who always fulfil the expressive and integrative needs, and hence the religious ones, in society. It is more convincing to argue that the circumstances of their lives in modern societies are experienced by them as more dependent on chance and the wills of other people than those of men. Similarly, it should be possible to establish independently those kinds of uncertainty which each social group experiences as being the most worrying, and to see if they are reflected in the kinds of reassurance which are sought in religion and elsewhere. For example, Stouffer (1955) found that anxiety about health, and the cost of being ill, was the overwhelming concern of a large number of Americans, and the religions of a "new thought" type which offer a solution to disease and which are commoner in American middle-class life than anywhere else are presumably a response to such an anxiety.

The difficulties involved in explaining religion as a response to uncertainty are similar to those involved in explaining it as a response to feelings of deprivation. Uncertainty must be defined from the respondent's viewpoint, which makes it difficult to create objective measures. We must also distinguish between a personal uncertainty, which may be resolved by entirely private means, and points where a social group faces an uncertain future but where a given individual sharing in the religious response may himself feel quite unconcerned. Religion may relieve uncertainty, but it is often argued, especially by psychiatrists, that it creates anxiety rather than solving it. This may be more true of the stringent moral demands of certain forms of Protestantism common among their patients than it is of many other religions.

## 4 DURKHEIM ON RELIGION

Sociologists must assume a model of human personality, but the distinctive characteristic of a sociological explanation of religion should be that it relates religion to other social patterns and institutions. Comte and Spencer had argued that sociology had a distinct subject matter which was ruled by its own causal laws, independent of those of individual psychology. Durkheim devoted his life to demonstrating that this was indeed the case; that scientific generalizations could be made about social processes which worked independently of the consciousness of men. His study of religion, *The Elementary Forms of the Religious Life* (first published in 1912), is the most influential single work in the sociological and anthropological study of religion.

Though Durkheim's views on religion have been less distorted than those of Max Weber, they have been over-simplified so often as to make a recapitulation of them and of those of his school useful. His main intellectual debts in the study of religion were to De Coulanges, who traced the political and legal structures of the city of classical antiquity back to the religious beliefs and practices which underlay social organization, and, most of all, to Smith's *Religion of the Semites* (1889). On the basis of observations from tribal life in the Near East, Smith claimed that primitive religion was a social entity; men do not choose a set of beliefs which explain things, rather they are born into social positions where certain religious acts are learnt along with everything else. In a tribal society, a private relationship with a god cannot exist. The communal acts of feasting and sacrifice bind men together in a union with the deity which sanctifies the community itself.

Durkheim believed that social control, and social existence itself, could only be based on shared ideas. These ideas, both descriptive and normative, together made up the *conscience collective*. The most fundamental ideas were the categories of space, time, causation, etc., with which we think. Logic is neither universal nor extrinsic, but created and reinforced in each society by religious ritual and by myth. In his work with Mauss on primitive classification, Durkheim argued that conceptual ordering systems varied between societies and originated in specific forms of social organization. Because all belief-systems are in part cosmologies, they are religions—or religions are cosmologies. Religion provides us with the "categories of understanding" without which we cannot think. All religions are "systems of ideas which . . . give us a complete representation of the world".

Such an explanation of religion by-passes any discussion of the truth of religious ideas. No human institution, Durkheim argued, could be founded on errors and lies; the strangest myths and rites cannot be attributed to faulty understandings. Religious ideas express and fulfil a social need; consequently, they are no more "unreal" or untrue than any other thinking which is not based directly on sense-data. (It is here that the great strength, and at the same time a weakness, of the functionalist method lies. It is impossible to exaggerate the advances that functionalism made possible when it insisted that all social facts be taken seriously and their explanation looked for in the role they played in the social structure. However bizarre or foolish beliefs or behaviour may seem, unprejudiced examination will usually discover cogent reasons for them. But the explanation can become too easy; odd behaviour can also denote masking ideologies, or automatism in the face of change, or fundamental conflict.)

At first Durkheim argued (1899) that religious beliefs and practices were to be defined by their *obligatory* nature. Law consisted of obligatory practices but not beliefs; scientific beliefs were not obligatory but sensible. (My summary of this early paper, and part of the discussion, is based on Lukes, 1968.) In the *Elementary Forms*, he took the argument considerably further by showing that the compelling force of religion, and its association with the most fundamental forms of thought, comes from its origin in society. The essence of religion lies in the rigid and elementary distinction made in all societies between the profane and the sacred realms; the sacred are "things set apart and forbidden", the object of rites.

Durkheim's conclusions were based on material about the totemic religion of the Australian aborigines which had been appearing in the 1890s. He used the evolutionist argument: if Arunta society was the simplest form known, then its totemic religion must be "the most primitive and simple religion", which would exhibit most clearly the essential features of all religions. (Even at the time at which he wrote, his assumptions were factually wrong; Codrington had described the operation of an even simpler religion, that of *mana*, a belief in impersonal power, in Melanesia; and Goldenweiser objected that totemic religion was not always found in conjunction with totemic taboos, exogamy, and the other features of social organization which Durkheim considered to be essential.) Durkheim argued that totemic religion was directly and obviously related to social organization. Totems symbolize kinship groups, and are particular to them. The totem and what relates to it are sacred. Men and their possessions bear an intimate relation to their totemic emblem; in part they are it, and thus in part divine. Beliefs and rites express the relationship of the group to the sacred, and it is their *collective* nature which distinguishes religion, which is always embodied in a cult or a church, from magic and from science. The divisions and concepts of the sacred world create those of social life; only religion can do this. It is the rite which is the socially important part of religion, and not the theology; Durkheim shared Robertson Smith's view that myths are created to interpret existing rites.

Durkheim went on to argue that collective worship binds men together and "takes them out of themselves". From this union, they derive their strength and confidence. In the case of totemic religion, the division of the natural world into totemic categories provides the aborigine with the concepts of hierarchy, conflict, and order arching above all, by means of which he not only *comprehends* social relationships, but *expresses* them. The compelling force of the categories comes from society; the periodic assemblies for worship both redefine the sacred and the social group, and kindle an energy among the supporters which they sense comes from society. Thus the believer who feels a moral force outside himself, communicating with him and regulating his social relationships, is correct—it is society. (Here Durkheim was drawing on contemporary studies of crowd psychology, except that he considered the "collective effervescence" of crowds to be normal and not pathological.)

Durkheim adopted the by then conventional evolutionary schema of the way religion develops as society increases in size. He argued that as societies become more complex, the individual's experience becomes unique, and increasingly men will create private ideal worlds and religions to embody their experience. Major religions were bound to lose their close connections with individual experience. Though social unity could only be based on a shared religion, since the functions of religion in explaining the real world were being taken over by science, religion could not be revived. Instead, he suggested, the collective symbols which denote existing social groups—flags, charters, the expressive activity at meetings of trade unions— could be used to unify those groups and to reinforce appropriate moral norms. The religions of reason and patriotic cults established after the French Revolution had been attempts to do this, and had transformed secular concepts, such as reason, into sacred ones. But the strength of the cults lay in popular enthusiasm, and when it waned they lost their power to sacralize and unite. There is an important gap in the explanation: how do some religious ideas become embodied in ritual form and retain adherents, whereas others do not? It may also be objected that religious rituals have markedly decreased in modern societies. However, there are very many quasi-secular rituals—civic ceremonies, memorial days, marches and celebrations, degree ceremonies, etc.— where, although there is little or no emphasis of religious ideas, there is a very strong emphasis on defining the social group of the participants and unifying it.

Durkheim was consistent with his general methodological premises in offering a purely social explanation of the nature and functions of religion. The most influential parts of his argument have been the definition of religion by its function, the emphasis on rites and collective acts rather than beliefs, and his demonstration that religion functioned by binding man closer to society, by enabling him to *comprehend* reality and right social relations, *communicate* with other men on a basis of shared concepts, and to *specify* and regulate ideas and social relations so that men perceived them as absolute and obligatory. The commonest criticisms of his work attribute to him views which he did not entirely hold.

The earliest and most persistent criticism is that Durkheim ignores individual religious experience, that because he cannot explain non-institutionalized religion, he cannot account for the rise of new religious leaders. Bergson (1935), for example, divided religion into "static" (or, as he assumed, Durkheimian) and "dynamic" parts; the dynamic part came from the mystical intuitions of the exceptional man, and was the source of all change. It is true that personal and innovatory beliefs are not strongly emphasized in Durkheim's system because he believed that although men, especially in modern societies, would create infinite numbers of private religious worlds, unless these corresponded to the conceptual and existential needs of the society or of a part of it, they would not become general, and so would lack any social effect. He was trying to replace the anti-positivist relativism of Bergson and his school by an explanation of why it is that social relations and fundamental categories are overwhelmingly experienced not as being in flux, but as absolute and unquestionable. Thought creates reality, and it makes a superior reality, which is society. The mythologies which guide us in the social world are produced from within society, but because of this they are absolutely compelling on us. (Durkheim has not really hacked his way out of the relativist wood; to explain why it is that men experience and accept beliefs as true does not demonstrate that they *are* true.)

By defending religion as true and fulfilling an important social need, did Durkheim imply it to be a necessary part of all societies? At times, he argues that the functions which religion performs will be taken over by other institutions, so that in modern societies science will provide the knowledge of the natural world and ultimately of the social world, and morality will be transmitted via education. But he did not work out exactly what would happen to social cohesion in an advanced society, where the coexistence of several religions must mean that religion would unify subgroups rather than society as a whole. Consequently, he has been criticized for assuming that, by examining a small and simple society, he could produce a theory which could also explain how religion functioned in a differentiated society with several specifically religious organizations. We cannot assume that religion is caused in the same way, nor that it fulfils the same functions (Eister, 1957). The identity between religion and cosmology, so characteristic of primitive societies and so confusing to ourselves (for some good examples, see Forde, 1958), is lacking in advanced society where religion is associated largely with morality.

The most forceful criticism of Durkheim has been anthropological, though it is ironic that after condemning for so long his generalizations about religion in all societies on the basis of one society, it is now anthropologists rather than sociologists who are concerned with general theories of myth and ritual. Most of the attack on Durkheim's theory has been on his theory of totemism. Lowie (1924) and Goldenweiser (1917) argued that aborigine society and totemism were not the simplest known social structure and religion, and totemism is not always associated with either social organization or social gatherings. Radcliffe-Brown's re-examination (1952) of Australian totemism corroborated Durkheim's analysis, if not all of his facts, but he considered that totemism was simply too varied, in both its importance, which ranged from the complex social and religious whole of the aborigine to the simple and apparently unimportant symbols of the Iroquois, and in the beliefs and practices it was associated with, to be treated as a whole. Since it seems to serve very different cultural and psychological functions in different societies, it cannot be considered as a single institution (Radcliffe-Brown, 1939). In particular, there is no agreement on why certain objects should be treated as sacred. Forde (1958) and Worsley (1956) show that many religious rituals and classifications are not connected with social relationships but with environmental conditions, such as securing an adequate supply of food. Here totemic rituals merge into the category of magic, since power is attributed to their performance alone. The criticism can be reformulated on a general level; Durkheim's theory of the relationship between religion and other social institutions is generally over-determined. Since he asserted that religious rituals and sacred objects *must* symbolize social relationships, he could offer no proof that they did so (Goody, 1961).

Lévi-Strauss's theory of totemism (1969) is in many ways like that of Durkheim. Human relationships are characterized by symmetry and exchange; totemism is one of the systems by which groupings and oppositions are established in society so that an orderly exchange of goods and women can occur. But whereas Durkheim tried to match beliefs and social groups and described man's view of the natural world as a social creation, Lévi-Strauss saw totemic concepts as an attempt to relate the social to the natural world (R. Robertson, 1970). All forms of belief, not just specifically religious ones, were part of man's attempt to bridge the gulf between nature and culture. Since we see the world by homologies and associations of ideas, totemism is something which is "good to think with".

Despite Durkheim's attacks on the evolutionary sequences— magic, religion, science—of the English anthropologists, in the last section of the *Elementary Forms* he argues that science will develop out of religious cosmologies and succeed them as the mode of integration in advanced society. However, science, lacking both the reinforcing power of a cult and the absolutist status of religious doctrine, is both more flexible, effective as a means for dealing with reality, and is less capable of creating social consensus than religion is. Some authors (Birnbaum and

Lenzer, 1969) believe that Durkheim saw a scientific consensus to be as compelling as a religious one. Whichever view we take, Durkheim still assumed that before the establishment of science as an institution, men thought in a non-scientific way about everything. Thus he was caught once again in the toils of the "pre-logical mentality" issue, which he had tried to avoid by discussing religion not as beliefs but as ritual and its effects.

## 5 FUNCTIONALISM, ANTHROPOLOGISTS AND RELIGION

As more sympathetic observers spent much longer periods of time among primitive peoples, it became evident that although their overall explanations of the natural world might not be scientific, most of their behaviour was governed by a utilitarian outlook. Malinowski, one of the first anthropologists to have lived for a long period in a simple society, argued that, without knowledge based on sound observation and reasoning, men could not have survived or organized a society at all. Religion and magic were not more primitive forms of knowledge but supplements to scientific knowledge; they fulfilled a psychological function. Scientific knowledge could never be wholly adequate; the uncertainty and danger involved in fishing and hunting, the ever-present fear of disease and death, left man aware of his impotence and drove him to create ritual or magical barriers "in those gaps and breaches left in the ever-imperfect wall of culture which he erects between himself and the besetting temptations and dangers of his destiny" (1925). Religion and magic were both responses to emotional stress, but the acts of religion were collective, not ends in themselves but means to an end. Religion has its origins not in society itself, but in the necessity for a stable society to find an answer to men's emotional needs as they realize anew the "conflict between human plans and realities". The most important function of religion is in creating "valuable mental attitudes" in connection with death, for strong personal attachments are broken by death, and only an over-riding assertion of human immortality will enable the bereaved to continue living in society. The ritual connected with death serves to bind together the survivors and to protect them from the meaninglessness which would corrode social life. The other important religious rituals of primitive peoples are similarly concerned with sacralizing the crises of human life. Religion is the most powerful agent of social control not because it derives from society, but because it offers men the answers and the modes of conduct which they need in periods of crisis.

Malinowski's psychological functionalism led him to argue that, although most religion is experienced collectively and concerned with the community, even among primitive peoples some religious experiences are private because they are caused by individual as well as social needs. Religion becomes internalized and is experienced as moral promptings, whereas the euphoria of collective action can often have no religious meaning, but be undertaken in an entirely secular spirit. Not all of society's traditions and myths are sacred, but the most important ones are "the very cement of the social fabric", on which morality and psychological well-being depend. Consequently the anthropologist will find that these, as well as ritual actions, are rigidly enforced.

The most consistent and clear exposition of the functionalist model of society is to be found in the work of Radcliffe-Brown. Malinowski's functionalism relied on postulating that *men* had biological and psychological needs which culture must satisfy for a society to remain stable; Radcliffe-Brown replaced this with a social functionalism in which *societies* themselves were to be treated as organisms, with sets of needs which all stable cultures would have to satisfy. The distinction between Malinowski and Radcliffe-Brown is brought out in their discussions of the functions of religious ritual. Whereas Malinowski thought that ritual functioned to soothe individual anxieties, Radcliffe-Brown thought that the anxiety itself was due to social conditioning; concern and grief are demanded of us at certain social junctures, and ritual is a symbolic method of expressing this. Our anxiety is consequently displaced from the original situation on to our abilities to perform the appropriate rituals, and this results in the large number of "secondary rituals" of purification or expiation which must be carried out when we fail to act correctly (Homans, 1941). (In fact, Gorer's excellent empirical study [1965; and see Aries, 1967] of mourning in modern Britain, where ritual connected with death has become both perfunctory and uncertain, supports both hypotheses. Relatively elaborate mourning rituals do seem to help the grief of the bereaved, but a fixed pattern of behaviour for mourning and treating the bereaved allays the anxieties of those who are not really grieved themselves, but are uncertain about how they should behave.)

By the 1930s, the study of religion in primitive societies had become less general and speculative for several reasons. The call for close and detailed fieldwork to record the structures of rapidly disappearing cultures made the general syntheses, which it was vaguely assumed would follow, seem less urgent, and the material which was being accumulated provided an endless series of counter-examples to all the generalizations which had previously been made. Theories of religious evolution, or of the origins of religion, were replaced first by diffusionism, and then by an ahistorical functionalism. In the general retreat from "speculative history", anthropologists used purely functional explanations to account for the specific form of religious beliefs and rituals as they operated in context. Great stress was put on the unique nature of each society, and the consequent difficulty of generalizing.

The function of religion, as of any other institution, is separate from the formal beliefs of which it is made up and which members of the society can readily explain to strangers. Anthropologists realized the extent of the gulf between the intellectual accounts of societies and the way that life was organized inside them. The gulf led them to restructure their methods, not only of gathering material but of deciding what to look at. The elaborate or bizarre contents of religious beliefs impressed them no longer; the important aspect of religion was the activities it directed, and the functions that they served in defining and unifying various social groups.

Societies, if studied as systems which organized behaviour, rather than as made up of men guided by beliefs, were controlled and bound primarily by kinship systems, and the emphasis in religious activities on rites of passage made religion seem largely subordinate to the needs of kin solidarity. "For the social anthropologist, religion is what religion does" (Evans-Pritchard, 1965).

## 6 RELIGION REDEFINED

The overthrow of intellectualist theories of religion seemed complete. The studies of primitive societies which were being made paid less attention to religious beliefs than formerly, but enough to show that it was wrong to assume that social knowledge could be divided into a practical, universally understandable, sensible sort which men used to think about everyday life, and another realm of thought, general and mystical, which produced the non-rational behaviour known as religious. Not only were many activities that were irrational to the observer—the *potlatch* of the Vancouver Indians, for example—not connected with religious beliefs at all, but religious beliefs often lacked the qualities of universality, generality and ethical content which those from middle-class Protestant or Jewish backgrounds had assumed that they would have. The definition of religion in terms of a feeling—of mystery or awe—put forward by anthropologists following Durkheim or Lowie (1924) was also impossible to maintain. Some peoples threatened or abused their gods when things went wrong, or regarded contact with the supernatural as a most ordinary and commonplace event (Benz, 1959).

It is easy for the observer to infer that people are distinguishing between the natural and the supernatural, but are they? The intellectualist theorists had divided religion from magic by distinguishing between trying to *manipulate* the world by supernatural means, and trying to *commune* with what was outside it. But closer attention to religious rituals and behaviour showed that whilst the custodians of a religious tradition might decry magic, the bulk of their followers were probably using religious rituals in an unintellectual, manipulative, and hence magical, way. To maintain the distinction led to serious distortions—for example, the claims that village Buddhism was "debased", and really represented a survival of animistic or Hindu beliefs, whereas Buddhism was only found among monks (Leach, 1968).

Ultimately, the intellectualist definitions of religion foundered, simply, on the enormous diversity of religion. They were progressively widened until they lost any meaning. The evolutionary theories of religion had been able to cope with the diversity, but they had been demolished because their stages seemed increasingly ethnocentric, or to be analysing primitive religion from too external a stance. Part of the effect of functionalist theory was that religion came to be analysed only in the context in which it was found; comparative analyses of the role of religion in different societies were abandoned for the time being.

# 7 RELIGION AS FUNCTIONAL

The influence of Durkheim and Malinowski on the sociological study of religion has been so fully absorbed that we no longer realize the immense changes that the functionalist viewpoint implied. Usually, we combine the social and structural functionalism of Durkheim and Radcliffe-Brown with the psychological functionalism of Malinowski, and assume that the primary cause and purpose of religion is its *integrative* function for the individual and society. A quick glance at elementary textbooks of sociology shows that the functionalist interpretation of religion is the reigning orthodoxy of Western sociology, even when the author may be doubtful about the applicability of functionalism to other institutions.

For example, a whole generation of sociology students have learnt from Kingsley Davis (*Human Society*, 1949, chapter 19) that all societies need to maintain agreement on ideas and emotions among their members, which is done by deriving them from ultimate ends, which are justified by reference to another world. In particular, Davis explains, certain symbols relating to social groups are made by social training and ritual to appear holy and to represent a supernatural world, and so make the ends and values of the social groups come to have a real and compelling hold upon their members. And so "religion makes a unique and indispensable contribution to social integration". In addition to this, the core function, it compensates the individual for inevitable frustration and sorrow by means of the release and solace of ritual, and the promise of future happiness. These functions of religion cannot be replaced by the rational explanations of science, for scientific explanations cannot define ultimate ends. Secularization can consequently result only in social disorganization. (Davis thought that such disorganization would lead to the formation of new religious sects, which would again reinforce unifying beliefs.)

Talcott Parsons has developed an even more widely influential functionalist model, which is ultimately rather similar to that of Davis. He criticizes the *Elementary Forms*, Durkheim's most functionalist and idealist work, as still being too positivist. He has reformulated the Durkheimian theory of religion on a more abstract and idealist model. Parsons considers that religious symbolism is not a representation of society or of empirical reality in any form, but that it refers to aspects of significant human experience which are outside the range of scientific understanding. Religion, because it is the only method of grasping the non-empirical, is a necessary basis for human action. Since the ultimate values which religion represents determine social action, religion is not a social phenomenon; rather, "society is a religious phenomenon".

For an analysis of which significant experiences lay outside scientific understanding, Parsons, and most recent American sociology, has turned to Weber. The satisfactions which the individual seeks are on the level of *meaning*. If suffering, injustice, etc., can be not solaced but *comprehended*, our reactions to it can be made part of a system of experience which enables us to express our sufferings to our fellow men and to receive comfort from them. On the cultural level, the problems recur in a cognitive form—why?—and must be answered if the moral standards of the society are not to be weakened. But Parsons has wrongly assumed that ultimate problems, such as death and pain, come from outside society. Not only does scientific knowledge affect the nature of the problem, and consequently the immediacy with which we feel it, but the growth of "scientism" is leading to a general optimistic conviction that science can ultimately solve the problem, which leads to a devaluing of religion even before this happens (Robertson, 1970; Parsons himself approaches this view in his discussion of death, 1963b). By trying to avoid the reduction of religion to social factors, Parsons seems to have reduced it to psychological ones—the need for understanding, and so on. One of the greatest strengths of Durkheim's model was the focus on variations in religious belief and their relation to different societies. Because Parsons takes the non-empirical and extra-scientific aspect of existence as fixed and given, he cannot explain changes in religious belief except in terms of a generally increasing sophistication, abstraction and morality.

The difficulties connected with functionalist explanations have often been noted, but the study of *religion* inside a functionalist framework has perhaps been more successful than that of any other social institution, and the schema is falling from favour less because it is inadequate in explaining religion than because functionalism as a general method has been devalued. The anthropological study of religion, in particular, has been living on the "conceptual capital" of functionalism (Geertz,

1966, 1968). The reasons for the decline of functionalism can be quickly listed: the impossibility of defining specifically enough the societal needs which must be met (particularly important in the case of religion, since many societies do seem to manage without a religion in the conventional sense); logical circularities, such as the explanation of institutions by functions and functions by institutions; the existence of much which can be seen only as entirely dysfunctional, and the failure to look at the causes of this; the implicit conservatism and static nature of the model, which make it especially difficult to apply to complex societies with internal conflicts and fast rates of growth; the failure to specify causal factors. Although religion undoubtedly does reinforce common values, the real task is to show how it actually does it, and why it is so effective.

A more important objection is that the "high-level values" which functionalists assume only religion can provide may not be necessary for social cohesion. Much—perhaps all—can be achieved by rigorous socialization and clear social expectations, which will produce "unselfish" behaviour without any underlying cosmic justification. (For example, study of professionalism as a work ethic which controls expectations and behaviour demonstrates the power of very limited, low-level ideologies. There is another powerful set concerned with not grumbling, taking it, bearing up.) This point will often be returned to in the course of this book, because it is an important qualification to all statements about the role of general values in society. When Parsons attempts to describe the general values of American society, he does so in such a general way that the situational exigencies which actually govern behaviour obviously could not be derived from his general values. Sometimes, beliefs are seen as being specific and concrete enough to be guides to action, and sometimes they are seen as general enough to provide unifying structures and to survive the constant small changes in patterns of everyday behaviour which occur in modern societies. Over time, we see clear and powerful organizing concepts— "the great chain of Being", "one nation under God", "the survival of the fittest"—come into existence, and other beliefs, both more and less general, have to be accommodated to them. But these powerful concepts are not necessarily extra-societal, ethical, or religious.

It is commonly observed that sets of beliefs which are often referred to and scrupulously obeyed may be relatively detached from the "grand design" of beliefs about a culture; for example, beliefs about sorcery, the causes of tuberculosis or about the relations between the sexes. A belief may be very *general* and yet not influential.

Another set of difficulties in the functional explanation of beliefs centres on the substitutes in secular societies for religion. Most functionalists accept that modern societies are less "religious" in some sense, and assume either that secular ideologies have replaced religion, or that only those who need solace and meaning acutely now need to seek religion. But religion is not a passive factor in the process. If the society has been so far divided that no set of common values can regulate relations between groups of men with different interests and experience, religious institutions may have exacerbated this by identifying themselves with one position rather than another, *causing* secularization because they come to be attacked as merely justifying the position of one social group. Religion may become attached to certain secular concepts, as for example in late nineteenth-century England it came to denote the crucially important social category of the "respectable", a concept derived from ordinary routines of behaviour but which was generalized to carry a far wider meaning.

Some attempts have been made at a stringent comparative analysis of the functions of religion. W. J. Goode's (1951) comparison of material on the role of religion from five societies was a sophisticated exercise, and his results did bear out functionalist assertions about the role of religion. It did tend to regulate and limit economic production, support the existing political system by endowing its agents with symbolic powers, and parallel the relationships and sanctions of the kinship system. But Goode insists on the limited applicability of his findings; religion acts to integrate a society by restraining self-interest, but it can be dysfunctional when in doing this it inhibits technical or economic innovation or divides loyalties. So the greater economic dynamism of Western society and its more rapid rate of change means that conclusions drawn from the study of the functions of religion in simple societies cannot be extended to it. Religion is too intertwined with other forces and motives, too varying in its operations in a complex society, for it to be considered as an independent factor there. (One might add, that this seems likely to be true of primitive society as well.) Integration is not always positively functional; a disruptive force in the present may become the basis of future stability.

Some of the earliest attempts at systematic inter-societal comparisons had used statistical pairings of the rates of occurrence of various beliefs and institutions in an attempt to determine the relationships between religious beliefs and social forms. The method was criticized by both functionalists and historicists because of the falsification which was inherent in taking a cultural item which can be indexed, for example monotheism, from its context, and comparing it with other beliefs and institutions similarly divorced from context. But unless we abandon the search for universal sociological theories, comparisons of this general kind must be made. Swanson (1960), for example, tried to test Durkheim's theories on the relationship between social structure and religious concepts by comparing the form of the supernatural and of the polity in a large number of societies. His results are frequently statistically significant, but sometimes hard to interpret—for example, the association of *monotheism* with a complex ruling *group*. But the strong associations which he found between supernatural sanctions for morality and the presence of social classes and other institutions which denote permanent inequalities of wealth and power, do point to a functionalist (and Marxist) conclusion about the role of religion as legitimating and enforcing existing social divisions.

The safest conclusion about the value of the functionalist approach is that it varies; it is more applicable, both to aspects of modern America and to simple societies, than it is to the older, more openly divided societies of Europe, or to many rapidly modernizing nations, where the complex of beliefs and attitudes which the traditional religion supports are those which the political modernizers are trying to change. Demerath (1965) suggests that functionalism is a suitable model for the analysis of middle-class religion in the United States, but that working-class sectarianism is better explained by a Marxist model. But if we try to specify his theory more closely, we can see that its truth depends on the aspect of the individual for which religion is said to be functional (his social integration; to subgroup or society; tension-release; or explanation of and compensation for lack of worldly success) and on what level of society we are considering social integration. The Marxist "opiate" theory entails in any case that religion is highly functional for social stability in that it prevents political or economic revolt among the workers; Demerath has in mind a more optimal model of society, in which working class sectarianism is dysfunctional because it prevents able individuals from accepting the ruling values of the society and rising within it. Demerath is using the psychological and cognitive functionalism of Parsons, and it is true that many middle-class Americans, who have lost traditional ties and have no strong personal links, do resort to religion quite explicitly for social contacts, psychological help, and "meaning".

A final weakness in explaining religion in terms of function is that explanations of the rise of new religious groups are consequently bound to become *ad hoc*. For example, Wallace (1956, 1966) claims that all new religions are revitalization movements, which arise when their predecessors have lost the power to satisfy the needs of new social groups. Others (for example, Catton, 1957; Lang and Lang, 1960) explain new religious groups or revivals purely in terms of psychological needs. But until the essential needs of a society or an individual can be exactly specified beforehand, such explanations can never be more than *ex post* descriptions. A more sophisticated version of these theories employs deprivation, or relative deprivation, as the explanation of new religions (see next chapter). But these theories are subject to the same disadvantages as other functionalist explanations. Their core is the distinction between objective conditions of deprivation and feelings of deprivation, the latter being those which find an outlet in new social, political or religious allegiances. But since we cannot specify a "reasonable" level of rewards (Durkheim's original definition of anomie was, after all, the tendency of men in non-traditional societies to infinitely broaden their range of comparisons, and so find their wants becoming insatiable), nor can we find many groups in modern societies which do *not* believe that they are being unjustly deprived in some way, it is again impossible to avoid the theory becoming an *ex post* explanation (Aberle, 1962).

Whilst the difficulty of reformulating functionalist theories of religion as predictive or falsifiable statements has been widely recognized, such theories have become the dominant, if not the only, perspective in the sociology of religion. That men have a psychological need for certainty, identity and socially confirmed ideals, and that religion can apparently satisfy this need for many of them, is indisputable. The sociological explanation must go beyond this, but it must also be rooted in it. Considerable amounts of research find that the intensity and variation between groups of religious beliefs is much as the functionalist would expect. In this respect, there is a continuous intellectual tradition from Hume to Parsons in the explanation of religion, in that although the explanation may refer to the links between particular religions and social structure, its implicit reference is always to the needs which all religions satisfy for individual human beings.

# CHAPTER III

# Max Weber and Religion as Meaning

Outside the protean outlines of the structural-functional approach to the sociology of religion, very little remains. But if the evidence is reviewed from a different angle, a different but more fragmentary pattern of inquiry can be discovered, stemming from Karl Marx and Max Weber. They were alike in viewing religion subjectively. They took religion to be what the men in each society said it was; consequently both thought that future industrial society would be increasingly irreligious, and both avoided the tortuous redefinitions of the central values of communist and other secular societies as "religious". They were interested in historical religions and their relations with different groups in complex societies, rather than in the role of religion in society in general.

Weber and Marx defined religion as what the religious say religion is; and most men think of religion as being about beliefs, not behaviour. Weber and Marx emphasized the central role of belief and *meaning* in religion and society. Religion is important because it causes men to see things in a certain way and to establish certain goals and values; sociologists and historians discover these by subjective identification. Once we operate with a historical definition of religion, rather than with a constructed definition which already gives it a specific role in the social structure, the relationship between religion and other social institutions becomes problematic.

Both Marx and Weber were concerned with the varying relationship between religion and political and economic institutions, and both emphasized that the relationship was often one of conflict, tension, or gross maladaptation. Both authors take the general framework of religious beliefs as given; from then on, by causal and historical methods, they show how religious ideas respond to social pressures and, in turn, theologies independently exert pressure on individuals. Weber has generally been credited with initiating sociological research on these themes, and many sociologists would consider an extension of his ideas as the most hopeful future for the sociology of religion (see, for example, Yinger, 1957; Demerath and Hammond, 1969).

## 1 KARL MARX

Marx was less interested in religion than in other social institutions, and his views on it were not very different from those of other contemporary radicals. His widespread influence has come about because those who accept his views on ideology extend them to the analysis of religion. To him religion was made by man and corresponded to nothing eternal or super-empirical; it was only a sign of the alienation of man in a society which oppressed and dehumanized him, and in which religion was therefore "the sigh of the oppressed creature, the heart of a heartless world, the spirit of a spiritless situation". A liberated man would feel no need of metaphysical explanation. His early work was concerned with the political and economic effects of religion as a means of intellectual and moral control. The ambiguity in the early Marx caused by his arguing both from specific social circumstances and from the essential nature of man is equally present in his views on religion. Man is religious because of his "priestly nature", but at other times he is religious solely because of his experiences in specific and doomed kinds of society. At one point, he suggests that Protestantism is a more effective form of repression than any previous religion, because authority is internalized. The punishing deity has moved inside man; he is controlled from within (1963).

Marx regarded religion as all but dead, and intellectual attacks on it as useless; it would only change with changes in the relations of production, and consequently, like antisemitism, would be defeated by the birth of a new social and economic order. It was "true", in the sense that it accurately embodied the feelings of men in a world which was wrong. (Christianity, with its doctrines of an abstract and a sinful man, suited an alienated and enslaved world the best; earlier religions had reflected the bond which still existed between men and nature.)

Men at home in the world used no religion. The rising bourgeoisie of France and England were objective and materialist
when they were attacking reactionary and feudal regimes.
Their support of materialist philosophy and the natural sciences
would have led them ultimately to scientific socialism, but when
they attained domination and the class antagonism between
them and the proletariat became acute, they renounced free
thinking and began to use religion as an opiate for the masses
(Marx and Engels, 1957). Religion not only reflected the suffering of the proletariat, but offered a fantasy escape from it; the
reward in heaven was to compensate the poor for the nature of
their life on earth. Even the fantasy was marked by the society
in which it had arisen; in capitalist England, theology was the
moral economy of the distribution of heavenly rewards (Birnbaum and Lenzer, 1969).

Marx's views on religion have never been accepted by bourgeois sociologists. Their very simplicity, and their "old-
fashioned" mixture of the theme of "reason and science against
superstition" with speculations on the "origins of religion", tell
against them. The issues Marx raised were extended, challenged
and refined by Max Weber. But many of the empirical studies
of the operation of religious institutions in modern societies
suggest that they do—or rather did—fulfil the role Marx
claimed for them, that of adjusting people to a social order from
which their material gains are so small that a political, even a
revolutionary, response would seem to be the only reasonable
alternative. Many manufacturers have explicitly supported
religion as a means of subjugating the masses, and keeping them
sober and working, before the era of high mass consumption
lent other attractions to the industrial order. (See Pope, 1942;
MacIntyre, 1967; Underwood, 1957; Yinger, 1946. Tressell
stressed this from his observations of the Hastings labourers in
*The Ragged Trousered Philanthropists*.) Whether religion acted to
keep the poor of industrializing Britain quiescent or not, it
was certainly widely assumed that it did by both radicals and
conservatives.

The exact nature of the connections between established
churches and political and economic interests has never been
properly studied, but there can be no doubt that influence is
exerted by members of secular élites on churches to control their
most outspokenly liberal and radical members and to support

the *status quo*. The pressure will vary according to how much influence the churches are felt to exert. The Catholic church, in South America in particular, is currently accused by radicals among both laity and clergy of supporting the established order, and the worker-priest experiment involved at one level a conflict between anti-clerical priests and an anti-communist Vatican (De Kadt, 1970; Poulat, 1959). The fact that religion tends to support the *status quo* on the ideational level has diverted attention from the study of the equally important material constraints on religious institutions.

Although it is easy to show in a general way that religious beliefs reflect social relationships, few scholars in this tradition have attempted a more subtle analysis. In particular, a crude materialism obscures both the elaborate interplay between organizational forms, theology and the world-view or views of the members of a church, and also the internal development of theology in relationship to other *ideas*. An important exception is the excellent study by Goldmann (1964) of the growth of rationalist thought in seventeenth- and eighteenth-century France, when theological and social trends intersected at a point at which the sacred became devoid of concern for men. The god of Thomist theology, miraculously intervening in the natural world, accessible by faith rather than by reason, had corresponded to the affective bonds of a stable community. The growth of capitalism, which altered the relationship between men, and relied for its rationale on the concept of the solitary, contract-making individual interacting with others on the basis of reason, led to changes in both science and theology which made the universe come to seem infinite and self-governing, with a god who neither interfered with nor was accessible to men. He had no personal reality.

The Marxist influence on the study of the origins of new religious movements has been rather more fruitful. It was Engels who elaborated on the role of new religions as precursors of revolutionary social change, or (as with the peasant war in Germany) millenarian movements which were forms of attack on a social order which was largely controlled and justified by religious institutions (Marx and Engels, 1957; see also Birnbaum and Lenzer, 1969). A millenarian movement, coming from those ill-used by society, often expresses ideas which will be taken up at a later stage by political institutions; it is pre-political. A series of studies have been conducted on this topic, particularly in connection with the ghost-dance of the American Indians and the "cargo" cults of Melanesia and South America, in which the revolt against the oppressor takes a religious form (Worsley, 1957; Lawrence, 1964; Burridge, 1960; see also Talmon, 1962, and Lanternari, 1963). Kautsky (1925) had applied the analysis to Christianity; Cohn (1957) and other more conservative historians are likely to see the movements as proto-fascist rather than proto-communist.

## 2 MAX WEBER

The direct influence of Marxist ideas on the sociology of religion has been slight, because the questions which they raised were taken over as the central focus of the work of Max Weber. It is his presentation of the issues which has been the prism by which the Marxist tradition has been refracted. (See R. Robertson, 1970; for a general account of the theory, T. Parsons, 1937; for an account of the empirical research, Bendix, 1960.) The simplest way of characterizing the points disputed between them is to say that Marx saw history as ultimately determined by material or technological factors, whereas Weber saw it as the working-out of the forces of great men and ideas; even though this ignores statements by both of them denying that they held such positions. Weber, as a pessimistic liberal, disagreed with Marx fundamentally in that he viewed religion as answering significant problems of meaning. He insisted that social behaviour—"action"—could only be understood from the viewpoint of the individual actor. At this level, we all experience the drive for an answer to problems which we know have no scientific or causal-historical answer—"why must there be suffering?" as opposed to "why is he feeling pain?" Religion is the answer to such problems. Marx's view was that in a better society, such problems would be greatly reduced, and would need and could expect no answer. Weber was less optimistic. He considered that religious solutions were no longer being accepted by intellectuals because they were too out of keeping with other kinds of knowledge, but he feared the effects that this might have on man's attachment to society and obedience to group norms. Our attitude to opiates must depend on whether we think the pain is bearable or curable.

On the general level, the issue raised is central to ideological debate in sociology between Marxists and Parsonians. If religion provides common values for a society, which men accept, social order can be achieved in large part by ideational rather than coercive or remunerative means. Many sociologists, including Weber, believe that a society without consistent values could not survive. But the growth of more skilled and efficient methods of control, the mass media among them, used by unpopular but apparently secure governments, has led some Marxist sociologists to a more radical conclusion. Perhaps societies can survive without religion or common higher-order values by means of a judicious mixture of bread and circuses and coercion. Both materialists and neo-idealists hedge their bets by introducing an indefinite time-period.

To study religious belief from the viewpoint of the individual actor raises the question of its intelligibility to the observer, and hence of its rationality. Weber treated this by delineating kinds of rationality—that governed by tradition, that where both means and ends are rationally chosen, that where rational means are adopted to reach a given end, and that which is rational on the affectual level. Religious belief or action can be rational in either the first or the last two senses. Much confusion has been caused by his statement that the Protestantism of the early entrepreneur involved a rational approach to the world, because he failed to see that the rationality of the acts of methodical accumulation and investment which he described was context-dependent. Even in industrial society, economic conditions have changed, so that hard work and thrift have sometimes become irrational themselves. Farmers in the American Midwest who believed strongly in the value of hard work, individualism and independence, and the prevention of illness by willpower, were puritans in an economic environment no longer favourable to them. Their dislike of debt led them to try to pay off mortgages when the funds could have been more profitably invested in farm machinery. Their use of machinery was not economically rational, because their this-worldly asceticism made them too readily prepared to work very long hours (Goldstein and Eichhorn, 1961).

The opposite position is that where apparently irrational spending might in context be perfectly rational. Burmese peasants spend money lavishly on Buddhist temples and religious feasts while living poorly themselves and never saving, and this behaviour is often taken to be due to Buddhist teachings, with their negative attitude to worldly possessions and striving. Spiro (1966b) considers that Buddhists *do* strongly desire wealth, luxury and enjoyment, but believe that one's future life is determined by the extent of charitable action in this life. Not only is lavish religious spending a sound financial investment in a future life, it is a source of social prestige. To save or invest money otherwise is risky, because of a combination of low income, endemic political and economic disturbance, and periodic government confiscation of private funds. The Burmese can control their future lives better than their future in this life; lavish spending on pious objects demonstrates a concern for the future over a far longer term than Westerners achieve. But Weber would argue that however rational their actions might be in their own terms, they do not form the basis for an economically rational society. But perhaps the dichotomy is misleading anyway.

## 3 THE PROTESTANT ETHIC

The question of the contribution of religion to economic action has been hotly debated in the context of Weber's *The Protestant Ethic and the Spirit of Capitalism,* which must be one of the most misinterpreted books ever written. (See accounts of the debate in Fischoff, 1944; Samuelsson, 1961; Fanfani, 1935; Green, 1959.) This is partly because the work is arranged as a series of rather disjointed observations about theologians and entrepreneurs in America, England and Germany between the sixteenth century and Weber's own lifetime. He begins with the observation that the pursuit of gain is found in all societies; whereas capitalism is the rational pursuit of profit on investments, which relies on a rational organization of free markets, formally free labour, and scrupulous contractual relationships. Despite the economic and scientific achievements of Oriental civilizations, free-market organization had only ever occurred in the West. Despite the ingenuity and capitalist instincts of individual Jewish and Catholic merchants, a capitalist *society,* which could validate and encourage the pursuit of gain, could only emerge with Protestantism. In Germany, the Netherlands, England and New England, the dominant religions were Calvinist at the time when capitalism was developed; these societies had become not less but *more* influenced by religion after the Reformation. Calvinism was infinitely burdensome to the sincere believer, because it taught that men exist only for the sake of an inscrutable god, who is free to do with them what he wills. Very few inherit eternal life, and this does not depend on their actions, but is eternally fixed. Even belonging to the true church is no guarantee of being among the elect.

Weber considered that these doctrines had two effects on their holders. They cut off the customary avenues of pleasure and escape; friends, family, sensuous pleasure, spending on God's churches, winning favour through helping the poor, humanist learning—all were distractions. Magical means to salvation—prayer, confession, ritual—were useless. The puritan saved money because he could not spend it. He was torn away from his traditional obligations to kin and to society, and told that he was best able to promote God's will by labour in his chosen calling. For Calvin there was no guarantee or certainty of grace or salvation, but this doctrine was psychologically intolerable; the Pietists and Lutherans had adopted the view that grace lay in faith or the sacraments. Among Calvinists, to doubt one's salvation was a sign of insufficient faith, and hard work was recommended as a means of overcoming such anxiety. Thus only a planned life of this-worldly asceticism could satisfy the Presbyterians, Methodists, Quakers and Baptists who were influenced by Calvinist doctrines, and the wealth that resulted became reinterpreted by them as a sign of God's favour. But the juggernaut lost its transcendental justification with the passing of time; by Franklin's time, its religious basis had withered away. We are now forced to work by a machine-dominated civilization, and wealth has become an end in itself, stripped of all ethical or spiritual meaning.

As a case-study of the influence of religious ideas on behaviour, the *Protestant Ethic* is rather ambiguous. Weber argued that the effects of the theological ideas were limited in time. Therefore, criticisms of Weber which allege that we are now hard-working, but not devout Protestants, are misconceived. So, too, are accounts of hard-working non-Protestants before the Reformation; to Weber these were pariah-capitalists, those who could not sufficiently dominate a political structure for their hard work to become the norm for a society. Similarly, it is irrelevant to cite early puritan divines who regarded earthly activity as vain. The value of Weber's work is that it demon-

strates how beliefs become altered by the pressure of social and
psychological forces. Such unintended consequences have
created a set of moral responses far from the original dogma,
and these have economic effects.

The main attacks on the Weberian thesis have been from
left-wing critics of capitalism (such as Tawney, 1927; Macpherson, 1962; and H. M. Robertson, 1933) who argue plausibly that the entrepreneurs altered the emphasis of Calvinism
as a religious justification for their economic individualism.
They argue that society had already changed radically before
the rise of Calvinism. New economic opportunities, new techno-
logies, a new class, and consequently a new view of society and
obligations to one's fellow men, had already created the
capitalist impulse. Weber did overemphasize the importance of
ideas on men's behaviour; one puzzling omission from his
theory is any explanation of why, if Calvinism offered its
original adherents so little, they came to believe in it. We do
not know how *strongly* the entrepreneurs held religious beliefs;
the apologists and theologians who wrote about them undoubtedly felt more strongly than the rest of the population. Weber
denied that Calvinists were innovators just because they were in
a religious minority, but the theory of marginal man as striver
and as capitalist has had many supporters.

Perhaps the most important critique of Weber is that which
accepts the association of Calvinism with capitalism, but denies
that the connection is causal. There are many alternative
possibilities—that Calvinism is the rationalization of capitalism;
that the development of the scientific world-view produced
them both; that religious freedom or the break-up of the
church's control over economic life was the cause of both; that
societies with political decentralization produced both Protestantism and capitalism (Swanson, 1967; Samuelsson, 1961).
Even if we accept that it was Protestantism which produced
capitalism, the connection might not be Calvinism's this-
worldly asceticism and emphasis on labouring at one's chosen
calling. (Means [1966] suggests increased literacy, the growth of
the natural sciences, or laissez-faire, which are also associated
with all Protestantism.) Powerful qualifications have been
made as a result of the study of the religion of the Tokugawa in
developing Japan (Bellah, 1957); of communism and nationalism as forces for modernization (Apter, 1963; Bellah, 1958; von

der Mehden, 1968); and of the effect of the Enlightenment and
the new science of political economy on late seventeenth-
century Europe (Samuelsson, 1961; Bryson, 1945). All these
intellectual and political movements broke up traditional social
orders which had been ruled by centralized governments in
which the interests of industrialists were not represented. By
weakening family and community ties, they released modernizing forces, creating, in the West at least, a different, inner-
directed and achievement-oriented kind of man. Some students
of modernization (Lüethy, 1964) argue that Protestantism is
important because of its effects on politics in the transition to
liberal democratic societies and that these are the effects which
allow free-enterprise economies to develop (see the discussion
in R. Robertson, 1970). The effect of Protestantism on
economic development can be attributed either to its doctrines
concerning the individual as sole authority, or to the way it
detaches men from traditional bonds, or to the fact that Protestantism tends to fission, and consequently a Protestant society
has more than one church and control is decentralized. Eisenstadt (1968) argues that Protestantism is a modernizing
influence only if it does not become so dominant as to be
incorporated in the state.

Weber undertook his later studies of religion in China, India
and ancient Israel in order to establish that such societies,
although possessing many economic and social preconditions
which might have led them to become capitalist, lacked the
essential ideological and theological ingredients. Both his
methodology and his findings have been debated at length.
The "Weberian thesis", in the crude form in which it has been
understood, has on the whole been rejected, both as a historical
account of what happened in industrializing societies and as an
explanation of why other societies did not or do not modernize.
However, the central Weberian statement—that men's actions
are to be understood in terms of their own goals and the means
which appear to them to be available—is increasingly widely
accepted. His argument means that the knowledge and
resources which are available to any society are less important
for social change than the structure of motives and the context
in which the knowledge is interpreted. For example, students
of the advanced scientific cultures of both ancient China and
India are inclined to agree that it was because science was the

province of the literati that it was never used for technical or industrial purposes. Needham argues that the Buddhist concept of *maya*, the insubstantial nature of the only apparently real world, powerfully inhibited the development of the applied aspects of Chinese scientific thought. The eventual acceptance of Western science in such societies is probably not so much because the thought-world of their members has changed so that they now see such knowledge as "true", but because some have come to admire or fear Western culture as a whole. Western technological achievements are based on science, and science is accepted *because* of this, not because it now seems intuitively true.

(There is an interesting study by Hsu [1952] of which people resorted to scientific, magical or religious means of control of an epidemic in a small town in China. Those who accepted inoculation were not the most educated, but those most closely in contact with, or economically dependent on, Westerners; the transmission of modernism depends not on intellectual but on personal links.)

## 4 RELIGION AND SOCIAL GROUPS

The other aspect of Weber's concern with the relationship between beliefs and action was his study of religious leaders and their social effects. Of the three Weberian types of authority, only the charismatic is capable of engendering major social change. Since charismatic leaders are often religious ones, new religious movements are a permanent potential for major change. The prophet can define a new way of life as the legitimate one, and the strength of his followers' commitment to him can lead them to break away from their previous frames of reference and adopt new goals and means. The sociologist must then study the two general variables which determine how the views of an individual come to affect social processes. Which groups in society will they appeal to, and why? And what form will the organization which comes to embody them take?

These two questions have been the basis of perhaps the most fruitful and interesting research in the sociology of religion. The many studies which have been made of small religious groups in Western societies and the kinds of members that they attract have demonstrated that there are characteristic connections between different levels of education and wealth, and different kinds of religious organization and theology. It is this approach to religion which has been the most fruitful in the study of modern societies; the attempts, originating with Durkheim, to trace religious beliefs or practices to the general character of social groupings or relationships founder on the enormous *variations* in experience, and consequently in perceptions, between members of a large and differentiated society. In such societies, social classes are major determinants of "life-chances", of social experience, and consequently different religious groups have different class profiles.

Weber described new religions as always appealing strongly to urban artisans and small-scale merchants (called "lower middle class" in the English translation), rather than to the wealthy or to peasants still bounded by traditional ties and magical routines. The very poorest, who see their lives as dependent on exterior social forces rather than their own efforts, will be influenced by revolutionary or communitarian doctrines, and thus susceptible to magical or emotional religious appeals. The privileged require a religion which legitimates their life-pattern and enhances their *being*; the underprivileged seek a religion which promises that one day they will become something. "... every need for salvation is an expression of some distress ..." (Weber, 1965). In the Judaeo-Christian religions, *ressentiment*, an expression of a desire for vengeance and a justification of suffering as meritorious, appears for the first time. But the need for salvation and ethical religion is shaped not only by social circumstances, but by the particular needs of intellectuals from the privileged classes (among whom Weber included priests). The intellectual's search for salvation is based on an inner need; as his knowledge demystifies the world for him, he searches for a meaningful order in it.

## 5 RELATIVE DEPRIVATION

In this way, Weber anticipated the development of the concept of relative deprivation. Relative deprivation was first used to explain why levels of morale among soldiers did not seem to be correlated with the objective unpleasantness of their conditions. It has been very widely used as a mechanism to relate together the position of a group in society and their resort to new movements—religious, political, economic. It is a truism that the least privileged are more acquiescent in their lot than those who have rather more, and it is evident that we must look at men's *expectations*, or the gap between how much they have and how much they expect to have or consider that they should have.

Glock (1964) has used the concept of the subjective gap to explain the *origin* of religious sects among certain groups, whose members *feel* various kinds of deprivation by comparison with their internalized standards or their reference groups. Deprivation, according to Glock, exists in five forms, but each new religious group is likely to be based on more than one form of deprivation. Men can feel themselves to be deficient in economic or social position, health, a justifying value-system or personal philosophy. Aberle (1962) has an alternative list of things one can feel deprived of: possessions, status, desirable behaviour, and total worth. Religious solutions are said by Glock to be resorted to where the deprived are mistaken about the nature of their deprivation, or where they feel that they lack the power to remedy it, but they can only assuage the feeling of deprivation, rather than remove its causes.

This sort of interpretation of the origins of new religions has been very common; many, including Marx, have used it unconsciously and unsystematically. It views religion as consisting essentially of *meaning*; this is its function for believers. It is difficult to avoid the assumption that religion is an inefficient psychological compensation for deprivations which could be removed permanently by political or economic changes, and many authors would not wish to do so. Thus some (Hobsbawm, 1959; Lawrence, 1964; Worsley, 1957; and see discussion in Talmon, 1962) have followed Engels in analysing various new religious movements as *pre-political*. It is possible, for example, to explain the constant stream of new religious movements originating among the poor in America as due to their lack of effective political outlets; in England, by contrast, after the rise of Methodism deprivation found effective political channels, and there have been no new working-class sects of any size. Although it is true that many new religious movements have preceded economic or political mobilization among the same group of people, it is not clear that, for the individuals concerned, religion must fulfil the same functions as secular movements, nor that religion is always less efficacious in ending deprivation. Essien-Udom (1962), for example, thinks that the

*[handwritten margin note: Meaning]*

situation of the American Negro is one in which he can achieve little by political or economic action, but where the symbolic restitutions offered by the Black Muslim movement can provide what he most badly needs. And some of the commonest and bitterest forms of deprivation—old age, ill health, loneliness, various kinds of personal stigma—can be alleviated by religious means, but not always by political or economic ones.

The theory of relative deprivation resembles that of evolution by natural selection in that it is essentially a convincing narrative rather than a testable proposition. Since probably all men feel some degree of deprivation about something, and the theory refers not to their objective situation but to how they feel, it is an *ex post* explanation. It would be possible to avoid this if we could predict that one type of deprivation would always result in a distinct response, or predict the necessary level of deprivation which would produce a movement (Aberle, 1962). But empirical attempts to distinguish between actual and felt deprivation show the difficulties. Some groups and their reference groups are more distinct than others. The Black Muslims, for example, had a distinct ideology which appealed to a defined group which undoubtedly both was and felt deprived. But many religious and social movements are very diffuse, in both the explanations and the compensations which they offer for evil and injustice, and consequently those they appeal to are not all deprived in the same way. Such movements may, by their very generality, attract members with a wide range of dissatisfactions, though they may not keep them all for long.

It is obvious that situational factors are all-important in determining whether movements will be formed. Do those deprived in the same way have any contact with each other? Do they see themselves as a group? What range of social response is open to them? To answer such questions further, we must know more about how individuals come to join religious groups, to which very little careful attention has been given. Lofland (1966; and Lofland and Stark, 1965) has outlined an approach similar to Smelser's value-added theory of social change. The person who joins a minority religious or political movement is exchanging the majority perspective for a minority one, and for him to do so not only must the movement build up ideological and organizational defences against the outside world, but the prospective member must possess certain

*[handwritten margin note: Groups / World view ↓]*

characteristics which have predisposed him to respond to his
initial contact with the movement.

One of the limitations of the existing work on why people join
new movements is that it has been concerned with movements
which are relatively small and distinct, and hence extremist in
religious or political terms. This has led researchers to cate-
gorize those who join such groups as "seekers"—that is,
sufferers from psychological malaise, searchers for security
rather than reality. Generalized "tension" can be solved in
three institutionalized ways in modern society: the psychiatric,
the political, and the religious. Social scientists are strongly
prejudiced in favour of the first two, and especially the first, as
"correct" and commonsense solutions. Lofland (1966) reminds
us that, from the point of view of the *actor*, a deviant (in this
context, religious) perspective frequently explains events better
than a "commonsense" one. In particular, the general circumstances of the poor and uneducated make them responsive to
very different kinds of explanation, especially religious ones,
from those which would appeal to the sociologist. Once they
have contacted the religious movement, a series of situational
contingencies—having reached a block to, or the end of an old
line of action, losing affective bonds with outsiders and developing or possessing them with members, intensive contact with
insiders—may draw new members in and make the costs of
leaving the movement increasingly high (Festinger *et al.*, 1956;
Lofland and Stark, 1965).

A study of social movements in late nineteenth-century
England (Budd, 1973) suggests that "seekers" do not move
randomly between religious and political movements, but
follow definite paths or circuits, defined by a common theme or
obsession; anti-cruelty, asceticism, anti-collectivism, are among
many possible themes. More research on changes in political
and religious beliefs and allegiances, and how they are related,
would be invaluable. (Pickering [1961] documented shifts in
religious membership in two English industrial towns, showing
how they formed a cycle, which might have been linked with
social mobility, as movement between denominations is in the
United States.)

## 6 MILLENARIANISM AND SYNCRETISM

One consequence of the contact and invasion by members of industrial societies of the more primitive societies of North and South America, Africa and Melanesia, has been the formation of new religions among the subject peoples (see Lanternari, 1963, for bibliography). Such religious movements are characteristically millennial—that is, they expect "imminent, total, this-worldly collective salvation" for their people (Talmon, 1962). They occur not only in simple societies affected by advanced ones, but also among the poor in advanced societies, where they are often based on eschatological passages in the Bible. (B. R. Wilson [1959a] calls them "revolutionary" sects—for example, Jehovah's Witnesses, Seventh Day Adventists, and Christadelphians. They are opposed to social reform, waiting for God to act in his own good time.)

From the exterior, rationalist point of view, such actions are puzzlingly ineffectual. It is customary to interpret such movements as pre-political or non-political, limited in their appeal to the politically passive or unfranchised. Some authors (Cohn, 1957; Lawrence, 1964; B. R. Wilson, 1961) interpret them as outlets for anxiety, which, because they prevent rational solutions, create malintegration on a societal level. Others (Worsley, 1957) see them as integrative, both individually and socially, largely because by bringing men together, often under a leader who already has political aspirations, such movements may facilitate the shift to political action.

Both theories are in danger of ignoring the perspective of the people themselves, and of assuming that religious beliefs as such can have no independent causal effect on actions, and no internal evolution. Belshaw (1950) emphasizes that, from the viewpoint of the Melanesian, a new cult is the traditional means of gaining mastery over a situation in which he is torn between admiration of European styles of living, obtained by apparently magical means, and rage at a people who deny him such abundance, destroy his culture and fob him off with their religion (which lacks the miraculous powers which fundamentalist missionaries may claim for it). The Melanesians' symbolic mimicry of important European activities is, to them, the best chance they have of controlling them. The distinction between religion (seen as an expressive activity) and politics (seen as an instrumental one) is a Western one, which is not obviously applicable to societies where a separate political realm with secular parties neither exists nor is likely to exist, even in the post-colonial future.

Religion and politics are not separate and distinct activities, even in advanced societies. Many religious movements among colonial peoples show a mixture of religious and Marxist elements in their eschatology; for example the Ras Tafari of Jamaica blend together vocabulary and concepts torn from the two (Simpson, 1955; Smith, Augier and Nettlefold, 1960). In South-east Asia, the first nationalist movements were originally infused with native religious movements and then formed into sectarian political parties. But in some instances, the new political systems were then racked by struggles between attempts to recreate the pre-colonial society by essentially religious means, and Marxist methods and goals, which the nationalists had also seized upon as an explanatory framework (von der Mehden, 1968). Cultural nationalists may attempt to restore certain aspects of the social framework as they were before colonization, and this may mean that nationalist leaders deliberately reject the divorce between religion and the state and the attempt to create a separate political realm. In such a context, new religious movements are as effective a form of revolt as new political ones.

The "rationality" of the political response as opposed to the religious can also be challenged on the ground that a superior power may tolerate resistance in a religious, but not in a political form. The Black Muslims are tolerated as the Black Panthers are not, and new religious sects are perhaps more common among contemporary South African Negroes than anywhere else (Sundkler, 1948; B. R. Wilson, 1971).

What determines the form that resistance to an intruding culture will take? Among American Indians, for example, active resistance has not only led to messianic millenarianism, but to retreatist movements, and also to physical resistance, and to depopulation (Barber, 1941). Three apparently similar tribal societies in western New Guinea reacted to contact with the West quite differently. One produced a classic millenarian movement, led by a messiah who promised to recreate the good society; another incorporated the foreigners into their existing religious ritual and mythology as other descendants of their superior ancestors, and blended these beliefs into the Christianity these descendants brought them; the third was the site of an unsuccessful experiment in community development, which seemed to block a religious reaction. The reaction to the West seemed to be determined by whether social conflict had existed within the society previously (van der Kroef, 1957).

Although many studies have been made of the origins of new churches and religious movements, there has been little study of syncretism, which is an equally common phenomenon when a universal religion associated with a conquering culture comes into contact with an indigenous religious tradition (Heise, 1967). The picture which is sometimes presented is that of a line between the two poles of the religion of the subordinate culture and the religion (usually Christianity or Islam) of the conquering culture; syncretism is then seen as a new religion, or mixture of the two, which can be located somewhere along the line. There is some truth in the picture. Religions are also cosmologies, theories of knowledge, intimately related to social order and social divisions; the rapid changes brought about in colonized societies, even though both colonizers and colonized may be trying to prevent them, mean that the organization and explanatory resources of the traditional local religion become inadequate. Its theories of disease and practitioners of healing, for instance, are challenged by Western medicine in the way that Western religion once was. But the process is two-way. It is a truism that every religion changes, over time and between cultures, to fit into an existing pattern of beliefs and practices. The Christian missionaries who strove to convert the heathen modified their theology toward the indigenous religion in the very effort to explain and translate Christianity into terms which would be locally comprehensible. To the outsider, the result is a tangle of old and new elements, but the uneducated in particular are not likely to distinguish religious beliefs and practices as belonging definitely to one religious tradition or another, nor to expect that a tradition will be internally consistent.

In some cases, the syncretic process has been more self-conscious and gone much further, and an effort has been made to create a systematic theology. Voodoo is an obvious example of a blend of Catholic and African religious symbolism, and one which has been deliberately fostered as part of a political négritude (Courlander and Bastien, 1956). As its political

fortunes have waxed and waned, so has its scholastic interpretations; "barbarous magic" was replaced by the "religion of Black
Africa" and finally by the "Core of Haitian identity". Haitian
voodoo is only one of the many "fetish cults" which have
flourished among Negroes in Cuba and Brazil, where Catholicism coexists with a system of priests and gods which is essentially
African. The Christian saints, themselves originally correspond-
ing to the local godlings of the areas where they originated, have
changed again into the forms of gods of Dahomey or the
Yoruba people.

But syncretism is not always explicable in terms of movement
along a line. Religious traditions are often weakly articulated.
A system of sorcerers who identify and heal spiritual sickness
may be left while other parts of the religion are abandoned.
(The increase in accusations of sorcery and witchcraft, which
has been reported from many societies that have been under-
going rapid change, shows that if stress has not lessened and
even increased then it is very unlikely that a method of coping
with it will be abandoned just because a religion that deals with
cosmic, moral and socially public procedures is disappearing.)
Alternatively the religion of the conquerors may be transmitted
—especially to the "modernized" élite—in a relatively pure
form. Indeed, its function for them may lie in enabling them to
identify themselves as closely as possible with the culture which
brought it. Christianity in Africa may have become national-
ized, and have an indigenous clergy, but it is not thereby
Africanized; the new religions may appear syncretic, but may
be ultra-Protestant in the behaviour they advocate and be
embraced by rising commercial strata for reasons similar to
those of seventeenth-century puritans.

There are few detailed studies of how a universal and a local
religion alter and combine. Messinger's excellent account
(1960) of the fusion of evangelical Christianity and the indigenous religion of the Anang people of Nigeria in the Christ Army
Church is an exception. The members of this syncretist church
were conscious of the hostility of the wealthy and powerful
mission churches, which attracted the young and ambitious.
They justified their own practices, such as faith-healing, women
clergy, glossolalia, and the separation of preaching, healing
and teaching functions, by reference to justifying passages in
the Bible. Their teachers showed great skill at finding Old

Testament passages which supported polygyny, ritual drinking, animal sacrifice, killing twins, and other practices which had been outlawed by missionaries.

The relationship of traditional religion to social stability was shown in the rising rates of sorcery and immoral (by both local and Western standards) behaviour among the Christianized Anang. Previously, oath-givers, the custodians of a powerful avenging spirit, had been used to great effect in the law courts, but the missionaries protested and swearing on the Bible was substituted. As a result the courts became corrupt, and litigants were forced to resort to sorcery to achieve their ends. The Christ Army Church flourished because it warded off and healed the attacks of the devils roused by such sorcery. These devils were vividly described in the book of Revelation and thus ratified by Christianity. General immorality had resulted from substituting a god who forgave believers for a god who never forgave and who punished the smallest mistake. The wearing of crosses and attending of confession was believed to ensure the new god's forgiveness. There are few clearer demonstrations of the way in which religion is an important part of social control in simple societies, and one which cannot be replaced by an alien religion, however superior its morality, in a way which will correspond to the existing social structure and pattern of expectations and so make its precepts effective. In complex societies, new religions can readily be absorbed because religion is related to morality and social control only in a very general way, which allows for considerable ground-level redefinition.

Fernandez has proposed (1964) that new religious movements in Africa can be classified along two dimensions, according to whether their symbolism derives from the old religious culture or the new, and whether they are concerned with instrumental or expressive gains. The instrumental reaction which takes the symbolism of the new culture are the churches which have split away from those controlled by Europeans, the dominant group. The Aladura (Peel, 1968) and the Ethiopian churches of South Africa (Sundkler, 1961) are examples of this kind; both are concerned to be accepted by the orthodox Christian churches, because this gives material and symbolic advantages. The new religions which reject Christianity and European culture may do so purely symbolically, or may create a compensatory world; they metamorphose into other forms very rapidly, and in particular seem to move toward instrumental and political forms of action as these come increasingly under the control of the Africans themselves.

## 7 RELIGIOUS ORGANIZATIONS—CHURCH AND SECT

Another aspect of Weber's interest in the complex relationship between belief and action was the way in which individual beliefs and actions become incorporated into religious organizations, just as he described rational-legal activities in secular life becoming embodied in bureaucracies. The organization which grows up around new religious leaders alters the nature of the religious message and the bond between the church and its members. Organizations have a dynamic of their own. Weber's pupil, Troeltsch (1931), took Weber's interest in the different organizational forms of modern society and applied it to religion.

On the basis of his studies of Christianity at the time of the Reformation, Troeltsch concluded that Christianity had always taken either the form of a distinct church or sect, where the collectivity was holy in itself, or had existed as a set of mystical doctrines about the value of *personal* religious experience and arcane knowledge, which might become focused in a cult. If the organization itself was holy, it would fall somewhere on a line between two opposites, the church, which accepted and legitimated existing social arrangements and sought to encompass everyone in its sacraments, and the sect, which, because it was opposed to much of secular life, was exclusivist; members had to fulfil fairly exacting requirements to enter and to remain.

Both church and sect believe that only their members have access to salvation; but whereas the church will baptize as members even those (such as children) who cannot rationally assent on the ground that the sacrament has a saving power, the sect is likely to reject all the immanent and magical aspects of grace, and to insist that baptism and salvation are dependent on a rational assent and a personal contact with the divine. Both church and sect thus divide men into members and non-members, and the latter, being spiritually outside grace, are likely to be treated as second-class citizens in other ways. The church sees its place in society as infusing all institutions with its own power, as is most evident during civic ceremonies. The sect is more likely to condemn secular society as corrupt and probably short-lived—its members are the "gathered remnant" who through an intense internal life form a separate society of their own, either shunning outside contact, or seeking it only to proselytize.

Both churches and sects have failed to maintain these rigid positions over time. The sectarian commitment dwindles as charisma is routinized, and the values, definitions and temptations of society are hard to resist; the organization must usually compromise to survive or grow. The church is afflicted from within by attacks on its worldliness and corruption, and the growing universalism of morality jeopardizes the claim that men can be saved by sacraments rather than by works. To save the typology, the denomination and the established sect are introduced to cope with the religious bodies created by religious pluralism, in which neither churches nor sects have been able to maintain an exclusive claim to salvation, and both have moved to a half-way position on baptism, the sacraments and the role of the priest, and to a tolerant and pluralist view on religious liberty and salvation. (The category of the denomination has been elaborated for the English context by D. A. Martin [1962], and see Gustafson [1967] for a critique of Troeltsch for confusing separate variables.) Further research has shown that religious organizations are far more complex than Troeltsch had thought.

Religious bodies differ from each other not only along these lines: *within* each organization there is often a struggle between inspiration and formalization—the pressures making for bureaucracy in secular organizations are also present in religious ones. The difference between them, however, is that in the religious context, considerations of efficiency or effectiveness are almost always seen as contrary to the spirit of true religion. Few detailed studies have been made of religious organizations, perhaps because most attention has been paid to sects, where organization is relatively underdeveloped, but perhaps also because discussions of careerism, red tape, and other features of bureaucracies, would be uncongenial to church officials, who are more interested in using the sociology of organizations to analyse the structure of their congregations (Fichter, 1954; Ward, 1961; but see K. A. Thompson's [1970] account of bureaucracy in the Church of England). Harrison's

(1959) excellent study of the way in which authority and power among American Baptists, who emphasize the democracy of all believers, have become concentrated among the executive of the American Baptist convention largely because legitimate leaders have tried to deny the fact of power or not to seek it, shows the interesting results which can be obtained from such studies. At the other extreme from the Baptists, some religious bodies emphasize the structure and hierarchy of the religious organization, and claim a sacred significance for it; this is true not only of established churches, which may claim a divine origin and power for their institutions, but of some sects, for example the Salvation Army (R. Robertson, 1970). (Much of the material on the churches as institutions is summarized in Moberg [1962]. Winter [1968] discusses administrative centralization among the three major religions in America.)

Most studies of religious organization have been concerned not with the internal structure of religious bodies but with the broad organizational differences between them. Troeltsch described a situation in which universal churches, supported by political and legal institutions, were confronted by sects who were denied social legitimacy and supported mainly by the poor and the marginal. But few modern sects are as persecuted as those which he studied at the time of the European Reformation, nor do they draw their membership so exclusively from the very poor. Thus his antitheses are no longer so far-reaching or important.

In America, where no church is established, none could claim an automatic allegiance, nor an organizational monopoly of the means to salvation. Niebuhr (1929) reinterpreted the American case as one where a series of *denominations* recruited among the poor in the disorganized society of the frontier and reflected their values of spontaneity, cooperation and concern with suffering and salvation. They gradually changed as congregations grew wealthier and accommodated to the society. A denomination resembles a sect in that it uses subjective rather than ritual means for the attainment of grace, but is like a church in that it automatically accepts children as members and does not demand repeated proof of a strong commitment.

Niebuhr described an inexorable process by which sects would inevitably accommodate to the world. As their members grew richer, their commitment would become attenuated, they would then press for a more ritual and less emotional form of service, and for formal entry qualifications rather than constantly renewed signs of grace such as spirit possession, glossolalia, or being saved. This transition has been observed among some religious bodies, especially among British and American Methodists. (Chamberlayne, 1964; Currie, 1968; Brewer, 1952. See Whitley [1955] for the Disciples of Christ; Mann [1955] for Canadian examples; Pope [1942] for Southern Protestantism. Dynes [1955] found an empirical link between the sect-to-church transition and the upward social mobility of congregations.)

In Canada, the struggle between sect and church reflected not only the emotionalism and anarchy of frontier society as opposed to the stability of the wealthy established community, but also the evangelical fervour of the native Canadian and American ministers who led the sects as opposed to the formalism of the educated British clergy, whose churches were supported by the Canadian government in their efforts to civilize and control the frontier. Each wave of westward expansion was followed by a burst of fundamentalism (S. D. Clark, 1948).

The movement from sect to church or denomination is by no means universal. New religions occasionally arise among the wealthy, and if they do they are likely to be cults, especially the cults which focus on gnostic knowledge. Some religious groups originated as churches; that is, they were always formal, ritualized and accommodated to the world; this is especially true of the schismatic groups in American and European Jewry (Steinberg, 1965; Sklare, 1955, terms them "ethnic churches"). Some sects seem to remain permanently isolated from the world and able to demand a strong commitment from their members, which has resulted in their being termed *established* sects (B. R. Wilson, 1961). This does not seem to have prevented the members of some of them (the Seventh Day Adventists or Mormons, for example) from becoming wealthier (Sargent, 1962; Davies, 1962). The Salvation Army in Britain has moved from denomination to sect to established sect (R. Robertson, 1970).

One of the most important theological differences between churches and sects on the one hand, and denominations on the other, is that the latter are non-universalist, that is, they are tolerant of other churches and denominations as an alternative means to grace (D. A. Martin, 1962). (Established sects resemble denominations in this respect.) It is interesting that the same religious group may be a sect or church in one society and a denomination in another, so that its doctrinal emphasis will differ between two social contexts. In the United States, for example, a large number of competing religious groups and a norm of religious equivalency and tolerance places pressure on groups which are universal churches in other societies—for example, Episcopalians, Catholics and Greek Orthodox—to abandon control of their members in affairs which the society considers secular, and to modify their doctrines on the authority of the church so as to become like denominations. If they do not do this they can only retain church-like claims to authority if their members are drawn from relatively isolated social or ethnic groups. If they are not isolated, their members will find a constant conflict between the general social definition of the part that religion plays in life, and the much greater demands that their church is making of them. As Luckmann (1967) points out, in a competitive situation, the monopolistic privileges of church or sect will be hard to maintain.

In practice, churches differ between countries and even congregations in the demands that they make on their members. The way in which the Catholic church in particular has been able to combine a theoretically universal and sacred authority with, in practice, enormous differences between the kinds of control exerted in, for example, a congregation in rural Ireland, an Irish congregation in Birmingham or Chicago, or a cluster of Catholic intellectuals around a university chaplaincy, is remarkable, and deserves detailed study.

The transition from sect to denomination to church is by no means automatic. It is more important to try to specify the kind of sect among which and the circumstances under which the transition begins (B. R. Wilson, 1959a). Another line of attack is to distinguish between different types of sects; the cult sometimes appears as one type. Berger (1954), Johnson (1957), Yinger (1970), S. D. Clark (1948), B. R. Wilson (1959a), J. Wilson (1968) and Dynes (1955) have suggested various schemes. E. Goode (1967), Eister (1957), and R. Robertson (1970) have criticized schemes that are based on a single defining variable, because we do not know if other important factors which have been incorporated into the definitions are always correlated with the original variable in the same way. Analysis is handicapped because so few studies have been made of churches, in comparison with the large number of studies of sects. The typology was developed on the basis of Christianity, and is not particularly appropriate to other religions, though R. Robertson (1970) and Yinger (1970) outline how it can be extended to them. It may not be very illuminating, however, in other societies, where the distinction between national and folk religions is often the more important one.

Some sociologists of religion feel that the study of organizational forms in religion has reached an impasse (see, for example, Eister, 1957; E. Goode, 1967). The implications of each general form of religious organization have been well established, but with an increasing interest in ecumenicalism, the churches themselves are trying to play down their differences in theology and organization. The membership of sects is a small proportion of the population, and only they are likely to be conscious of the links between dogma and organizational structure. Churches are now affected less by sectarian tendencies than by the argument that the existing structure of meetings for worship in specialized buildings ought to be abandoned entirely, and that religious institutions should abandon their separate identity. Studying religious organizations limits us to studying the influence of religion on their members, and excludes the rising numbers of non-members.

Part of the fascination of the study of sects is that they preserve much closer links than cults or churches do between the religious organization and the lives of their members. Their ability to monopolize the spare time and energy of their members, and to reverse the separation of family, work, political and other roles which has occurred with industrialization, means that they must be able to exert considerable control. Consequently, their theology and organization must "fit" rather more closely with their members' experience and needs than is necessary in denominations, which make fewer demands. Festinger *et al.* (1956) showed the control a sect can exert over its members because of the difficulties that they would face on leaving; not only would they lose friends and a pattern which gave meaning to life, they would be forced to reject much of their previous lives as useless and erroneous. The ways in which sects can exert control on formally free members and how they come to taboo certain ways of behaving, has been mainly studied in isolated communitarian groups, where the demands are most severe, but where the boundary-maintaining factors are correspondingly strong. More attention needs to be paid to the sects which have difficulty in maintaining "a unified and internally consistent interpretation of the meaning of the world" because their members have access to other world-views. (Bittner, 1963, discusses some of the mechanisms; B. R. Wilson, 1961, and J. Wilson, 1968, discuss some examples.)

## 8 CONCLUSION—RELIGION AS MEANING

Weber, and after him Malinowski and Parsons, have seen religion as a form of knowledge, something which answers pre-existent and eternal problems of meaning. Suffering, and problems about it, are taken as given—they are thought of as "frustrations"—and religious beliefs are symbolic resolutions of problems that cause suffering.

The dangers of this position lie in intuiting other men's problems from their beliefs; Weber thought that suffering was the central problem, but others have identified it as the search for a right relation between men and god, or for the means of redemption. And whereas Weber understood that specific social structures and experiences make the content of religious beliefs different for each social group, many sociologists have built on his initial statement about religion as meaning to reach a remarkably idealist position. Talcott Parsons, for example, describes the religion of each society as expressing the most ultimate level of values—that which ultimately endows all human activity with meaning. He implies a hierarchy of values in which the normative exigencies guiding specific actions are derived from general values and, in turn, support them. But the examples that he gives of general cultural values—such as "instrumental activism" for modern America—are too general, and *must* be too general, for the ends and means which actually govern behaviour to be derived directly from them with no other constraints on the process.

In a remarkably meliorist and evolutionary treatment (T. Parsons, 1963a), he describes Christianity in modern America as a belief-system of great refinement and generality operating in a society with very high moral standards, which has already become so obedient to Christian values that they have largely become internalized. He sees a growing distinction since the Reformation, not only between the administrative and sacramental aspects of the church, but between the demands of the church and the individual's dependence upon God as the ultimate source of truth. So various denominations can coexist in a Christian society because there are two layers of religious commitment, one to a specific institution and the other to the general moral community for all members of the society, religious or not. "To deny that this underlying consensus exists would be to claim that American society stood in a state of latent religious war' (1963a).

It can be argued that this way of thinking simply takes religion too seriously. Weber's consciousness of the way in which religious ideas are constantly reshaped by social and psychological pressures and by the religious organizations themselves has been subordinated to an extreme idealist position, in which the most abstract and general Christian aspirations and values are assumed to be the ones which actually operate. What we need are studies of how far men's religious beliefs are actually operative; when do they perceive a situation as being governed by norms derived from religion? It may be that societies can have many religions without being in a state of religious war, not because men share underlying religious values, but because religious values do not affect their lives very much. Their day-to-day behaviour is governed by quite other exigencies, in particular simply the examples and precedents set by their reference groups and those significant for them. At certain points—death, the outbreak of war, marriage, etc.—reference may be made to supreme values, couched in religious or quasi-religious terms; but it is difficult to prove that these values underlie the rest of behaviour in any important sense. Religious motives, like others, are ambiguous and confused; a man sentenced to death for his part in the anti-Catholic Gordon riots said when questioned, "Damn my eyes, I have no religion; but I have to keep it up for the good of the Cause" (quoted in G. Rudé, *The Crowd in History*, 1964, p. 232).

The phenomenologist also bases his definition of the study of religion on its meaning to the individual and thus how it influences his ongoing social relations. I have argued in this chapter at various points that we would learn more about religion if we paid more attention to how individuals perceive religion, and to the structure of their beliefs and the way in which they are related to myths or general systems of belief. ". . . to study history is first of all to try to *understand* men's actions, the impulses which have moved them, the ends which they have pursued, and the meaning which their behaviour and their actions had for them" (Goldmann, 1969). Although Weber argued for these *subjects* of study, he spent most of his life trying to devise an objective *method* of studying them, and would undoubtedly have rejected the programmes of Berger and Luckmann or Garfinkel for sociology. The methodological issues are both complex and familiar, but a good empirical reason for rejecting an entirely subjectivist position is that churches and their organization, theologies, and social contexts are objective facts. Individuals may perceive them in different ways, just as they may have very different views of politics and levels of commitment to them, but the structure of parties and churches continues more or less regardless of their perceptions. Not entirely so, of course. Religious and political systems are affected if the nature and extent of participation in the system changes. The power of a system is affected by the degree of confidence in it, and if we look only at actions and not at perceptions we cannot assess confidence. This is why the study of secularization is so difficult; the structure of religious institutions continues long after perceptions of them have changed in ways which will ultimately change them.

But, even if perceptions change structures, outside of structures, perceptions have little or no social existence. A personal set of perceptions outside a shared structure does not become the basis for social interaction, and so it is outside the realm of sociology. Marx and Durkheim were agreed on the importance of structures, which can continue to exist for a time independently of the changes in individual perceptions. But in the end, they change. It was primarily Weber who showed us how to analyse how and why they change.

# CHAPTER IV

# Religion—Some Evidence

The previous chapters have set out the major sociological ways of thinking about religion and the traditions of work which have resulted. It is clear that satisfactory models have been created for the study of the differences between religious organizations, and for the study of certain sorts of minority religious movement, and that these stem from Weber's work rather than from Durkheim's. These movements are for the most part small and relatively isolated, and thus are distinct from the beliefs and activities (religious or secular) of the majority of members of the society in which they are found. An immense area of ignorance is thus left untouched. Does religion operate in the same way in every society? Does it embody widely accepted social norms, or unifying values, and if so, can we identify these, and show the processes by which they govern behaviour? Can we observe them being conveyed to individuals? Who is most responsive to them? How, in turn, do social changes lead to changes in theology? Can we compare the role of religion in two societies, or between two periods of time, with any exactness?

These questions raise another and a more basic one. Is religion a single phenomenon, a "thing"? The question is partly one of a correct definition of religion. If we take several definitions, the answer that they all seem to suggest is that religion is not a single phenomenon, and consequently that research to establish what religion "is" or "does" is vain.

For example, if we take the view that every human society faces a set of questions about "ultimate meaning", then it is clear that there is a diminution with modernization in the number of questions to which a magico-religious answer is sought. Rather than trying to equate aspects of science and politics (which now provide the answers, or at least redefine the questions) with religion itself, it would be more fruitful to discuss why and how certain dilemmas and problems are seen as having passed out of "religious" control. If religion is defined on a psychological basis, as having to do with feelings of awe, sacredness, "rightness", etc., then the power and frequency of these feelings, and the symbols, sacred or secular, with which they are connected, vary not only between individuals, but vary greatly between cultures. How can we decide, for example, if the veneration of the idea of the progress of mankind is a "religious" feeling?

These considerations suggest that we cannot talk about the "role of religion in society". It is too complex and varied, even within a single society. (Consider the very different role played by religion in the lives of two white Protestant Americans, one a middle-class Episcopalian whose beliefs are effectively agnostic, but who sees the church as a source of social contacts and psychological warmth; the other a poor white Appalachian farmer, whose fervent adherence to Southern Baptism enables him to combine Catholics, communists, Negroes, atheists, intellectuals and liberal Northerners into a composite outgroup, threatening him economically and politically but shortly due to wither beneath the wrath of a Mighty God.) Like kinship structures or political activity, religion varies enormously in its salience, its elaboration, and its power over decisions and other institutions. But to say that religion is not a single "thing" does not mean that we cannot generalize about it or attempt to explain it in sociological terms.

Religion can be defined, either in the way that each society or its religious tradition itself has defined it (the basis of the Weberian school), or in a way that makes it accord with a general theory of the role it plays in society (the basis of the Durkheimian school). The difficulty with the first sort of definition is that we cannot compare two religious traditions. Indeed, to try to describe village Hinduism in terms of abstract beliefs or the moral precepts which structure ritual in the terms which we would use to describe, say, Protestantism, would be to misunderstand it. The history of misinterpretations of the religions and cosmologies of simple people, by observers who thought of religion as something equivalent to the middle-class Protestantism which had formed their ideas of religion, emphasizes the importance of this point. Perhaps the Reformation—

or rather the myth of it—has been most responsible for providing us with an implicit model of how religion should operate in the world, which has affected most English and American sociologists and theologians. Our conception is of religion as something structured by beliefs; as transcendent; as offering a standard by which the world is judged; as being internalized in each individual by religious education, and thus providing each of us with a mode of judging our experience which is essentially moral. (Thus, in discussing secularization, we look for something which can replace these features.) It is difficult for sociologists, even if they realize that this is a very *Protestant* conception of religion, to eradicate the assumption that other religions must have features analogous to these, or that they will become more like this model. The great virtue of the Durkheimian school lay in breaking out of this mould.

The second method of defining religion, the Durkheimian or functionalist one, because it is no longer constrained by the definitions of the believer, means that we are unable to choose between competing definitions of religion; and, more importantly, are led to facile equations of all sorts of activities concerned with values, crowds and ritual behaviour, or social bonding, with "religion". A harder but more fruitful way of defining religion is to try to discover what is "religious" and what is "secular" for each society and each group. The shifting boundaries are the clue to secularization. At the same time, part of the function of religion in all societies is inadmissible to the participants; to admit that we go to church because we like to be thought well of, or want to meet useful business contacts, is to jeopardize our legitimate reasons. Similarly, religious institutions cannot function like secular ones in that, like aspects of the law and of old-fashioned armies, they operate with the notion of an ultimate and unchallengeable authority. This affects ways of settling disputes and of discussing change so that the integration of the pragmatic, decentralized and shifting authority systems of the rest of modern society with such relatively fixed systems becomes rather a delicate matter.

These considerations mean that the first task of the sociologist is to find what religion means to any social group. At what points in their lives and arguments do they refer to it? Which values and norms are generally considered to have a religious backing? What power and influence do religious institutions have, and by what are they influenced? Does religion embody or parallel other social divisions (political, economic, racial), and if so, how do the institutions interact? How are value-structures sustained and personal losses borne by those without religious beliefs? Speculation about religion in society can be interesting only if it uses at least some knowledge of such matters, which are largely concerned with the less institutionalized part of religious experience.

The following three chapters discuss some of the evidence that we have about the role of religion in people's lives. The evidence is almost all taken from Britain and the United States. This is partly because they are sufficiently similar, both in their religions and in the nature of the society, to make it possible to discuss and compare without the complexities of comparisons between many very different entities, but it is mainly because the overwhelming bulk of *sociological* studies of religion are American, or English to a lesser extent. There have been many excellent anthropological studies of the role of religion in smaller societies and communities, but they are not concerned with the features of religion and society which are crucial to the questions asked here—the internal *variation* in religion and the reasons for it, and the relation between it and social group or class. The other major source of modern factual material which has been omitted is the French studies of religious practice. All but the best of these are very much "market research for the churches", for example variations in practice are discussed mainly in terms of geographical areas, and so they have little bearing on the theoretical questions outlined.

Chapter V describes religious *beliefs* in terms of what men actually do seem to know and believe. Chapter VI discusses religion in relation to social *group*, and Chapter VII considers religion in relation to *secularization*.

# CHAPTER V

# *Religious Beliefs*

Within any society there is a range of individual religious experience. Not only are some people much "more" religious than others; they have different beliefs and use them in different contexts. Even in simple Polynesian societies, *mana* can be experienced either as a set of taboos, or as a metaphysical concept about impersonal powers and their right relationships to men. Moreover, some people use religious beliefs in contexts—relations with workmates, family life—which other members of the same society would consider wholly secular. Hence the shamefaced resentment which many English and Americans feel toward members of fundamentalist sects, who may continue inconveniently to insist that bawdiness at the office party or knocking off some stationery is sinful.

That resentment gives us an insight into the relationship between religion and "ultimate" values in our culture. Almost all members of English or American society concede the claim of religion to define moral actions and judgment in terms of absolute values. But this does not mean that in concrete and specific situations, they will "refer" to religion nor even to moral values. In new situations, we learn how to behave, on the whole, not by referring to values at all, but by observation and imitation in balancing our own wants against what is considered reasonable or customary. The research into the operation of reference groups illuminates the way in which concepts such as "fairness" and "justice" are built up for specific contexts, and a standard of acceptable behaviour established. It is this which produces such widespread inconsistencies between beliefs, between actions, and between beliefs and actions. The more educated we become, the more we seek to justify ourselves on a general level of reasons and values, and thus we are encouraged to identify and reconcile our inconsistencies.

(Though it is hard to deny that our narcissism is only possible because social reality is structured by the preconceptions of the educated.) But adolescents and the less educated are by comparison confused—by the gaps between exhortation and reality, or between other people's moral judgments and their own reactions. The mass media reinforce contradictions and confusions, as well as stereotyping. The statements of religious spokesmen may or may not coincide with the pragmatic morality of our peers and may be very unspecific; those who preached against drink or blasphemy at least provided an unambiguous guide to behaviour, where their more sophisticated successors, trying to reinterpret religious values for a shifting culture, are plagued by their indefiniteness.

Alongside this contextual way of learning and using morality there are structured world-views, self-consciously possessed and used by only a few people. Some are religious and some secular, but it is those which are not conventional for the *milieu* of their holders which are likely to be most deliberate and defined. However, for the majority of people in Britain and the United States, the religious beliefs which they were taught and have never rejected bear an uncertain relationship to the beliefs which actually govern their behaviour.

## 1 WHAT DO THEY BELIEVE?

Religious beliefs are notoriously hard to define. People are reluctant to answer questions, especially if they are neither orthodox believers nor self-consciously secularist. The populations of both countries seem surprisingly confused and ignorant, perhaps because it is hard for them to make their beliefs explicit. The surveys have not been able to show which beliefs are important to them or affect their behaviour, but are nonetheless very revealing.

In Britain, the separation of religion from regular church-attendance (less than a quarter of the population attend church; nearly all say they believe in God and are "religious") has resulted in increasingly heterodox beliefs. This has been most fully documented by Gorer (1955). In a large, if unrepresentative, sample, he found that nearly all his respondents described themselves as Christian, but three-fifths believed in neither hell nor the devil, and under half in a life after death. Only 12 per cent of those who did believe in an after-life saw it as consisting of a scriptural hell and heaven, with allocation to them depending on behaviour in this life. In fact, nearly as many believed in reincarnation. The commonest picture of the after-life was as a universal state of untroubled leisure and rest, a common theme in popular American religious works (Schneider and Dornbusch, 1958). Images of heaven reflect our experiences of want on earth; earlier English heavens and utopias offered a lavish abundance of meat and drink and freedom from toil. Mass Observation (1948) also found that the Londoners whom they questioned were inconsistent; some of the doubters prayed to a god about whose existence they were uncertain, and went to church; half the firm believers did not attend.

Church attendance is highest among Catholics and members of the smaller Protestant sects, but is also affected by social factors. It is commoner among women and the young upper-middle classes; many of the latter still fall into the category of public-school education, political Conservatism, and active Anglicanism. As in America, the upper-middle classes are the most likely to attend church, but the least likely to pray. In traditional and old-established communities, this class maintains a pattern of sporadic attendance; most of the population attend church only for weddings and funerals. The most sceptical of religion are the young, urban, married men from the prosperous working class; the most fundamentalist are the elderly and poor (Gorer, 1955).

But unless we know the connections that people make between their beliefs, and their roots in teaching and experience, it is easy to see coherent world-views as contradictory. This is even more true in religion than in politics, since religious beliefs are less discussed, and now kept less within bounds by catechisms and the orthodox religious teaching which defines the "right" beliefs. D. A. Martin's accounts (1968) of religious traditions in England suggest general ways of thinking and feeling which are derived from church traditions but no longer controlled by them; Zweig (1952) sees them as even more unregulated, as "personal religions". But even though individual religious beliefs may bear little relationship to official ones, there is no doubt that the attitude to social order, "respectability", how much one can expect from life, and so on, is permeated for most people by metaphysical ideas about providence, guilt, retribution and mystery, which come from an old religious framework. Loudon (1966), for example, discusses the way in which misfortune and madness in a rural community in South Wales are attributed to either supernatural or natural agencies. There is almost no other research in this area.

The metaphysical and moral frameworks that people possess may bear little relationship to the present theology of their church. Such frameworks are rooted in more than formal religion and change very slowly. The simplified versions of dogma and morality that are taught to children are generally far more old-fashioned than those prevailing among the clergy. The shifts in formal theology leave these underlying strata exposed, much to the embarrassment of progressive clergymen. Stewart Headlam, for instance, a nineteenth-century Christian Socialist who found the doctrine of a literal hell repugnant to his moral sensibility, preached against it to his poverty-stricken flock in Drury Lane. A "small but decent milliner" was quick to connect this with her underlying notion of what right conduct was about. "Oh, Mr Headlam, if that be so, where is the reward of the righteous?" Even more strikingly, on another occasion Headlam was putting forward his new high-church conceptions of the mediating and interpreting role of the priesthood, when a working man rose at the back and cried, from the passionate Nonconformist tradition which he had abandoned, "Atheist as I am, sir, atheist as I am, no man shall stand between my soul and my God" (Bettany, 1926).

These underlying frameworks are still prevalent in a society where a clear conception of religious dogma has become very rare. Belief-systems have become fragmented and contingent; even those who are not religious may refer to a religious order underlying the world, and materialists and orthodox Christians are both capable of a belief in ghosts and various aspects of the occult (Loudon, 1966; Abercrombie *et al.*, 1970). But these magical beliefs are scarcely a body-blow to the dominance of science; indeed, Spiritualism and New Thought are curious demonstrations of the prestige of science, of the power which is attached to its vocabulary, so that hitherto transcendental explanations of spirits and healing are given a quasi-scientific explanation, just as Scientology pays homage to the impressive intellectual apparatus of physics and psychiatry. Superstitious beliefs are most common among the very poor, who are the most likely to experience their lives as being powerless in the grip of imponderable forces. Gorer found that about a quarter of his sample, including the most actively religious, believed that their future was predetermined and knowable.

Religious belief in the United States seems as eclectic and confused as it is in Britain. Religious knowledge seems extraordinarily limited. This is surprising since, although there is little religious teaching in schools, nearly half the population regularly attends church, and virtually all identify themselves as members of a religion.[1] Nevertheless, only two-thirds of all Americans who were Christians knew where Christ was born, only a third knew who ruled Jerusalem at the time, and less than a third knew who delivered the Sermon on the Mount (Stark and Glock, 1968). Catholics have rather more knowledge of liturgy and Protestants of the Bible, but neither knew much more about Christianity than did Jews. Even among the actively religious, knowledge of the Bible is very limited, and many respondents accepted as authentic statements completely opposed to Christ's teaching, but couched in Biblical language. Most Americans do not seem concerned about salvation, either because they are not convinced of the existence of an after-life (more of them believe that good works are essential to salvation than believe in salvation!—Glock and Stark, 1969) or because they are satisfied that they have achieved salvation already. A large number believe that religion has nothing to do with economic or political life (Stark and Glock, 1968; Herberg, 1955). The peripherality of religion is felt by some of the more educated to be regrettable but inevitable; four-fifths of a large sample of college students felt a need for a religious faith or philosophy, but less than one-fifth felt that religion was going to provide them with much satisfaction in life (Goldsen *et al.*, 1960).

[1] Comparison of rates of various kinds of religiosity for Great Britain and the United States, taken from various sources, 1948–52.

| Percentage of the population who : | Great Britain | United States |
|---|---|---|
| Belong to a church | 21·6 | 57 |
| Attend church weekly | 14·6 | 43 |
| Pray daily | 46 | 42·5 |
| Believe in God | 72 | 95·5 |
| Believe in after-life | 47 | 72 |
| Can name four Gospels | 61 | 35 |
| Claim church affiliation | 90·5 | 95 |

Several sorts of explanation have been produced for these facts. The first tries to distinguish between "true" and "conventional" religion. People with strongly held religious beliefs, who are actively devout and attend church regularly, hold opinions which are rather more in keeping with the theological interpretation of the ethical demands of Christianity than those of the conservative and authoritarian religious majority. Allport (1966) and Allen and Spilka (1967) consider the former as truly religious and the rest as Laodicean. But we cannot assume that beliefs in keeping with one interpretation of Christian ethics are more truly religious, nor does this view offer us much help in analysing the content and the causes of "conventional" religious beliefs.

Another explanation hinges on a distinction between different kinds of religiosity. There do seem to be consistent differences between a personal and a church-oriented kind of religious experience (King, 1967), or between a religion which is *associational*, or centred only on a church as a centre of purely religious interest, and a religion which is *communal*, or part of a total way of life which is lived out among co-religionists. (Lenski, 1961, in a pioneering study, established the importance of religious subcultures.)

The most recent attempts at explanation of the disjunction between religious beliefs and practice have been the most successful (Fukuyama, 1961; Glock and Stark, 1965; Stark and Glock, 1968; and Demerath, 1965). They have described *dimensions* of religious behaviour and experience, and tried to discover how widely each one is found and how they are interrelated. They have found that there is a difference between the amount that Americans *know* about their religion and the extent to which they *believe* what they know, and that these differ in turn from how actively they *practise* religion, either in public, such as by going to church, or in private, such as by prayer and Bible-reading, and this in turn differs from whether or not they have *experienced* any contact with the transcendental.

This research has opened many promising avenues for exploration. It needs refining and repeating in Britain and in other countries, and extension beyond active churchgoers, but it offers not only a way of sorting out the confusion of random beliefs and behaviours which various surveys have presented for England and America, but also a way of accurately assessing the way in which people are affected by different religions and kinds of religious experience. The conclusions of the research so far are very interesting; they show that the association between the dimensions is not very strong, but that *belief* is correlated more highly with all the other dimensions than they are with each other. The variations among different groups between the dimensions confirm many intuitive assumptions. Women *know* less about religion, but believe and experience it rather more (Fukuyama, 1961, on the basis of a Congregationalist sample). This must explain their higher reported rates of private prayer and Bible-reading. Religious *beliefs* steadily increase toward old age; but is this a function of ageing itself, or of an increasing contemporary ignorance of and indifference toward religion? But religious *practice* rises from a trough in young adulthood to very active churchgoing among young families, only to fall again in late middle-age. This is explained by the finding (also from a Congregationalist sample) that those joining the suburban churches are the parents of young children who wish to commit themselves as a family to a nearby church congregation which will emphasize "belonging" generally; they are relatively indifferent to issues of belief (Berger and Nash, 1962). A surprisingly large proportion of a population which on other indices seems to take religion lightly, reports direct experience of supernatural and transcendental forces (Stark, 1965; Stark and Glock, 1968). Such experiences are almost universal among members of denominations such as the Pentecostalists or Baptists, where they are expected both theologically and socially; members of liberal Protestant congregations who report such encounters come from the congregational "core" who have communal as well as associational ties with their church.

## 2 EXCEPTIONS AND VARIATIONS

The overall surveys of religious belief obscure the enormous variations in religious experience in both British and American society. The exceptions to the general picture of unstructured and unexamined confusion at both the individual and the social level are too small to affect the general picture, but nonetheless provide milieux where beliefs and action are related together in a far more stringent way. The deliberately anticlerical or atheist faction has been weak in both societies, except in its impact on intellectual life; it is discussed as part of secularization. On the other side lie the members of those religious sects who are considerably affected in all their social relationships by their religious beliefs. In both societies, the small fundamentalist sects comprise only one or two per cent of the population, and their members are largely drawn from the very poor, isolated, or socially marginal. But the attraction of sects for the sociologist of religion lies not only in the often bizarre and striking beliefs and activities of the sectarian, but in their distinctiveness. The enclosed social world of many sects makes it possible to distinguish the interconnections between the beliefs, the organization which is formed and the way it copes with the pressures of a hostile or indifferent environment, and the characteristics of the kind of person that is attracted. New sects—Scientology, for example—can act as pointers to a kind of strain which is being felt in the part of the social structure from which the members are recruited. In larger and older religious bodies, beliefs and needs are more diffuse and more varied. A practical advantage in studying sects is that their fundamentalist beliefs are sufficiently removed from the agnostic or liberal religionist beliefs of the sociologists of religion to enable them all to share a common view of the beliefs of the sectarian. The nearer theologies come to home, the more perceptions of them are likely to diverge, and so make professional discussion difficult.

What kinds of need are these exceptional religious organizations linked to? One kind, the religious community, appears to have been a search for a totally supportive society, as a reaction either to the dangers and insecurity of life in the recently settled areas of nineteenth-century America, or, more recently, as a reaction to its individualism, though the communes now springing up in the United States among predominantly middle-class people show no signs of the staying-power or economic success of some of the older religious communities, many of which were staffed by peasants used to a communal and self-sufficient mode of life (Bestor, 1950; O'Dea, 1957; Desroches, 1955). At the other extreme from the all-embracing world of the utopian sect lies the loose communion of the gnostic cult. Cults in both England and America seem to attract a floating population of "thrill-seekers", many of them elderly women without family ties, who avoid the corporate links of a congregation. Explanation of their attraction to cults has often suffered from a facile psychologism; the cult has bizarre and unusual beliefs, and so it is easily assumed that it attracts bizarre and unusual people (Catton, 1957; Buckner, 1965). But this is to divorce belief from context. Festinger *et al.* (1956) and Lofland (1966) studied two cults whose members had severed their ties with society because they expected the world to end almost immediately, a striking example of a belief which flouts commonsense assumptions. Both studies emphasized that the process of becoming committed to the group and its members enabled men and women to over-ride the repeated postponement of Doomsday. The challenge that these delays provided to the cult was far less, for most of its members, than the challenge that leaving the cult would have involved. More generally, bizarre beliefs when held in company are confirmed by experience just as our commonsense ones are, in many cases rather more so—for every piece of good or bad luck, every random happening, has its meaning. The positivistic commonsense which sociologists think of as the norm blinds us to the explanatory capacities of odd belief-systems in our own society (Bittner, 1963; and see Lurie, 1967, for an acute exposure of the mores and motives of two fictional sociologists studying this sort of group).

Cults collect members by random processes; they seem to have no other basis for common action, and so explanations of how members come to join them focus on psychological needs and the satisfactions of belief and ritual that the cult provides. But intense religious activity is also found at the other end of the social integration scale, among those who are identified with and interact with each other because of non-religious factors. The community aspect of the religion is very strong, and membership has a wide social significance. The Protestants and Catholics of Northern Ireland are a classic example. The intensity of religious activity in these cases can be explained in several ways. The group may be using the religious meeting to express and resolve tensions which are a function of their social experience; the church congregation may become the basis for community action of all kinds; and the wider society, in defining men as "Catholic" or "Hindu", may throw them back on a religious identity which they would otherwise have felt less strongly.

There are many examples of communal religiosity of this

kind in both Britain and the United States; the working-class
Catholic communities in large English cities (Hickey, 1967;
Ward, 1961) or the Jewish community in Leeds and elsewhere
are old-established religious and social identities, but recent
immigrants from Pakistan and the West Indies show such
communities in a process of formation. The first Hindus and
Muslims in a Christian society had to form their own congregations, which became a basis for social contact and for political
mobilization. Those successful within English society are more
likely to move out of both ghetto and religion. The West
Indians had expected to be received into the English denominations of which they were already members—but some of them
were already dominated by ethnic minorities—as, for example,
Catholic congregations often were by the Irish. The services of
the others seemed too cold and not reverent enough; the modes
of worship and styles in ritual had become attuned to the low-key
and withdrawn emotional needs of the English. And vicars
found that actively welcoming West Indians was likely to
offend their less active white parishioners (Rex and Moore,
1967). In many towns, Jamaicans founded ecstatic Pentecostalist churches whose activities seem a successful response to
the difficulties felt by their members (Kiev, 1964; Calley, 1965);
but more ambitious Jamaicans joined English Pentecostalist
groups, where the emotional rejection of the world has become
attenuated.

In the United States, the groups most clearly excluded from
the assimilation process have been the American Indians and
the Negroes. Both initially reacted by creating a religious
identity. The Indians found their traditional religions dis-
integrating under the impact of missionaries and the circum-
scription of their political and geographical freedom, and
reacted with a series of religious movements, the Ghost Dances
and peyote cults, which countered symbolically the overwhelming power of the white man (Slotkin, 1956; Mooney, 1965;
Kluckholm, 1944). The American Negro responded first to the
forms of Protestantism which stressed congregational unity and
the meaning of suffering, but as he gained more social autonomy
created a series of more radical political and religious movements, all of which were centrally concerned with trying to
re-establish a sense of identity in the face of a society which systematically alternated between denying him and encouraging

him to become like a white middle-class American. The religious protests, from Garveyism to the Black Muslims, have been seen as less threatening than the political protests, and so have been tolerated (Fauset, 1944; Cruse, 1967). The Black Muslims seek to re-establish the Negro American's links with his African past, and to reverse the position of black and white. Like other religious bodies recruiting among the disorganized ghettos of the poor, they demand a life of rigorous puritanism and self-denial, self-help among themselves, and avoidance of contacts with the corrupt society which enslaves their fellows (Lincoln, 1961; Essien-Udom, 1962).

## 3 RELIGION AS SOCIAL LABEL

The cults described in the previous section are examples of religious movements where church and group are unusually closely allied; only members of a particular ethnic group may join a church. But more generally, religion seems to serve a *labelling* purpose in American life. That is, it is argued, religious allegiance is not an integral part of the moral or intellectual structure of the society, which is profoundly secular, nor does it correspond to individual beliefs, since many active churchgoers are either ignorant of or dissent from the theology of their churches; religious allegiance is used as a social label to denote something about the group which it defines. The explanation has been used in two ways: to explain the support for religion from the American establishment, and to explain the persistence of subcultures.

Religion in the United States is often said to be important as a repository and symbol of the central values of the society: individualism, hard work, personal freedom and private enterprise. In its general existence, rather than in its theology, it supports the American way of life by marking it off from godless communism. General Eisenhower's dictum that American society was founded on a deeply held religious faith, and that he didn't care what it was, is much quoted in support of these views. Bellah claims that there is conventional religion and a civic religion, a set of ceremonies and beliefs which reaffirms and legitimates action in the public sphere, and which is important in guiding foreign policy, where moral values rather than *Realpolitik* have been influential. He outlines the mythopoeic events in American history which lend its institutions a god-given quality (Bellah, 1967; Herberg, 1955). A small American town, disrupted by increasing contact with the larger society, used a civic religion in just this way on a small scale to create a public image about the nature of the community, and to conceal the conflicts within it (Vidich and Bensman, 1958).

Much of the special role that the Christian churches have in the formally secular society of America is to mark off an intellectual and social opposition to atheistic communism; the political system defines itself by reference to the religious system. The liberal Protestant clergy, who tried in the Depression to involve the churches in radical social change, met with a violent reaction which accused the Social Gospel of being not only a socialist but a *Jewish* plot (Carter, 1954). Identifying the churches with the political establishment is dangerous if opinion diversifies, since mild dissent will be seen as sacrilegious and so outside the normal political processes of adjustment and compromise. And thus both right and left will be more readily alienated than they would be in a society where established values and procedures were not so firmly identified with the correct national way of life. In Goldsen *et al.*'s study (1960) of American college students, the religious had, and felt that they had, wider agreement with central American values.

Religion has not only been used to define the nation as a whole, it has been a shorthand way of describing and marking off the cultural cleavages within it. The social history of American society is that of waves of migrants, from a wide variety of cultures and with different religions (even the same denomination had become very much altered among the peasants of each society). Each wave of immigrants found their attributes resisted and disliked, and chief among them were the national churches to which they clung to help them create a cultural identity. It is cultural, rather than economic, divisions which have been the major points of dissension since the wholesale migrations during the last century from Central and Eastern Europe (Gusfield, 1966). The formal separation of church and state did not prevent hostility between the older-established Protestants and the Catholics, Jews, and European Protestants who challenged their supremacy.

The interweaving of political, social, economic and religious identities in the United States created a social *meaning* for each denomination which is so precise that it is an aspect of social mobility, and even varies from place to place by the origins and nature of the local élite, in a way which scarcely exists else-where. A brief sketch of American social history shows how the connections between social position and denomination were built up.

The first clash came between the Federalists and the liberals. The wealthy and conservative Federalists, identified with the Episcopalian or Congregational churches, succeeded in estab-lishing one or the other in each state. The liberals, who were Deists, formed an alliance with the other Protestant colonists who were Baptist, Methodist and Presbyterian, and disestab-lished the churches. But the social opposition between the two groups was submerged by their common anxiety at the irreligion of the disorganized conditions of the frontier and of the rapidly-growing towns. These were periodically transformed by waves of revivalism which finally reached into the religions of the élite. Even the strongholds of Deism, the New England colleges, abandoned Unitarianism and Universalism for ortho-doxy, and the Presbyterian, Baptist and Methodist churches flourished on emphasizing their differences, united only in their opposition to Catholicism and new Protestant sects. But the old social élite in the cities of New England remained Congrega-tional or Episcopalian; the new towns of the Midwest, founded and run by migrants from Scotland or Northern Ireland rather than England, were likely to consider the Presbyterian church as the church of the élite. In the favourable climate for evan-gelical religion, the Methodist and Baptist churches grew rapidly (by 1850, two-thirds of American Protestants were Methodists or Baptists), and worldly success and antagonism to European immigrants led them to be absorbed into the political, economic and social establishment and to become Republican (see Table 1).

The nineteenth-century movements for moral reform—temperance, the abolition of slavery, sabbath observance—were identified at first with the old Calvinist denominations, but after the new middle class had become more conservative they were taken over and more rigorously pursued by the evangelical denominations. The reform movements were essentially "symbolic crusades", attempts to reassert a certain way of life on behalf of a cultural class against the working-

Percentage Occupational Composition of each Religious Group in the United States

| % distribution of members of each religious group across seven socio-economic categories | Total no. in sample | Professional | Business | White-collar | Service | Skilled and semi-skilled | Unskilled | Farm |
|---|---|---|---|---|---|---|---|---|
| Roman Catholic | 2,332 | 7·1 | 6·6 | 23·0 | 13·6 | 35·3 | 5·8 | 8·6 |
| Methodist | 2,053 | 10·8 | 7·8 | 19·6 | 11·0 | 23·0 | 5·1 | 22·7 |
| Baptist | 1,344 | 6·1 | 5·7 | 14·5 | 15·5 | 29·2 | 6·7 | 22·3 |
| Presbyterian | 923 | 19·7 | 11·2 | 20·7 | 7·9 | 20·2 | 3·3 | 17·0 |
| Protestant, smaller bodies | 845 | 9·0 | 6·5 | 15·3 | 12·9 | 27·8 | 9·6 | 18·9 |
| Lutheran | 720 | 6·1 | 7·4 | 17·8 | 11·6 | 26·9 | 4·0 | 26·2 |
| Episcopal | 571 | 17·1 | 14·5 | 25·2 | 10·2 | 23·3 | 2·3 | 7·4 |
| Jewish | 515 | 14·4 | 21·7 | 36·5 | 4·3 | 22·3 | 0·2 | 0·6 |
| No Preference | 453 | 11·7 | 8·2 | 23·2 | 10·5 | 28·3 | 7·1 | 11·0 |
| Undesignated Protestant | 439 | 9·3 | 7·5 | 19·8 | 11·4 | 33·3 | 6·8 | 11·9 |
| Christian | 365 | 9·9 | 6·3 | 14·0 | 9·5 | 25·5 | 5·5 | 29·3 |
| Congregational | 362 | 19·6 | 13·3 | 19·3 | 5·8 | 21·0 | 1·4 | 19·6 |
| No Answer or "Don't Know" | 305 | 9·2 | 6·6 | 16·4 | 7·9 | 31·1 | 9·5 | 19·3 |
| Latter Day Saints (Mormon) | 167 | 9·0 | 5·4 | 15·0 | 6·5 | 15·6 | 19·8 | 28·7 |
| Christian Scientist | 134 | 13·4 | 9·7 | 35·1 | 8·9 | 18·7 | 1·5 | 12·7 |
| Reformed | 127 | 7·1 | 11·0 | 23·6 | 8·7 | 26·8 | 3·1 | 19·7 |
| Atheist/Agnostic | 16 | 31·3 | 12·5 | 31·2 | 0·0 | 12·5 | 0·0 | 12·5 |
| Total number in sample: | 11,671 | | | | | | | |
| % of total sample in each socio-economic category: | | 10·5 | 8·5 | 20·4 | 11·2 | 27·2 | 5·5 | 16·7 |

Source: H. W. Schneider, *Religion in Twentieth-Century America*. Cambridge: Harvard University Press, 1952, p. 23.

class, Catholic, drinking, urban, and potentially socialistic immigrants who threatened it (Gusfield, 1966). Evangelical religion was a weapon in the fight against Catholicism and the "godless social-service nonsense". In the same way, the Southern white élite defending slavery and a pre-industrial life-style saw themselves as Protestants defending the region from the polyglot, drinking population of the North—the Know-Nothing party and the Klan originated as anti-Catholic movements. It was inevitable that the new European immigrants, especially the Irish and German Catholics, would turn to the Democratic party, which became the defender of liquor, free immigration, and the poor.

The structure of the connections between politics, moral outlook, ethnic group and religion stamped the churches in America with more than theological identities, which still persist. The fervent and fundamentalist Protestantism of the South, among both black and white, still shapes a cultural resistance to the liberal and industrial North. The white churches struggled against the North's polyglot influences— Darwinism, Catholicism, the social sciences, drinking, gambling, Sunday opening and civil rights—just as they continued to champion the Confederate cause even after political and economic resistance had come to an end. Because of this, the Southern Protestant clergy and the churches are more powerful, doctrinally orthodox and fundamentalist than in the North, and can expect higher public and private commitment among their congregations. But as the region industrializes, leadership is beginning to pass from them to the industrial and professional élite. The Negro congregations have always been important as centres of resistance; the slave rebellions that did occur were led by preachers, and the black congregations of Baptists and Methodists found potent arguments in the Bible against the hypocrisy and oppression of their masters. At the time of emancipation, the large churches split between South and North, with the Southern Methodists, Baptists and Presbyterians continuing to hold that slavery was a civil and legal matter outside the churches' concern. The deterioration of race relations and increasing separation of blacks and whites in the late nineteenth century led to Negroes being allowed to establish their own denominations and, by 1945, 94 per cent of all Protestant American Negroes belonged to all-Negro denominations.

Since the church was the only social institution which they were able to control, it became a centre of social and political resistance, and becoming a preacher was the main avenue of social mobility. The civil rights movement of the fifties was first mobilized by middle-class congregations and led by Negro ministers; those dissatisfied with their meliorist approach to change and the little it achieved turned to secular alternatives.

In the North, successive groups of European immigrants turned in a strange land to their churches, only to find that they had not yet been established, or that they were dominated by another cultural group. The confusion of ethnic and religious ties led to considerable change. The gulf between the Catholicism or the Methodism of, say, German immigrants, and the existing American Catholic or Methodist congregations was all the greater because the newcomers were mainly of peasant origin, whose religion contained large "folk" elements unique to each area. Among the Protestants, the language that services were to be conducted in created difficulties. Some denominations allowed separate congregations to be set up on a language or national basis; others refused this, and the immigrants themselves set up separate bodies. In the extreme case, national bonds proved to be more powerful than religious barriers, and Catholics, Muslims, Protestants and Orthodox from Syria united in an Arabic-speaking church union. The Catholic church found that each generation of immigrants became the next generation's priesthood, resenting the new inflow from a different country. The old English Catholics were disturbed by the influx of Irish, who aroused prejudice against themselves and in consequence against all members of their religion. By the mid-nineteenth century, the priesthood was mainly Irish and trying in turn to prevent Germans, Italians and Poles transferring the features of their village Catholicism to the American church.

Historians are undecided as to how far the churches that acted as a source of identity and mobilization for new immigrants were rejected for the older American churches by the second and third generations of immigrants in their attempts to become assimilated. But all three major religions are now responding to strong social pressure to become a simple label, *alternatives* in a unified American pattern, as cultural differences between their congregations are smoothed away. The general characteristics of the new religion are taken from middle-class Protestant denominations, and the Jewish and the Catholic hierarchies are under pressure to make the patterns of their worship more compatible with this, that is, concentrated on the Sunday-morning service. Among Catholics, family churchgoing to Sunday Mass has increased as attendance at evening and week-day services has decreased, and the control of the Church over affairs that Protestantism defines as secular—science, books and films, marriage and divorce—has been widely resisted. Conservative and Reform Judaism have been founded and have grown just because they are *churches*, in which the observation of religion has been moved from the private and family rituals performed at home to the service at the synagogue, where the rabbi has metamorphosed from scholar to head of the community. Judaism in America has shifted from a primary concern with observing the Law to a public profession of faith; the successful middle-class business families who have abandoned Hebrew and the *mitzvot* which stamped them as abrasively different in secular life, have become more assiduous than their parents in attending synagogue (Sklare, 1955; Sklare and Greenblum, 1967).

These changes in Judaism and Catholicism appear to contradict the earlier argument that religion should not be treated as it is in functionalist analysis, as a single *thing*, because whatever its theology, social pressures will force it into the shape that is needed for the overall equilibrium of the society. Here is a case in which, part consciously, part unconsciously, changes are being brought about in two religious traditions by priests and congregations to make them fulfil the same societal and psychological needs as a third.

However, the pressure to converge is being applied by those members of all three faiths who are in the same general social position—middle-class families, predominantly business, living in the suburban communities of the North. Their experience is increasingly the same; the pressures on them for social conformity, for a church as a community institution, are great. Under such circumstances Jews and Catholics are likely to respond to efforts to make their religious observance move toward a general equivalency with that of their neighbours. No one is suggesting that they adopt the fervent fundamentalist Protestantism of the poor or the South; and indeed, among the poor, where pressures to conformity are less, ethnic and religious differences continue to stand out sharply.

Religious beliefs are both a function of and an influence upon social experiences. Experiences differ widely, even in quite small societies; in modern societies, the major way of categorizing and examining the differences is to examine the differences in experience which make up the distinct worlds of different social classes and ethnic groups. These differences make the psychological, cultural and social expectation and experience of religion different for members of different occupational and ethnic groups, even though in some cases they may be members of the same religious congregation.

# CHAPTER VI

# *Religion and Social Group*

The discussion of religion in relation to social group derives from the work of Weber, and ultimately from Marx. That there are correlations between the membership of different churches and different social classes, or that religious beliefs and practices systematically vary by social class, is indisputable. Even amongst Catholic congregations working in a fixed tradition, Pin (1956) has described the variations according to the class composition of the neighbourhood of mood, decorations, and way in which priest and congregation are related to worship. But what general significance do the correlations have? In Europe, opposition to the established political and economic order has entailed opposition to the church with which the establishment was identified. Though structural differentiation has attenuated the link between churches and political life, this general constellation of class and religious antagonisms, though muffled, is still there; in the United States it has never really existed, since cultural conflicts were between different religious groups rather than between dominant church and anti-clerical sect or political party.

As a consequence of this, research into the interrelation of religion and social group in the United States was originally centred on the role of religion in social mobility. America, a society of immigrants with no established church, contained an unusually large number of churches each of which was associated with a particular social group or small number of groups. These groups have had very differing success in American life. What part has religion played in this process?

## 1 SECTARIANISM AND SUCCESS

The Protestant denominations and sects of the United States originated among the poor; but many of them have found that

as their congregations grew wealthier, their organization
became more routinized, formalized, and church-like (Brewer,
1952 and Chamberlayne, 1964, of Methodism; Davies, 1962, of
Mormons; Harrison, 1959, of Baptism). Men seem commonly
to move between denominations, prompted by their rising social
status to move to the church which locally enjoys higher status
and a wealthier congregation. Weber (1946) observed that New
England businessmen appeared to belong to certain Protestant
sects not only because their theology ratified capitalist accumulation, but because to belong to such a sect was an invaluable
mark of financial integrity and provided necessary contacts
with business associates. Moving between churches for these
motives may be no commoner in America than elsewhere but it
is certainly more explicit.

For those sectarians who did become wealthier, were the
values and behaviour given to them by religious experience
necessary causes, or was their success due only to an open
economic environment allied to the purely material benefits of
sectarian membership which Weber had described? As many
authors have argued, the enclosed social world of the sect,
where contact with the unredeemed is avoided and worldly
goods despised, may handicap the social mobility of members
by leading them to devalue the world and to devote their
energies to attaining office within the sect. "The real blue-
bloods are those who are firm in their faith," said a poor agri-
cultural worker, a member of a Californian revivalist church
(Goldschmidt, 1947). The utopian sects (such as the Shakers,
Harmonists and Amish) which form enclosed communities,
although they may require hard work and abstemiousness from
their members and while the community as a whole may
prosper, insulate their members from the world so that they
cannot succeed within it; if they leave the sect, they forfeit their
property. But the Seventh Day Adventists, despite many
stringent rules, such as a Sabbath on a Saturday, which might
seem to interfere with business success, have shown upward
movement as a social group because the sect values worldly
success (Sargent, 1962). The Moravians provide an excellent
test of the effects of theology versus those of economic and social
environment. The same theology led Moravian communities to
capitalist enterprise, in the shape of Bethlem Steel, and upward
social mobility in Pennsylvania, where the group had bourgeois

H

leaders and hard work could result in economic success in a society where it was admired, but it also led to economic stagnation in Saxony, where the community was led by aristocrats without a commitment to hard and profitable work, and where, in an isolated farming community, it could bring little improvement in economic reward (Gollin, 1967).

The religions of the dispossessed, marked by emotional release, fundamentalism and contempt for the unredeemed, offer their members a refuge from the scorn and hardship that they experience in the world (Pope, 1942). In particular they appeal to the poor migrants in big cities, entering at the bottom of the wage market and living in disorganized neighbourhoods, who seek the security they offer. But whereas Holt (1940) thought that the migrants from the Southern United States who joined Holiness and Pentecostalist churches were reacting in a negative way to cultural shock by seeking a religion which defended old rural values rather than developing more functional ideologies, Johnson (1961) and A. Parsons (1965) argue that Holiness and Pentecostalist churches *do* encourage their members to adopt the secular value-systems of individualism and achievement. They emphasize the enormous importance of the gulf which the lower-class sect member must cross in separating himself from the disorderly life of the urban or rural slum, with its traditional masculine pleasures of gambling, drinking, smoking, sports, profanity and a lack of scrupulousness over money or time. Stephenson (1968) vividly described the conflict in an Appalachian village between the self-indulgent lives of the unredeemed and the hopes of their wives, who urged them to get converted, become respectable, and get on in modern life. The ascetic behaviour that members of the community of the elect must adopt trains them to forgo gratification now for the long-term goal of salvation, and the emotional, erotic, or magical aspects of their religious experiences do not detract from the economic consequences of their changed behaviour. Indeed, by providing opportunities for releasing tension, the services strengthen their commitment to the sect and to a routinized and disciplined life-style. As Weber and Pope pointed out, the saved make good workmen, if not good entrepreneurs.

Most Protestant sects in America gain a wealthier and more established congregation in time, but not only because their original members become wealthier. It could also be that the congregations themselves inevitably change over time to a more established and ritualist form of worship in which they are less attractive to the poor, or they may actively try to recruit wealthy members and discourage poor ones. As the status of teachers in a small town in California fell in the local pecking-order, they were no longer expected to attend the élite church, but were made welcome at those of the next rank (Goldschmidt, 1947). The changing theology of congregations is less important than their general atmosphere in attracting or repelling their members; they are described as homey and fervent, or decent and decorous. A Pentecostalist congregation in a neighbour-hood that was growing more affluent changed its beliefs in several predictable ways; material wealth and secular concerns came to be seen as consistent with, rather than a barrier to, full spiritual life; science, whilst still subordinate to divine purposes, was no longer sinful but useful; women could still demonstrate their spirituality through emotional outbursts at meetings for worship, but men were now seen as more fitting leaders of prayer meetings. Those members of the church who were marginal to society, who had previously found release from their sense of failure in mutual confession in an atmosphere of warm empathy, now found that their outbursts were seen as not quite respectable. The increasing accommodation of the church to society had made it more successful, but had led to conflict between its members over basic beliefs (Young, 1960).

Small sects can change their theological emphasis and ritual as the status and needs of their members change. But do they help their members to achieve upward social mobility and, if so, is it the religious *beliefs* which are the agents, or some other consequence of being a sectarian? The studies so far suggest no conclusion. Churches cannot shift nearly so easily, and in any case, their membership is drawn from a wider social group. Can their theologies affect their members, or is it other factors associated with membership of a particular religious tradition which give Protestants, Jews and Catholics very differing worldly success? Is it Judaism, or the effects of antisemitic prejudices, the middle-class composition and aspirations of Jewish communities, a characteristic pattern of encouragement and reward for some kinds of success which mothers give to Jewish sons, which makes Jews more successful?

## 2 PROTESTANTS AND CATHOLICS

Considerable research has been carried out in the United States on the classic Weberian problem: the different rates of worldly success on the part of Catholics, Protestants and Jews. However, the research has not so far resolved whether the difference is due to different religious *beliefs*—this-worldly asceticism versus living "ethically hand to mouth".

The most important study is still that made in Detroit by Lenski (1961), which established a marked difference between white Protestants and Jews on the one hand, and Catholics and Negro Protestants on the other, in that the latter two were more embedded in family controls, less aspirant for a college education, especially a scientific one, less likely to go into business, and less successful if they did. (See also Mayer and Sharp, 1962. Vaughan *et al.* [1966] showed that few Catholics became scientists, and if they did, tended to leave the church.) However, Greeley (1963; and see Greeley and Rossi, 1966; Wagner *et al.*, 1959) argues that the Catholic church is not opposed to scientific knowledge, and in his study found no evidence that Catholic students studied science less frequently, lost their faith if they did, or were less interested in economic achievement. (He did, though, find that Catholic students avoided the social sciences, the area of knowledge where conflict with a traditional religious framework is now strongest, and which is overwhelmingly the province of agnostic Jews.) He believes that typically "Jewish" or "Catholic" attitudes have nothing to do with Judaism or Catholicism, but stem from the different social situation of the two religious groups; the Jews as sophisticated migrants from urban areas, the Catholics predominantly peasants. He found that the socio-economic status of Catholics rose with each generation that their families had been in America.

Further studies have complicated rather than solved the issue, and show how elaborate the ramifications of religious belief, membership and social-group ties are. The social and economic status of Catholics, and of the Catholic church, has been rising in America since the last war (Glenn and Hyland, 1967; Fichter, 1961). But Catholics are concentrated in the large cities of the North, where the opportunity to move upward is greater than it is for the Protestant populations of the rural areas or of the South; and the most successful social group is still composed almost entirely of Protestants, Jews, and the irreligious. Mack *et al.* (1956) found no relationship between religion and aspirational levels, or religion and social mobility, whereas Veroff *et al.* (1962) found considerable differences in achievement motivation between Protestants and Catholics which they linked with other studies of child-rearing practices suggesting a "Protestant" pattern of guilt, or reliance on internalized controls by threatening loss of love, and a "Catholic" pattern of shame which rested on the external pressures of concrete reward and punishment. (However, few of the studies appear to have controlled adequately for the influence of different class environments.) Yet further studies (Abramson and Noll, 1966; Kosa and Rachielle, 1963) find significant differences in levels of aspiration and achievement between the ethnic groups *inside* Catholicism. Italian Catholics were considerably more secular, and had higher and more "capitalist" aspirations than the more devout, traditionalist and less ambitious Irish and German Catholics. (The Italians arrived the most recently, thus casting doubts on Greeley's original thesis about length of time in America as the crucial factor.)

But, unfortunately for sociologists, achievement is not a function of expressed ambition or wants. Ambition varies; not all its forms are equally effective. Turner's (1964) excellent but neglected study of ambition among Californian adolescents showed that poor boys were highly ambitious, but that they did not value either higher education or the strict interior discipline and the devotion to work as an end in itself, rather than as a means to money and power, which they would need in order to get highly-paid jobs in an advanced industrial society. And there is some evidence (Veroff *et al.*, 1962; Greeley, 1963) that Catholics are prone to adopt a materialist and external form of ambition—an interest in money and power—rather than the more effective internalized and idealized ambitions of Protestants. But even to reinterpret the greater success of Protestants in terms of different socialization patterns is to ignore the pressures of the external environment. Lenski's finding about the lack of success among Negro Protestants has been forgotten; if they lack the internalized ambition of their white counterparts, this is presumably because they realize it would be useless. Failure in business or the educational system is due to more than lack of theological or psychological motivation, though it may produce it.

The effect on men's lives of being Protestant or Catholic is produced not only by religious belief and experience but because religious affiliation is also a *label* for ethnic groups which have very different chances of worldly success. Though Catholics and Jews have gained considerable economic and political power in the United States, they are still largely excluded from the Anglo-Saxon Protestant élite—the heads of large corporations, educational institutions, and the military bureaucracy. The ruling group in many cities still use their membership of a small number of Protestant congregations— those imported from England or Scotland—to define, to both outsiders and themselves, their élite status (Baltzell, 1964).

The balance of power between Democrats and Republicans, and consequently between ethnic and religious minorities and white Protestants, determines the relationships between the churches in every community where the old ties between religious and political organizations still hold. Underwood (1957) traced the interconnection between economic, political, social and theological divisions in a New England industrial town. The Catholic groups were gaining power at the expense of the Protestants; political power had been the first to shift as more and more Catholic immigrants had streamed in to work in the Yankee paper mills. The Protestant clergy became increasingly angry as the Catholic hierarchy attempted to control aspects of the public life of the town, culminating in a prohibition of public meetings on birth control. But to the Catholic clergy, who came predominantly from the theocratic communities of Ireland, the church had a firm position on matters of faith and morality which it was their duty to uphold. The educated and upper-class Catholic élite, however, familiar with arguments in learned journals which were not reported in the Diocesan press, were better informed than the priesthood, more tolerant theologically, and consequently unreceptive to clerical guidance (see also Abramson and Noll, 1966). Some of the most acrimonious points of contact between the two communities were in the economic sphere, in the hiring of labour for the paper mills, which used to be determined by the religious affiliation of the foremen. But as the labour unions succeeded in rationalizing hiring processes, the churches were generally withdrawing from intervention in what was increasingly described as the "technical" world of work, and restricting their attention to "religious" issues. Structural differentiation meant that all the churches were less and less able to define public issues as legitimate religious ones.

## 3 RELIGIOUS EXPECTATIONS AND SOCIAL EXPERIENCE

The research discussed so far shows that there are links between different churches and social groups which affect the nature of theology and of religious experience. But large religious groups draw their membership from more than one social class, and so congregations vary in their social composition. How does social class alone affect individual religious experience? In both Britain and the United States, higher rates of *private* religious practice—private prayer and Bible-reading —are reported by the poor, and higher rates of *public* worship by the upper-middle class. Demerath (1965) distinguished between the associational religiosity which is marked by attending a church and formal involvement in it, and the communal religiosity, which is found more often in small sects, where friends are only found among the congregation, and which, since religion sets them apart from the world, spills over into other parts of life. These ways of being religious were correlated with social class as well as denomination; but in addition, it was found that the lower the social status of members of any given Protestant congregation, the higher the proportion of communal religiosity among members of each social stratum within it. In addition, those who were of discrepant or marginal social status were more likely to experience communal religiosity, though the association was explained by the fact that both social marginality and communal religiosity were more common among the elderly and among women. Among the religious, the lower class are generally more fundamentalist, lay greater emphasis on the importance of a literal Bible, sin and an after-life, and are more devout and more knowledgeable about doctrinal matters than the middle class. The religious upper-middle-class man sees religion as almost entirely an ethical matter, and in consequence attaches great importance to the right to self-determination of religious beliefs.

Theologies express the themes appropriate to the different expectations and experiences of each social group. Conversely, theology translated into practice creates for those born into a church or sect the "shape" which ever after religion will hold for them. In the United States, the denominations of the upper-middle class have a liberal theology with stress on individual ethical conduct; the denominations of the poor are predominantly theologically conservative. As the middle class grows, liberal theology will probably increase. One study (Stark and Glock, 1968) challenged a widespread view that the religious groups growing most rapidly in America are the fundamentalist sects. Their evidence was that among Protestants, those who had moved between denominations had moved in a more liberal direction, though they did not test whether the same individuals were part of the parallel movement into the middle class and the big cities. The conservative denominations had a more loyal membership, but were not recruiting; the liberal denominations were attracting new members, but their church attendance was sporadic, and they were likely to leave altogether. Higher education by itself increases the likelihood of agnosticism or extreme religious liberalism (Goldsen *et al.*, 1960).

Would these findings about variations in religious belief also be true for Britain? There is no research into different types of religiosity, but we know something about the overall class composition of the different churches, and so can speculate about the connections between their theology, the predominant social class of their adherents, and the structure of the religious sub-community. The connections are less strong than in the United States, partly because, ironically in a country with a state church, religion is considered to be an entirely private concern. The social necessity to be an Anglican, or a member of at least a religion, among those connected with government, politics, education and public morality generally has declined rapidly during the twentieth century, and so has the social differential between the churches. The links between theology and experience are complicated by the fact that the Anglican church, the church of the majority, is also the Church of England. Both because it *is* the established church, and has therefore to be responsive to more than internal pressure, and because it is deliberately amorphous in order to appeal to all of society, the theology of the Anglican church is probably less important than what it stands for. In small traditional communities, the "Conservative Party at prayer" jibe still seems accurate enough.

The community studies which are the only source of material on the links between religion, politics and social group have mainly been carried out in such communities—in villages or small towns with an established social and industrial structure. In nineteenth-century Glossop, a Derbyshire mill town, the ruling Anglican-Conservative connection of large manufacturers was opposed by the Dissenters, small mill owners and workers, led by two families of Unitarians. The rise of the labour movement only affected the structure by drawing away some of the more radical dissenters (Birch, 1959). In Banbury, an Oxfordshire market-town, the élite had also been the Anglican-Conservative group, strongly represented on the borough council and controlling some of the sports clubs. The old opposition was again the Free-Church/Liberal group, recruited here from among tradespeople who were Wesleyans, and artisans who were Primitive Methodists, labourers being either unchurched or Church of England. Outside this older social structure, a new group of manufacturers and workmen had appeared, less associated with the churches than with professional associations and trade unionism (Stacey, 1960). Again, a Cumberland village was divided into austere Bible-Christians, who formed the Liberal Club, and the laxer Anglicans, some of whom ran the Conservative Club. The different patterns of church and sectarian religiosity were marked, the Methodists attending service weekly, whereas Anglicans attended church in a pattern which corresponded less with Christian feasts than with the progress of the secular year, for example the quarterly rent days. The Anglican church was seen by everyone but the incumbent as general to the parish; it had become analogous to the religious institution of a simpler society, where scant attention was paid to belief, but the rituals of the church were used to mark social and personal transitions.

In these traditional communities, Anglicanism and Dissent are less alternative forms of *religious* belief or organization than they are part of the structure of different social groups; the established landowners or members of the old professions, and the old bourgeoisie of small manufacturers, tradesmen and artisans. Religion has a different meaning and role for the two groups. Old-fashioned Anglicans attached little importance to theodicy, and much to the aesthetic and rites of the church and its role in the community. Their missionary efforts among the nineteenth-century poor (a very different impulse from the evangelical one) meant that although skilled workers might become Methodists, the churchgoing poor, unless they were Irish, were likely to be Anglican. Even by the start of the nineteenth century, Dissent was recruiting mainly among the urban middle class and skilled artisans.

Originally, the new dissenters had been the vehicle of opposition in England to established religion and the squirearchy, and they had flourished among the relatively independent craftsmen, or in isolated mining and fishing villages. As such, among Primitive Methodists in particular, the religion was fervent, emotional and egalitarian; whole villages were unified under ministers, at once spiritual and secular leaders. But as the local chapels prospered in the towns, they became closed communities of skilled workers and tradesmen, and the poorer members sought, in repeated schism, for a renewed enthusiasm (Pelling, 1968; Currie, 1968). But as religious institutions declined in saliency and political ones increased, opposition to the established order shifted from religious dissent to political radicalism and socialism. The Dissenting tradition is still far stronger in Wales and in Scotland than in England; fortified, perhaps, not only by the greater religious observance characteristic of rural areas but by the role of defining the native resistance to the lax, Anglican, landowning English (Emmet, 1964; Pelling, 1968). But in Wales at least, the persistent ties between Nonconformity and radicalism have largely been broken as class divisions have come to seem more important than national identity. The urban workers in the new industries have lost their cultural ties with Nonconformity, though in the heavy-industry region of southwest Wales, the links between class, politics, union and religious denomination both provided the leaders for cultural, political and social life, and defined the churches in terms of a left-right political continuum from the ultra-democratic Congregationalist to the middle-class Presbyterian or Anglican (Brennan *et al.*, 1954).

Celtic dissent and small communities apart, in the new housing estates and large cities, life is not structured around the churches in England. The large suburban congregations of the United States are echoed, but much more faintly. In a privatized life, Durkheimian religion has no place; Weberian religion has no claim on those who never had it so good.

## 4 CULTS OF SUCCESS

It is easy to see the correspondence between most sects and the social experience of their members. Whether the stress falls on the equality of all true believers, their superior position in the next world, the meaning of suffering, or the comforts and ecstatic release in finding the Lord, the connection with feeling underprivileged is plain. But what does religion offer the powerful and successful in modern society? In a society with an established church, the church provides the image of a stable society and state united under God; the powerful may use it, more or less consciously, as a means of social control. But the theology of the church will not correspond to their world-view, because the churches are based on much older metaphysical structures. Weber pointed out that the successful in modern societies need theologies which ratify worldly well-being, base themselves on "science", and stress man's divinity and power through his ability to control.

Such individuals may adopt the secular ideologies of humanism, scientism, nationalism or, in communist societies, Marxism-Leninism. These world-views resemble each other in stressing man's *control* over the world, and enhance the self-esteem of those who use and create the knowledge on which such control is based. The outlook of these philosophies is optimistic; their model of man is of a being both good, social and rational. But many more upper-middle-class people have a more conservative metaphysic in which traditional Christianity or Judaism has given way to a more vaguely conceived set of beliefs of an optimistic and this-worldly kind. In both England and the United States, many of them may continue to attend a conventional church, especially if they are members of traditional communities or professions, because to do so is to them a part of social duty. But their private religious views are quite different.

In the United States, a series of intellectual currents spreading outward from the New England transcendentalists has produced a large body of popular religious literature, read by many people who may still attend orthodox denominations with their "theodicy of sin and suffering". But best-selling religious literature over the last century has described religion in terms of subjective experience, not eternal truths. More and more, it is something which eases pain, makes life pleasant and healthy, and possibly even wealthy (Schneider and Dornbusch, 1958). Religion has become more and more explicitly connected with health in this literature; by thinking rightly, men can overcome sickness and sorrow, and gain mental well-being by faith. (The popularity of Norman Vincent Peale and the religion of reassurance, and the religio-psychiatric movement, are part of the same syndrome.) Sin is often described in the literature as if it is something unreal, a product of the mind—"negative thinking" (Griswold, 1934; Wardwell, 1965; Braden, 1963).

Such a concept of religion has many appeals for the wealthy and successful. Its individualism, focus on human relationships, the immanence which justifies man's confidence, and the use of semi-scientific knowledge, combine to present religion as something which is a *means* to happiness in modern society. The lack of interest in dogma or ultimate ends ratifies a satisfied experience in the world, and provides wealthy people, who must move smoothly among those of different religious faiths, with an undogmatic creed which stresses good personal relationships. The religious instruction in a school in a wealthy Canadian suburb, which had to be acceptable to both Jew and Gentile, consisted "almost exclusively in the translation of pleasant small-group or primary-group experiences into a weakened vocabulary of traditional religion" (Seeley *et al.*, 1956).

The effects of transcendentalism were not only to shift emphasis in middle-class religion away from sin and suffering to positive thinking, adjustment, and well-being, but also resulted in some religious cults, the cults of success. Never attracting a large membership, they represented the world-view of the increasingly educated and wealthy professional and business class. The doctrine that the world is an illusion and reality lies beyond it is common to them all, but some—New Thought, Christian Science, the Church of Religious Science, Divine Science—stress that belief can heal, whereas others—Spiritualism and Theosophy—are largely occult. Scientology and Psychiana are modern versions of these cults, and reflect, significantly enough, a greater concern with mental than with physical health. The Ethical Culture movement, beginning as a schism from Reform Judaism, was based on the same idealist and transcendentalist theology cast in an agnostic form.

Not only the metaphysics but the organizational forms of these cults are suited to the needs of their members. Most of the healing and gnostic movements of modern society are cults; that is, relationships between their members are at a minimum. In some cases, members merely subscribe to the church for literature; in others, they may occasionally attend its meetings, but less to worship and experience the community of believers than to gain arcane knowledge or to submit to the personal powers of a teacher or healer. Membership is consequently very often shortlived (B. R. Wilson, 1959a; Berger, 1954). The cults seem to be especially appealing to middle-aged women, who form a large majority of their audiences and, presumably, for whom the problems of personal health and adjustment loom large. The emotional disengagement of these congregations, and their attempts to avoid and to deny, rather than to collectively surmount the problems of death and suffering, are of course the antithesis of religion as Durkheim conceived it. But the values and the circumstances of wealthy and successful people in modern society lead them to minimize collective emotion. For example, wealthy and educated Americans prefer simple funerals, seeking to suppress emotion as far as possible and to avoid the traditional theological consolations, in which in any case few of them entirely believe (Bowman, 1959; Kephart, 1950). Psychoanalytic theory and practice, identified as scientific, modern and effective, is the best consolation in a privatized life.

Cults of success attract few members compared with the large numbers who read popular religious works, or listen to radio preachers such as Peale, who stress that religion is a means to well-being. Theologians have reacted to this popular gospel of personal happiness and adjustment with considerable distaste. The liberals have no desire to see religion used to bolster the social complacency of the wealthy; the conservatives see the core of Christianity as Christ's power to redeem men from the very real sin, suffering and temptation which is part of the condition of mankind. The cults of reassurance by denying the existence of sin demolish the meaning of redemption. Some theologians (Schneider, 1952; Berger, 1961) think that the increasing popularity of church attendance in twentieth-century America is due to the appeal of religion as reassurance, and deplore it. Indeed, all religious organizations must choose between challenging and solacing their members' worldly experience. Glock *et al.* (1967) and Metz (1967) found that when clergy tried to build the large, financially viable and united congregations by which their superiors judged their success, they found that their original doctrines, usually sharply in opposition to many American secular values, were overcome by the values of survival. In a society where the churches are not viewed as set over against the world, and must compete for its allegiance, they must accommodate to society at large if their members feel that they have no quarrel with it.

## 5 CLASS AND CONGREGATION

This review of the findings about connections between the social class, doctrines and organization of religious bodies in England and the United States shows only the ramification and uncertainty of the connections. Sometimes the links between the needs which are clearly associated with the situation of a particular social group, and the dogma of a small church monopolized by the group, are obvious. Mainly they are far looser; the church was founded in a very different time, or recruits divergent members. And many members are less aware of the dogma of their church—how, for example, it interprets worldly inequalities—than they are of the "feel" of the local congregation; homey and fervent, or decorous and cool. Most of the findings are from the United States; similar studies are needed in Britain. In particular, the role of religious beliefs as factors in social mobility, and how the beliefs actually operate (if they do) needs more thorough investigation and subtle treatment. How do the laity perceive the theology of their churches, and when do they notice that it is at odds with their private beliefs? The community studies show that different congregations of the same denomination vary in doctrinal emphasis according to the social position of the congregation in the area, and with its links with local political parties and other institutions. How do congregations shift their positions? The research would require preliminary studies of the moral values and general expectations of religion in different groups of the population. Sensitive explorations of social variations in concepts such as human control versus fate or providence; the relation of this world to other possible worlds; or "proper" behaviour under stress, would illuminate a great deal.

# CHAPTER VII

# *Religion and Secularization*

Secularization is the most important issue, theoretically and practically, in the sociology of religion. Practically, because much of the interest of churchmen in the subject is because they hope to retard, prevent, or at least understand secularization. Theoretically, because if religion is disappearing in modern societies, it is possible for us to discuss what caused it and what it does by examining what antecedent condition has disappeared or been modified, and what behaviour seems to be taking over from religious behaviour. To put it crudely, if religion is *par excellence* ritual, collective behaviour, we should find new forms of this, or a reaction to its loss, in a secular society. If religion is beliefs, values, and ways of justifying them, we will find new values, or a situation where behaviour is not guided by large-scale belief-systems, in a secular society. If religion is a socially structured response to personality needs, we will find alternative responses to them appearing.

Since secularization, whatever else it is, is undoubtedly closely connected with modernization and industrialization, the *ceteris paribus* problem makes accurate discussion of the nature and effects of secularization very difficult. But there are other problems.

## 1 THE DEFINITION OF "SECULARIZATION"

Many problems hinge on the shifting meaning of "secularization". Like many other key concepts in sociology, its meaning has become so diffuse as to obscure rather than clarify, so that, for example, both the full churches of the United States, and the empty ones of England, are pointed to as evidence of its existence. (For discussions of the concept, see O'Dea, 1966; D. A. Martin, 1969; and Yinger, 1969.) Writers from within a religious tradition commonly mean by secularization a weakening of "true religion" in the lives of men, and thus large congregations are not incompatible with a "secularization of the spirit". The difficulty with such arguments lies in their assumption of a previous Age of Faith; did religious ideas greatly influence the mute unlettered majority? Sociologists generally mean by secularization something rather broader; "the process whereby religious thinking, practice and institutions lose social significance" (B. R. Wilson, 1966).

It clarifies matters if we distinguish between a secularization of individual beliefs (in which human beings lose interest in the supernatural, in providence, in luck, in guilt, redemption and atonement, and turn to purely technically rational means of organizing work and relationships) and a secularization in which individuals remain as prone to resort to non-rational beliefs and acts as they were, but where these are no longer formally called religious, nor (consequently) controlled by a church's authority or its theology. The latter position seems nearer to the state of affairs in modern societies. Thus, the churches lose their power to embody the moral consensus of a society, and are increasingly by-passed in national debates over social policy and morality, or it comes to be assumed that they will ultimately adopt the prevailing view. A radical decrease in the power of religious *institutions* coexists with private metaphysics which are not particularly secular. But because they are **no** longer mediated by theology and definite moral teachings, they become more disparate, more dominated by other areas of experience.

Another conceptual distinction which must be made at once and borne in mind is that between secularization proper, and structural differentiation. Some writers consider manifestations of the latter (the move from an educational system controlled by the church to one controlled by the state, for instance) as evidence of the former. Herbert Spencer, the originator of the concept, seems to have done. He used structural differentiation to describe the process by which secular roles and institutions became separated from religious ones. To him, the process was bound up with the rise of Nonconformity in English society; once the religious monopoly of the established church had been challenged, religion became a matter of personal choice. Consequently, the close organizational and ideological bonds between any particular church or set of religious beliefs and other parts of society, such as the family or the economy, would have to be replaced by a bond which could accommodate to alternative religions, and ultimately men would begin to interact in the non-religious areas of society without reference to their religious beliefs.

The nature of the links between religion, social control and social knowledge is altered when more than one religion proselytizes among the same people. If religions are defined as belonging to distinct, separate subgroups, they have little effect on one another, but once they become seen as universal, the cohesive world-view is breached. No church can control the changes of secular life, because it can no longer command the absolute adherence of its members. Competition between churches for membership makes resisting secular wants with spiritual values dangerous (Luckmann, 1967). Once churches accept, more or less explicitly, that doctrines must sometimes be modified to accommodate to secular changes, religious values lose the preeminence which it is argued that they can have in a traditional society. The statesmen of eighteenth-century England who argued forcefully against tolerating Catholics, Nonconformists and Jews realized this. Though they were themselves often Deists, they believed that the Anglican church would be able to maintain social stability only if it had a religious monopoly.

Despite this, many sociologists believe that structural differentiation does not entail secularization. They argue that it gives religion a limited but purer, and hence more powerful, role, since once the church has ceased to be involved with secular activities, it can be based more firmly on purely spiritual and internal premises. Although attractive to theologians (see Winter, 1961; Berger, 1969), the argument makes little sociological sense; making values pure and divorcing them from social contexts and pressures seems likely to weaken, not strengthen, the likelihood of them becoming a basis for action. Talcott Parsons is the most important sociologist to believe that structural differentiation does make religion more powerful. His views on religion, as on other matters, are hard to summarize accurately, but are approximately as follows.

The institutional subsystems in any society cannot function unless they are legitimized. The basis of all kinds of power is not force, but normative legitimacy. Thus, all social action is

I

ultimately moral, because it is oriented by a set of value-expectations which become part of our role-expectations and our goals. Society is therefore a moral enterprise, and its ultimate values are religious. Parsons argues that it is incorrect to see the United States as a society in the last stages of secularization. Rather, the role of religion is being redefined. Structural differentiation has meant that religion has lost its secondary functions and retained its "core" function, that of "the regulation of the balance of the motivational commitment of the individual to the values of his society". That is, religion maintains the balance between the roles that men must perform in society—their practical commitments—and the problems of their ultimate fate and the meaning of what they do. Confusingly, Parsons insists that the core functions of religion are not cognitive, but practical. Religion has lost control of the moral and intellectual spheres of American life, but paradoxically continues to represent ultimate values. He asserts that the increasing concern with the quality of inner experience, with problems of personality and personal obligation, is connected with alterations in the structure of personal values. Both changes make religion more central and important. The lack of interest in formal theology merely reflects the general lack of interest in abstract thought among Americans.

Both theoretical and practical objections have been made to this rather ambiguous position. Empirically, Parsons's view that religion in modern America shows signs of structural differentiation, *not* secularization, means that American religious institutions should be more concerned with the core functions of religion than they were; that they should have a clearer and more separate identity against secular institutions; and that this should entail a narrower conception of the role of the minister. Sykes (1969) argues that none of this is true, and that this is because there has been secularization. That is, the churches have become reflexive and secondary institutions. It is difficult to define "core" functions for any institution in a way that avoids them becoming identical with "residual" functions, which may or may not be "core". More generally, why should religious values be seen as "core", rather than the rules of thumb for conduct now discussed purely in the context of work, or of education, or family life? Parsons would argue, because they are the overall integrating values. But are they? And even if they are, are they used? Why should we accept the notion of a hierarchy of control, in which the sentiments and norms which guide interaction are governed from above, rather than a situation where changes in social structure and patterns of interaction bring about changes in role-values, and hence in ultimate values? (Parsons himself sometimes argues for this. 1960, p. 319.)

Secularization refers not only to the increasing separation of religious institutions, values and roles; it can also be employed to mean an increasing attention to proximate, short-term, or expedient ends. Weber, for example, feared such a "demystification of the world", in which men would become increasingly concerned with very limited, pragmatic, and self-interested ends, *not* because a framework of common values could be assumed, but because it could not be assumed. A world, for example, in which men went through the routines of rational material acquisition for proximate ends—wealth, status, social conformity—rather than for the larger ethical ends which had once made their activity a "calling". Parsons sometimes tends to the optimistic view, that the peaceful coexistence of different religious systems in the United States can only be because there is a universal commitment to an overall value-system which validates the social system as a whole. But at other times, he shows concern that particularistic values are becoming more dominant than general ones, and that ultimately this must entail a loss of adaptive power on the part of the social system. Conflict must ensue because the system will move out of equilibrium as proximate ends, based on different locations in the pattern-variables, fail to be mediated by overall values. The individual, for example, experiences potential conflict between the particularistic values of family obligations and the universalistic mores of his occupational ethics (as so often, Parsons takes an idealized version of professional life as representative of all occupational ideologies), and if the general sphere of values has lost its power to regulate them in a single system, insoluble disjunctions will result in behaviour.

Parsons, in fact, is operating with two distinct meanings of secularization—the increasing structural differentiation of the role of the religious professional and religious institutions from other areas of life, and the weakening power of general, integrating values, whether "religious", or scientific, humanist or

Marxist. The fact of structural differentiation is indisputable; the very efforts of radical clergy to combat it only reveal its extent. What is in dispute is how far it entails secularization in the more general second sense, "the process whereby religious thinking, practice and institutions lose social significance". Most sociologists would claim that structural differentiation does entail secularization; counter-claims rest on identifying religion with very general assumptions underlying all action. The way in which the process of secularization has affected other parts of the social structure is still largely unknown. The rest of this chapter sketches in the kind of evidence which has been collected to illuminate certain crucial junctures in the process.

## 2 BRITAIN—DISENGAGEMENT

For a long time, secularization in Britain was discussed as if it began with the explicit rejection of Christian dogma by various Victorian scientists and scholars. Only recently have popular religious beliefs, and dimensions of secularism other than beliefs, come to be examined. These show how mistaken it is to think in terms of a previous religious "baseline" away from which there has been a constant movement. Lukewarm commitment, reluctance to attend church, and resort to superstitious explanations have, if priests and parsons are to be believed, long been true of the English. Some of the very poor were already conspicuous by their absence from church as early as the seventeenth century (Hill, 1964; Laslett, 1965), and Swift and Cobbett were not the only observers to comment on the irreligion of country men and women, often thought of as more devout. Each generation thinks itself uniquely irreligious; attendance at church in a Cumberland village had been low for four hundred years, according to parish records, but each Anglican incumbent had thought that this was a recent trend (W. M. Williams, 1956).

A recent excellent study of popular beliefs in sixteenth- and seventeenth-century England (Thomas, 1971) enables us for the first time to assess in detail the relationship between the rise of Protestantism and various aspects of secularization. Thomas describes a history of constant oscillation between religion as transcendent and religion as magic. (His picture is strikingly similar to Hume's outline.) The medieval church had been forced to claim supernatural powers for itself in order to combat pagan beliefs, so that saints and relics and images had assumed a miraculous efficacy, prayers were used as charms, and the sacraments had magical powers (for example, the widespread belief in the magical powers of the communion wafer). The Catholic hierarchy tried to prevent religious powers becoming completely detached from the intentions with which rites were carried out, or from their moral meaning, but only defined as superstitious those beliefs which they disapproved of or which invoked the aid of the Devil. The Reformation saw a radical effort to divide magic and religion again, and to abolish all magical elements from the church, especially claims to *operate* the power of God.

Magic involved a kind of amoral automatism in the workings of the world—unbaptized children went to hell and God struck down those who inadvertently took his name in vain. The effect of the Reformation was to contest such automatism with the idea of the importance of each man's individual will and intentions, and his responsibility to seek grace and communicate with God. How, then, did men cope with fears and dreads in the interregnum between the discrediting of magic and the rise of the technical remedies of science, which were not apparent for another two centuries or so? Thomas describes the increasing drawing-apart of the world-views of the educated and of the superstitious. By the mid-seventeenth century, they inhabited two mental worlds. The superstitious still relied heavily on astrology, magical beliefs and remedies for sickness and trouble, and witchcraft. Though the material conditions of life had vastly improved by the end of the seventeenth century, and economic and social hardships were now understood by the more sophisticated to be due to impersonal causes, technical control had not really increased, nor had the basic problems that magic, etcetera, was concerned with been altered. But what had changed was the *aspiration* to technical control, and the appearance of *theories*, rather than techniques, which cast the understanding of the world in mechanical terms. At first, mechanical theories had coexisted with divine providence, and signs and portents of God's purpose were searched for along with natural causation. After the Reformation, to rely solely on divine aid was regarded as impertinent and superstitious. (Because the casting of lots had been a direct appeal for divine guidance, the Puritans forbade games of chance.)

By the seventeenth century it was no longer intellectually fashionable to see events as God's punishments or rewards, and so prayer as divination or as petition for specific ends was also out of favour among intellectuals, though it remained current among many clergy and laymen until at least the mid-nineteenth century. But the tension toward magic remained; during the Commonwealth, the sects which arose among the poor revived the wonder-working concept of religion, but educated society increasingly regarded these healing and prophesying messiahs as insane.

Despite the intellectual dismissal of magic, astrology, etc., and the diatribes of the clergy against them, the hold of orthodox religious views on the mass of English people was never more than partial. Orthodox theology was dominant because it offered *general* explanations, and had political authority on its side. But in the efforts of the clergy to break away from the magical aspects of traditional religion, religion itself was changed; the idea of a particular providence, of the link between guilt and misfortune, was abandoned, and religion became based on a general natural theology which could coexist with a mechanist philosophy.

In some ways, the influence of Puritanism strengthened structural differentiation between religion and the rest of society, but in other ways it eroded it. It altered religion by insisting, for example, that the Bible could and was to be interpreted by the individual's reason; *right* reason, or reason sanctified by grace, was available to all men (Hill, 1969). The magical and ritual part of religion which had paralleled the degrees of society and of the universe was sharply demarcated from the new tradition of natural religion, where the best guide to God's work was the scrutiny of nature and of the Bible. The new meaning of "reason" as not *a priori* logic but the resort to experiment created science as a separate establishment which could create, disseminate and use a rival form of knowledge. But science itself was not at this period as separate from magic as the nineteenth-century rationalists, who created the potent myths of science, believed. The great sixteenth-century scientists were the last of the magi, combining methods and a subject matter which laid the foundations of science with necromancy, or a search for the future of the world in the numbers in the Bible. In addition, those men who were Puritans were trying to *reintegrate* religious beliefs and their general activity in the world. By relinquishing magical and conventional beliefs and routines, seeking for rules of guidance by reading and listening to sermons, and trying to embody them in a life seen as a calling, they were making a thorough-going attempt to reintegrate religious beliefs and secular life. (C. and K. George [1961]; Thrupp [1948] documented the interdependence of secular and religious life in medieval London, and found that the influence of the clergy on the business community increased once the "double standard" had been abolished by Calvinism.)

The exact part that Protestantism played in the "birth of the modern world" is in dispute. Tawney (1927) followed Weber in arguing for the crucial role of Puritanism in transforming society from a stable, traditional and hierarchical form to a modern industrial state. He argues that Puritanism was a *symptom* of secularization; part of a growing opposition to the established church and state, at a time when the connections between the new industrial and commercial classes, and Presbyterianism, Congregationalism, and Puritanism generally were often commented on by contemporaries. The theocracy of early Calvinism, which Weber thought had triggered off the crucial psychological drive, the desperate search for a sign of grace, Tawney thought had had little influence on the English dissenting classes, who had altered their religious beliefs to suit their commercial activities. The chiliastic, levelling, collectivist strain in the attack on established religion and established society, briefly visible during the Commonwealth, was submerged again until the Evangelical revival.

The links between Puritanism and the transformation of the economy have been debated at length; Samuelsson (1961) provides a summary of and an attack on the Weberian view, quoting central Puritan texts in praise of poverty and moderation, and citing other, more plausible, intellectual influences for the development of capitalism, such as Enlightenment thinking, and, in the United States, Social Darwinism (Bryson, 1945). Another link has been suggested by Merton (1936, 1938), that between Puritanism and science. The Puritans found in science both a means of exploring God's creation, and a series of technical discoveries which benefited trade and manufacture. Puritans were certainly the major force behind the new science and modes of manufacturing, but even if their religious beliefs *were* crucial in creating new secular knowledge and roles, did they do so because the beliefs themselves were more "secular", or because they were more likely to divide the society into sacred and secular spheres?

The eighteenth century in Britain and America saw a rapid advance in the secularization of knowledge, concomitant with the first approach to scientific study of human affairs. The growth of religious tolerance (which was an inevitable consequence of structural differentiation plus religious pluralism) led to a turning from dogmatic theology and revealed religion to natural theology. The spread of liberal and humanitarian ideas assisted the slow and imperceptible shift from a system of knowledge where moral ideas were derived from God's intentions, and consequently monitored by priests, to one where theology was itself subject to morality, now seen as what it was reasonable to expect from averagely virtuous men rather than virtuosos. Walker (1964) has traced an important part of the process in the gradual modification, moralization and abandonment of the theology of hell, original sin, and a salvation governed by rules. The change began first in the seventeenth century among the Old Dissenting ministry, spreading to their congregations and to liberal ministers in other denominations. The changes took several centuries; Methodists only began to protest at hell-fire sermons in the 1870s, and children may still be exposed to scarcely attenuated versions of very outdated theology. But the whole structure of the debate inside theology changed; gradually, conservatives ceased to cite scriptural authority, and began to argue that the idea of hell was a necessary deterrent to immoral or subversive behaviour. Liberals argued for more ethical and liberal rules of salvation, or for hell "as a metaphor". Religious tolerance was resisted above all not because the doctrines of non-established churches were false, but because to end absolutist claims for one faith would break down moral and social restraint against wrongdoing until the concept of authority had itself become pluralist (Henriques, 1961).

## 3 SECULARIZATION, SOCIALISM AND SOCIAL CONTROL

In all societies, men have feared that those who rebelled against religion, or the reigning metaphysical orthodoxy, would also be immoralists and destroyers. And although religious rebels will usually try to escape or to transcend the existing social structure rather than directly to attack it, political rebels find that their revolt against existing structures cannot go very far unless it is justified and underpinned by a new metaphysic. The major example of a metaphysic of political revolt has been Marxism. Especially in the early phase of socialist movements, great stress is laid on the power of socialism to create a new moral world, and much antagonism is expressed toward supernatural religion, which is believed to protect the *status quo* by directing attention from worldly misery to heavenly rewards, and by preaching docility, acceptance, and other values which a ruling class might find convenient in a "slave religion". When, as in Britain, socialist or revolutionary leaders begin to argue that there is no real quarrel between their views and religion, that socialism is a purely *political* doctrine without its own ethics or metaphysics, the socialist movement is moving from a revolutionary position, the claim to be a counter-culture, to social democracy. The party no longer aims at total but at segmental transformation.

How true has this assumption been about the role of religion in social control? Does the confrontation of Christianity and socialism provide us with an example of two major belief-systems in conflict, or is the dispute about institutional allegiances and powers rather than ideas? Both systems of beliefs are very broad and discontinuous; many claim they do not even conflict. At the same time, to study their contact should tell us much about the relationship of power to ideology, and about the assumptions which are made in all societies about the "proper" place for religious and political considerations, and the role of religion in social stability.

Unfortunately, very little work has yet been done on the structural and intellectual aspect of the relations between religion and politics. (See the limited information on the influence of religious allegiances on voting in various countries, and MacIntyre, 1969. Desroches [1955 and 1956] emphasizes the intellectual continuities between some forms of religion and socialism.) Nationalism and socialism are the major contemporary "revolutionary ideologies", and both have ambiguous and varying relationships with traditional religion. Nationalist parties in their attack on the alien colonial power may sponsor the original indigenous religion against the religion of the alien ruler. Indeed, nationalist movements commonly originate within native religious movements as they try to mobilize support for resisting and reversing the changes brought about by the alien élite. But sooner or later, the nationalist movement will be partly taken over by Marxist rationales, and there will be conflict between the secular communists, interested in many aspects of modernization, and the supporters of the indigenous religion or of the new religio-political movement which was the first vehicle of protest. (Von der Mehden [1968] describes the process in south-east Asia.) But the role of the colonizers' religion is not only that of simple social control; it may itself provide a rationale for a limited revolt. The revolutionary priests of Latin America have attracted attention far outweighing their numbers (de Kadt, 1970), just as the worker-priest movement did when it became too identified with the industrial prole-tariat for the good of amicable relations between church and state (Poulat, 1959). Both groups dramatized and criticized the extent to which the religious hierarchy had become identified with existing institutional arrangements.

Britain and the United States, both marked by religious pluralism and a pragmatic intellectual tradition, never experienced the explicit intellectual opposition of a conserva-tive, churchgoing, ruling group and a radical, anti-clerical proletariat. The debate between the two groups in these countries rapidly became centred less on politics and economics than on morality. After the French Revolution, it is clear from popular writings in both countries that the areas the ruling classes thought to be in most need of supernatural reinforce-ment were respect for authority and existing property relation-ships. Arthur Young begged the Anglican church to pay more attention to the poor, for "the true Christian will never be a Leveller, will never listen to French politics or French philo-sophy". Contemporary radicals and Jacobins were indeed often Deists or atheists; the *Age of Reason* was circulated as widely as the *Rights of Man*, and both these brilliant populariza-tions of the ideas of the *philosophes* became permanent strands in English radical working-class culture. But they were less im-portant strands than those coming from Methodism. Method-ism was in many ways a revolutionary doctrine, but it called for changes in morality and feeling rather than in economic life.

It made the culture of early nineteenth-century radicalism strongly anti-clerical, but not antagonistic to all religion (but see E. P. Thompson, 1963).

The anti-clericalism of some radicals was not the most important change in the social position of religion. As the new industrial towns grew, first in England and later in Europe and the United States, the new urban proletariat failed to appear in church. Respectable Nonconformity in England, even by the beginning of the nineteenth century, was becoming confined to the urban lower-middle class and skilled artisans. A multitude of short-lived sects attracted some of the most destitute, and the Salvation Army, adapted in ideology, style and organization to the needs of the poor, was the most successful at recruiting them from the 1860s onwards. Together with the Anglican church, it dispensed a minimum level of welfare to the poorest; the refusal of many independent craftsmen to attend Anglican services lest they should be suspected of doing so in order to get free clothes and meal-tickets, illustrated the general attractions of this aspect of Anglicanism. By the mid century, only just over a third of the population had attended church on census day (Pickering, 1967). With some exceptions, the larger the city, or the poorer the area, the lower the attendance. Those in the churches were divided equally between Nonconformity and the Church of England; there were as yet few Catholics, for they were still pouring into London and Lancashire from Ireland, and the church, unprepared, had a shortage of premises and priests. (The nature of anti-Catholic prejudice in England would be an interesting study; it produced stronger Protestant congregations in areas where there were many working-class Catholics. See Pelling, 1968.) But from this time on, the majority of English people had ceased to attend church regularly, and consequently became increasingly unfamiliar with orthodox religious belief. The extent of this was not fully realized until the end of the century, when Booth's investigation brought to light many men like the poor crossing-sweeper who asked what god was.

Why this change? It was not the intellectual influence of materialist socialism, because the move from the churches antedated it. (As in Sweden; see Gustaffson, 1950, 1953.) European socialists did mainly become atheists, and the parties developed extensive secular rituals to replace supernatural religion, but English radical movements—Chartism, Owenism, later the I.L.P.—were internally divided. Some members considered that their new beliefs constituted a religion, and adopted some religious forms; Marx and his circle condemned the attachment of English radicals to secular ceremonies as abetting their fatal tendency to compromise with the established order. Others wanted radicalism to be associated with Nonconformity, especially Primitive Methodism, whose anti-clerical strain matched their own. (The similarity between Methodist and Chartist methods of organization has been commented on.) A few wanted entirely new, non-supernatural, progressive religions to be created to accompany the new political movements. The supporters and founders of these religions of progress had one common motive; by providing a *moral* rationale for sweeping social and economic changes, they hoped to win all men, and so to prevent the division of society into revolutionary and ruling camps. Their efforts now seem ludicrous. But perhaps they were right about the cause of secularization, of the emptying churches. Living when they did, they remembered what had been, or what the myth had described as, an Age of Faith, when religious institutions and ideas *could* represent shared experience for the society, could guide moral views, and, or so the legend of the Evangelical revival had it, could move the powerful and the dissolute alike to recognize their duties to society.

Similar liberal groups arose within the churches. The Christian Socialist movement in Britain, and the Social Gospel in the United States, were unique among radical movements in their belief in the powers of a general altruism which alone could turn men from a society which was selfish and individualist to create a future community, at once socialist and the Kingdom of God on earth.

## 4 CHRISTIAN SOCIALISM AND THE SOCIAL GOSPEL

Modern industrial societies have seemed to many to entail a possessive individualism, a lack of *communitas*, and some versions of both conservatism and socialism condemn this. One of the more sophisticated nineteenth-century arguments for the retention of Christianity was that it was the only possible way to keep society as a moral unity and to justify unselfish behaviour. But it has often been argued that the growth of working, living, and political arrangements which created separate worlds (largely class-structured) of experience made it necessary for men to find new institutions which would embody their now-separate concerns. Thus religion lost its most crucial role, that of providing a common structure of meaning and judgment for the whole of society. (See Smelser, 1959; and the industrial novels of Mrs Gaskell, the wife of a Unitarian minister who had had considerable experience of the slums of early nineteenth-century Manchester.) The argument that the breakdown of the common experience which makes religion possible gave rise to the empty churches is a convincing one. The takeover of the explanation of the world and of man by the see 128 natural and social sciences hastened the process of disintegration. For example, in 1853, the Presbytery of Scotland petitioned the monarch for a national fast against the cholera, a classic Durkheimian example of the use of ritual for social unification. Lord Palmerston refused, on the grounds that chloride of lime would be more use (cited in Thomas, 1971).

At first, socialism claimed to be the only way of restituting the old communal life, and the Christian Socialist movement was based on this claim (D'A. Jones, 1968). The various religions of socialism also enshrined a vision of a future society in which politics would wither away because conflict could not arise. Many of these movements were influenced by the writings of T. H. Green, the English idealist philosopher, who believed that if a moral rationale could be produced for progressive social change and enlarged state powers, all men would unite to bring them about. His work had considerable influence on many of his Oxford pupils, leading them both to a new conception of liberalism in politics, and to work amongst the London poor in University settlements. Amongst this group were the Fabians and the first theorists of the welfare state, which was to promote both social efficiency and the welfare of the distressed. (Richter, 1964, 1966. See MacIntyre [1967] who argued that Green was trying to reunite a shattered moral consensus.) The rise of the Labour *Party*, and the transition of progressive thinkers to political activity, marked the end of the interest in creating a quasi-religion to embody the new consciousness.

In England and the United States, the split between the

radical groups and religion never came. The ties of so many with religion were so strong that anti-clerical socialists tried to avoid religious issues. (Even Bradlaugh found himself relying on Nonconformist votes at Northampton.) Only in the industrial villages of Wales, Fifeshire and Yorkshire where Nonconformity had been part of the fabric of working-class radicalism was socialism directly presented as an alternative to the chapel. And in the United States, Deism lost contact with radical politics with the emergence of the Democrats, who relied on the immigrant churches. Support for a communist and atheist labour movement came mainly from Continental immigrants, importing their own conceptions of the relations between religion and politics. Their inadequate English, as much as their alien definitions, prevented them from having much impact on either religion or politics.

Another factor which has prevented the religious/non-religious dimension from being identified as a class-politics division has been the minority tradition of agnostic middle-class radicalism. Middle-class radicals usually support social reforms which have a largely *moral* content (for example, pacifism) rather than the economic and material concerns of working-class radicals. Because of the expressive, moral quality of these reform movements, which are not much concerned with gaining general social power, they rapidly become the rallying points for wider deviant perspectives (Parkin, 1968). Movements such as the Campaign for Nuclear Disarmament, or the anti-Vietnam War movement, come to focus a general moral protest. Movements for greater self-determination in sexual behaviour, or against apartheid and censorship, are largely supported by the middle class, though they are likely to find most political support within socialist parties.

The general philosophy which lies behind these movements is humanist; it stresses the autonomy of the individual, and the possession of natural rights and dignities by all human beings because they are human, rather than because they occupy a certain status or possess certain qualities. The extreme individualism and personal autonomy which are personal and moral goals for the "new" middle class are often seen as the "secular" consciousness *par excellence*, the creators of a personality and value structure so highly rational and open to change and uncertainty that it is devoid of a basis for religious experience. Is this so?

Durkheim (1898) argued, in a little-known paper, that individualism was in fact the religion of the intellectuals; " . . . la religion de l'individu est d'institution sociale . . ." He pointed out that individualism was itself a complex value-system, which had come to be the basis for many social institutions and customs in contemporary France. Since men's lives varied a great deal in a complex society, their common humanity, all they possessed in common, became what was worshipped, in the Positivist movement for example. "Dès qu'une fin est poursuivie par tout un peuple, elle acquiert, par suite de cette adhésion unanime, une sorte de suprématie morale qui l'élève bien au-dessus des fins privées, et lui donne ainsi un caractère religieux."

Conservative theorists who argue that individualism broke down rules and structures, that to prevent anomie it must be checked, have not realized that it is a religion—a set of collective beliefs and practices, which is rooted in social experience and learning. Durkheim argued that just *as if* it were a religion, it was implicitly invoked in the Dreyfus affair. Durkheim goes further than Parsons and many sociologists do when they claim that the quest for personal autonomy, satisfying relationships, and so on, is a religious one, or that the ultimate values of our society enshrine individualism, liberalism, democracy, and so on. Durkheim implies further, that these "individualist" values have a concrete institutional basis, and that they subsume social action, for the intelligentsia at least, in an explicit way— that they are socially recognized as the "right" values. He is surely correct in this view, rather than the one commonly attributed to him, that is that "modern" values such as individualism are somehow inimical to social stability and cannot become the basis for collective sentiments nor be expressed in ritual action. If this analysis were to be followed up, it might substantiate the charge of conservative churchmen that an interest in liberal social reforms is inimical to Christian belief, because the reformism stems from a largely concealed set of values which are radically individualist, and those of the secular intelligentsia. In this way churchmen may, by urging that the church become more involved in social reform movements, be admitting secularism in the bellies of these Trojan horses.

In the United States, to a much greater extent than in

England, the clergy themselves—or some of them—have been the leaders in claiming general moral reform to be a central part of Christianity. The Social Gospel movement originated in the 1860s among those denominations—Unitarian, Congregational and Episcopalian—with a relatively liberal theology, a middle-class laity, and the social outlook of churches rather than sects. In keeping with these characteristics, the general position of the movement was that the churches must accept the sovereignty of the state, but that their responsibility for public morality at a period when rapid economic change was dissolving the old relationship between master and man meant that "Christian law" must be applied to society. Just as the temperance and other social movements had been, the Social Gospel movement was taken up later by the Baptist and Methodist churches, which were more eschatological and lower-middle class, and they reformulated it more stringently. Man in society, and man's institutions, stood under divine judgment, and consequently a part of religious duty was to try to realize good in the contemporary industrial order, racked by strikes and appalling social conditions.

Ironically, the churches which were most affected by the Social Gospel—the older, liberal Protestant denominations—were those with the wealthiest and most conservative congregations. The Catholic church and the fundamentalist sects which recruited from the poor and ethnic outgroups were opposed to the Social Gospel. The cross-pressures of theology and economics resulted not only in conflicts between the more liberal clergy and their wealthy, conservative parishioners, but in a relationship between religion and political behaviour which operated independently of social class and worked against it. Middle-class people who worshipped frequently in liberal denominations were sometimes affected sufficiently by the social ethics of Episcopalianism and Congregationalism to vote Democrat; whereas working-class members of fundamentalist sects, if they attended frequently, were more likely not to vote, or to vote Republican (Johnson, 1962; in Oregon).

In the United States, as in England, the divisions of interest and of ideology which grew as industrialism progressed made it impossible to find a message to reshape an unjust society which could claim sufficient transcendental authority to compel those with different economic interests to accept the church as arbitrator. Members of the Social Gospel movement them-selves were torn between the Protestant demand to Witness, and the strong social pressure for the churches to reinforce an existing structure. The movement was at its strongest after the First World War, when a largely united and powerful Protestant church was able temporarily to espouse a wide range of movements for social reform. Then the attack came from several directions. The world of knowledge was becoming increasingly secular, and liberal intellectuals were abandoning the church for secular political movements. Organized labour disliked the Social Gospel churches, because they were mostly prohibition-ist. But the most powerful attack came from the Protestant fundamentalists, who regarded theological modernism as a betrayal of Protestant and American values. Jews were promi-nent in the socialist parties, and the fundamentalists suspected the modernist movement of being inspired by them. In the South, the strong nativist reaction into fundamentalism gave birth to the Ku Klux Klan, and to the campaign against the teaching of evolution by natural selection in schools. The campaign had a wider moral meaning; such modern knowledge, transmitted by education, was at the root of modernism and moral laxity; evolution symbolized not the challenge of science to the Bible, but the first onslaught of atheistic modernism. It also implied abandoning belief in original sin, redemption, and man's personal moral responsibility, which was believed to be bound up with them. In that evolutionary biology was atheistic, it seemed likely to be an essential constituent of communism (Gatewood, 1966; Carter, 1954).

The fundamentalist faction grew, and finally split off to form its own national council to oppose the socialist and pacifist tendencies of the National Council of Churches. During the depression and the Popular Front period, the Social Gospel movement grew by shedding its ties with Prohibitionism, and attacking militarism and the worsening race relations which were resulting in separate Negro congregations. But the alliance of pacifists, socialists, and liberal modernist clergy was frac-tured by, respectively, rearmament, Stalinism, and the rise of neo-orthodox theology in Europe. The new theologians condemned the Social Gospel as characteristic of American individualism and moral arrogance, as overlooking man's total dependence on god, and exalting science and social activity

K

rather than bearing witness to humanity's moral frailty. A growing social pessimism was evident in the theology of the late 1930s and 40s (Carter, 1954; Meyer, 1960).

The Cold War increased the tendency of neo-orthodox theology to see the confrontation between capitalism and communism as a "spiritual" conflict, in which orthodox Christianity became the moral rationale of capitalism and democracy. The strong revival of the fundamentalist sects in the 1950s, and the popularity of Billy Graham as a neo-fundamentalist and anti-communist evangelist to the white lower-middle classes, were part of the process of finding a set of values which would combat communism and modernist tendencies. The growing popularity of fundamentalism led to a further decline in the prestige of churches and their ministers among liberals and socialists. But with the 1960s, an increasingly unpopular war and a civil rights movement led to middle-class movements of moral protest which found no real place in organized politics, and the Social Gospel movement revived in consequence; the churches became the main centres to embody and focus the discontent. Stark and Glock (1968) claimed that by the late 1960s, the fastest-growing denominations were those liberal and moderate Protestant churches which emphasized the ethical and moral duties of their members to society. But their parishioners were not all in agreement with the shift from dogmatic theology to social ethics; public opinion polls found many Americans agreeing with the man who complained that when he was a child, he went to church to hear the preacher tell him about heaven and hell, how to deserve the former and escape the latter, whereas now he was only told about why he shouldn't eat scab grapes.

## 5 THE ROLE OF THE CLERGY

The declining prestige of the churches has affected the status of their ministers. In England, Paul (1964) and Coxon (1965) have documented the decline in numbers and relative pay of the Anglican clergy; their lesser social influence is both cause and consequence of the fact that they are being recruited from the lower-middle rather than the upper-middle class, from non-graduates rather than Oxbridge graduates, and from an older population. Despite their generally high status, the clergy themselves, especially if their congregations are small, express dissatisfaction with both their role, their training for it, and their parishioners' expectations of them (Towler, 1970; B. R. Wilson, 1966). The Anglican clergy find that they are expected to christen, marry and bury many who have no other contact with the church. More generally, they feel a lack of esteem in a society where religion is rarely the subject of private discussion, and where attempts to make it more relevant are resented. The most important exodus from the churches for them was not that of the working class, but of their own reference group, the middle class, who began to fall away in the first decade of the twentieth century (Wickham, 1957). In England, religion is generally felt to be a good thing; i.e. it is rarely talked about, and attack on religious belief is resented. But many surveys report a dislike of the clergy and of organized religion, perhaps because of memories of coerced attendance at religious services in schools, the army, hospitals, and so on, in a society where worship is seen as meaningful only if it is entirely voluntary. Clergy, as the agents of such restraint, are often disliked, and workingmen in particular are likely to associate them with hypocrisy, an "easy job", and the ruling classes (Zweig, 1952, 1961; D. A. Martin, 1968; D. R. Robertson, 1968; and Pickering, 1968). But efforts by the clergy to break away from these associations are strongly resisted by both church hierarchies and congregations; the minister must be "above politics".

Clergy in the United States find themselves in similar dilemmas, which have been rather better documented. Both societies are experiencing a rapid decline in vocations, and this is resulting in changes in the organization and objectives of religious orders and the minister's role. The increasing bureaucratization of society has affected the churches; ministers and rabbis alike find themselves forced into unsatisfying organizational roles, which both they and their parishioners feel are less important than those of the traditional pastor and preacher (Fichter, 1961; Sklare, 1955). In a period when it is professional counselling rather than spiritual power which is sought in a crisis, the younger clergy are redefining their involvement with the problems of their flock as based on psychiatric, rather than spiritual, knowledge (Berger, 1969). They are handicapped by their lack of expertise in the eyes of medical and welfare professionals, who are unwilling to cooperate fully with them, though in fact clergymen are extensively consulted by members of their congregations for all kinds of personal problems (Cumming and Harrington, 1963). The religio-psychiatric movement has had considerable vogue among the clergy, but far less among psychiatrists, since their knowledge stems from a determinedly secular and positivist tradition (Klausner, 1964).

Clergy may also try to make theological doctrines more living for their flocks by developing a stand for the churches on controversial issues, but here they are controlled by congregational pressures. The Episcopal church, for example, is ambivalent and uncertain on issues concerned with war, labour, and the present distribution of wealth and power, because its congregations are united and conservative. On moral issues concerned with human rights, racial equality and intermarriage, clergy can be outspoken and liberal because their parishioners are divided and uncertain (Glock and Ringer, 1956). The clergy are not merely Laodicean when they avoid taking a stand which may offend their parishioners. All churches at least, if not all sects, have as a priority retaining communication with sinners in the hope of changing their hearts. And if the churches are to ratify central values, to be identified with love and order, it is felt that open disagreement among the ministry is unseemly (Campbell and Pettigrew, 1959; S. D. Clark, 1948). Glock *et al.* (1967) and Metz (1967) point out that those who see the Christian message as a challenge to existing society, a challenge which has all too often been betrayed, have failed to notice the pressure on clergy from both church officials and parishioners to build large, united, and financially viable congregations, which entails that survival goals triumph over the original doctrinal ones. Radical clergy and religious can be accommodated in specialized roles such as that of the campus minister (Hammond and Mitchell, 1965), or in a radical religious order such as the Dominicans. One of the organizational strengths of Catholicism lies in its institutional sub-specialization.

Ecumenicalism is another example of a reform which can proceed fairly rapidly because most church members are either indifferent to it or regard it as essentially the province of the minister. The clergy are interested in reunification partly because they are more conscious of the theological imperative of a church indivisible, and partly because church unity promises to augment the power of the church organization and of the ministry. Particularly in denominations without a strong sacerdotal tradition, ministers hope to share the greater prestige of church clergy and the higher status of the functionaries of the older churches *vis-à-vis* secular authorities (B. R. Wilson, 1966). A thorough but unsympathetic account of the process of Methodist reunion in Britain (Currie, 1968) attributes it to the search for lateral growth by churches which had failed to maintain frontal growth, though Methodism did not in fact gain new members as a result of pooling resources.

The pressure for church unity is not only due to an effort to use resources more economically. The clergy are conscious that the theological and liturgical issues which once divided denominations are now less crucial; indeed, many of their parishioners may not be aware of them. Part of the reaction to declining congregations has been the rephrasing of absolute and specific ethical and theological dogmas in more symbolic, contemporary and general terms, which will express the spirit of the previous *fiats* and yet allow for the variations in behaviour and belief which are inherent in a complex society. (Ecumenicalism has proceeded fastest in the mission field, where the gains from cooperation are more obvious, and the challenge of alien religions throws into relief the similarities between all forms of evangelical Christianity. For similar reasons, the pressure for reunion has occasionally come not from the clergy, but from the laity; on the Canadian frontier, for example, where shared hardships and a populist tradition made the directives of the religious hierarchy and the theological colleges far off in the East seem unimportant.)

Currie's detailed study of Methodism showed the theological accompaniments of the process of division and reunification. The original schisms were either due to revivals of sectarian fervour among poorer Methodists, or to conflict between ministers and the central organization. Membership began to decline critically after the 1880s, and younger and more educated Methodists became increasingly impatient with the sectarian loyalties of the local chapels. The new Biblical scholarship was weakening the absolute moral and intellectual claims which had been based on a divine revelation, and thus the apparatus of discipline was sapped. The class meeting, once "to mark disorderly walkers", became a fellowship, and collective worship became more important than accepting detailed points of doctrine. The move from a theodicy of sin, suffering and salvation to a more cheerful and this-worldly communion was accompanied by the decline of inspired preachers before trained practitioners. On such a basis, ecumenicalism can succeed; doctrine has become flexible, the particularities of belief less important. Only changes in rituals and forms of worship are likely to provoke disagreement between clergy and laity; modernist theology can become many things to many men (S. D. Clark, 1948).

## 6 THE SECULARIZATION OF KNOWLEDGE

Underlying all the more specific changes which have been discussed in this chapter is the secularization of knowledge. This is still the main contender for both the cause and the definition of secularization; the other, much newer, explanation, that of the break-up of moral and experiential links between the classes in industrial society, only explains the downfall of the public position of religion and the role of the universal church.

Explanations of secularization are confused, as was said earlier, because the word covers more than one process, and they do not occur simultaneously. It is also difficult to break away from the evolutionary schema which assumes that earlier or primitive societies are more religious. Although it is true that their thinking is not often *scientific*, that is not deliberately aimed to frame open hypotheses which are universally experimentally refutable, this does not mean that it is necessarily religious or magical. Some simple cultures appear to resort relatively little to religious explanations (Douglas, 1970), and if magico-religious explanations were to be expressed as a proportion of all explanations that were commonly resorted to, it is likely that the proportion would fluctuate over time, rather than constantly fall. It has repeatedly been established, for example, that witchcraft (or accusations of witchcraft) increases under circumstances connected with modernization, either because of guilt that traditional charitable obligations are no longer being met (Thomas, 1971) or because of the tension and uncertainty produced by the breaking down of a stable social order (Marwick, 1965; Lewis, 1971).

Despite these caveats, knowledge in modern industrial societies is incomparably more "secular" than it was in previous periods in these societies. It is inaccurate to attribute this to a rise in secular consciousness, or to the increasing control over worrying uncertainties, since, as has often been remarked, most people now trust and believe in "science" without understanding it in the same way that they might once have assumed that "religion can explain it" or "god must have had a reason". They believe in the superior powers of science, in part because it *has* enabled men to control the world, but in part because of a myth in our culture about the power of science which is socially supported in much the same way as, for example, witchcraft is for the Azande, and part of the myth is about the clash between religion and science which was resolved in favour of science. As an institution, science has acquired higher prestige and greater usefulness; a sixteenth-century Englishman might attempt to create a penal system, or an explanation of feminine hysteria, "according to the laws of God"—a twentieth-century Englishman would hope to create a *scientific* explanation or system.

The neo-orthodox theologians argued that the liberal theologians of the thirties relinquished too much to the explanatory province of science, and it is true that most people believe scientific explanations to be superior to theological ones not because they have studied either, but because both scientists and theologians have told them so (Berger, 1969). Very little is known of the way in which scientific beliefs filtered down to the general population and were incorporated into their everyday perspectives. Ellegard's (1958) excellent study of the reception of Darwin's ideas at various intellectual levels, which was made by studying the book reviews in a large number of journals, is immensely revealing and a model for further studies. Popular interest in science grew rapidly in England and the United States in the last quarter of the nineteenth century. In England in the 1870s, local scientific societies spread rapidly.

They aimed at educating the general public, from the artisan upward. Popular theology, which had been the largest category of books sold until then, was ousted from first place by books on popular science. It has often been assumed that the new theories in biology and geology were themselves responsible for the destruction of religious faith. The examples of Frederick Gosse, and many eminent scientists who became agnostics, are often cited. But objections to Biblical religion on the part of non-scientists seem to have been based not on its untruth, but on its immorality. A group of workingmen and small manufacturers who became active anti-clericals reported that they lost their religious faith, not through reading Darwin, Lyell, or Strauss, but the Bible (Budd, 1967). Their objections were essentially those of Thomas Paine, and of sceptics from the sixteenth century on; the Bible was contradictory; it glorified savage and superstitious beliefs which a civilized age had outgrown. Members of the intelligentsia, too, rejected religion for ethical reasons above all. The intellectual objections were not new; what had changed was the attitude to authority, the capacity to oppose increasingly individualist and humanitarian moral standards to what had previously been seen as divinely ordered.

The opposition to religion is shaped above all by the social meaning religion has at any period. In Victorian England, the over-riding association had been between piety and respectability. The importance of being respectable for manufacturers, politicians, tradesmen and artisans cannot be exaggerated; even eminent and liberal scholars felt strong social pressure. Reformers in the churches tried to prevent this identification by urging Christians of the duty of social reform, and by begging the ragged not to stay away from church. But the churches which could retain close emotional links with the poor were those who felt themselves outside respectability: the new Catholic churches with their Irish priests, the Salvation Army, the poorer sects. As a growing number of eminent scholars, politicians and others were affected by the secular traditions of new forms of knowledge and left the churches, the strength of the identity between churchgoing and respectability was weakened. Members of the Establishment referred less often and less confidently to "Christian principles" in pronouncements on legal, educational, medical and a host of other issues. Finally religion became implicitly understood, in most areas of life, to be a matter of private concern.

It was the secular intellectuals who strove most self-consciously in Britain to replace a religious world-view by a scientific one; the influential popular writers on science have not merely reported it, but discerned a scientific morality and a metaphysical meaning in it. But the most challenging extension of scientific thinking has come with the growth of the behavioural sciences since the last war. They challenge not only the framework of a conservative religious morality—"guilt", for example—but also attack values that are derived from religion but that liberals find rather more congenial, such as the responsibility of the autonomous individual. But the implications and the outcome of the conflict between *Homo sociologus* and the values of our society are still to come.

None of the above should be taken to mean that people in England no longer believe in God, or do not use a framework of thought at many times which is a religious one. Rather, it is argued that they are religious in this sense, but that what is lacking is the public acknowledgment of and reference to such a framework. Because private beliefs cannot be attached to and reinforced by public ones, they become increasingly diverse and eclectic, and so such public reference points as do remain must become less specific—"responsibility in sex" replaces sexual monogamy. The diversity of the private myths and frameworks, and the generality of the public ones, mean that neither can be very influential in guiding social choices. The secularization of knowledge has weakened the influence of the religious framework in most areas of life to the point of disappearance; and it is in this sense that British society can be described as secular. In the United States, a framework of a kind does survive, and is frequently invoked to define certain boundaries—primarily political ones. What is disputable is whether the framework is acknowledged outside these very limited boundary-maintaining functions, and whether its response to secular pressures has not divorced it completely from the morals and metaphysics of the Christian tradition.

Considered in Durkheimian terms, religion has been replaced by science as the organizer and judge of knowledge for society; ritual is much truncated. In this respect, there has been profound secularization if we confine religion to its traditional definition—i.e. practices connected with supernatural beliefs. In Weberian terms, religion undoubtedly remains a source of private meaning. Is it less so than it was? It is easy to romanticize the "simple faith" of the worlds we have lost, but nonetheless there has undoubtedly been some decline, partly because changing societies generate new problems of meaning, and there may be no new theology to explain them; we look for scientific explanations instead. But because publicly religion is referred to less, and because it reflects social divisions in experience, it lacks social force—it has become "privatized".

# CHAPTER VIII

# *Conclusion*

The five preceding chapters have described, first, two traditions or series of questions which have been asked about the role of religion in society, and second, the empirical work which has been done in the two societies where sociologists of religion have been the most active. The gap between the questions, which are on a very general level of significance, and the research, which is mainly concerned with religious institutions and is limited in scope, shows how much remains to be done. In this concluding chapter, a few suggestions are made about future research.

The traditional large-scale theoretical questions will have to be modified or abandoned. Topics such as the role of religion in social order or economic life must remain unanswerable as long as sociologists go on hedging their bets in various ways by switching between definitions of religion—conventional, psychological, cognitive, socially functional. We cannot infer directly from religious belief to action, because one of the most important functions of religion is as a *label* with its own social consequences. Nor can we infer that the functions for the individual are the same as those for the group or the society. In modern societies, the belief-systems and rewards of churches are often at variance with those of secular institutions; the religious man may be integrated, but into a group which separates him from an effective role in the wider society. We must distinguish not only between integration for the individual and for the society as a whole, but also between different levels of integration and sources of authority. Religious ceremonies can help both to integrate the participants into society or to bar them from it. Religious views may neither support nor govern legal, economic, or political ones.

The part that religion plays in social order is unknown

because we do not know to what extent men do interact on a basis of common moral values. The diminished role of religion in industrial society is often attributed to the greater extent of calculative or self-interested behaviour, and the reduction and privatization of those situations connected with death and suffering which only a "religious" response can alleviate. But "self-interest" itself operates in a moral and social framework, which defines both what it is and in what situations it is legitimate. The moral codes which govern institutions apparently ruled by self-interest vary considerably (see Macpherson, 1962). To say that a motive is "natural" because it is self-interested is to ignore the subliminal patternings and social pressures which make certain ends seem desirable to us and certain means legitimate. In other words, to say that a "religious" framework of action has been replaced by a rational and calculative one is too superficial. It was partly developments in theology which aided the change, and these developments were an attempt to make religion less "magical", less immediately based on needs, and more "transcendent", that is, concerned to embody very general and abstract ideas. At each period, "religious" and "secular" metaphysics interact. Parsons is wrong to consider that religious values are by definition the "ultimate" ones; however, "ultimate" values are still related in most people's minds to dimly conceived "religious" rationales of meaning and judgment.

## 1 REALITY AND MYTH

It has been the argument of this book that the sociology of religion ought not to look at those beliefs and acts termed "religious", and add some secular equivalents, but to look at *all* the beliefs and structures of meaning which are "ultimate" in some sense to any group of men; looking at all their myths, symbols and rituals to do with both the universally "ultimate" —birth, marriage, disease and death, heroic action, good social relations, and so on—and also with what is important and problematic for specific cultures—cattle for the Dinka, technology for us. How do we think about these matters, and how do we express them and our feelings about them to each other?

Berger and Luckmann adopt this viewpoint when they argue that social reality is essentially *precarious*. Their view is that social reality is no more than the creation by man of an objective all-embracing symbolic universe. It is by religion that he can shore up this world of appearances against the encroachments of chaos and despair, because religion provides a realm of "ultimate meanings". Thus they are opposed to the view that religion is a separate institutional subsystem with special integrating functions for society. This cramps the sociologist of religion into concentrating on public, institutionalized behaviour which can be relatively objectively and clearly isolated; subjective religiosity is identified as an attitude, and studied by a different discipline. Berger and Luckmann argue that the latter is far more important, though they disagree as to whether *all* systems of meaning are religious (Luckmann), or whether the symbolic universe of science differs from that of religion in important ways.

According to this view, to create a concept of the self or to find meaning and significance in everyday life we require a religion. These elementary metaphysical structures are universal but not institutionalized. Personal religiosity, which is based on these general but private systems of meaning, may be threatened if it meets with a public religious establishment— "official religion"—which bends religion away from questions of concern and significance to the historical individual. To Luckmann, the contemporary decline of traditional Christianity signifies the replacement of "institutional" religion by the underlying "social" or "natural" form. Berger, and many contemporary theologians, urge the extension of the theology, ritual and worship of "institutional" religion to sanctify the areas of human life—sexuality, games, the city, political action—from which it has been separated. Without this, they argue, religious worlds are becoming privatized and hence precarious, based on each person's arbitrary selection of themes. These are selected from the media, literature, meanings generated inside the family. The fact that deeply moving or significant experiences, especially those concerned with self-realization or strong emotion, are commonly described as "religious" supports their argument. For example, people devoid of conventional religious belief often describe the effect of hallucinogenic drugs on them as "religious"—they describe their feelings by saying that they have experienced the holy, the supernatural. Recent sympathetic interest in the fantastic worlds of schizophrenics has revealed the precariousness of our everyday structures of reality, and the ubiquity of the myths that we use as bases for communication.

The view that we use ideas to order a reality which is meaningless and chaotic is attractively plausible, but perhaps only to intellectuals, who are notoriously both estranged from much of the social order, and prone to resort to ideas explicitly to order experience. It is easy to miss the myths that we use because we are looking for something more exalted. Warner (1959), in his brilliant account of Biggy Muldoon, the small garage proprietor and local wide boy in Yankee City, analyses how a person in whom "intellectuals" would be entirely uninterested defined the limits of the system and a mode of heroic but too-dangerous and hubristic action for a host of timid citizens, whilst enabling them to experience vicariously his outrageous exploits. Every group has its Muldoon; societies also have more "noteworthy" and public myths about tricksters—B'rer Rabbit, Anansi the Spider-Man, Reynard the Fox; the specific supports the public myth, and vice versa.

The argument that religion as a set of *ideas* enables us to order the chaos of experience is like the equally problematic humanist dogma that the value of great art is to enable us to transcend our personal situation and sufferings and, by comprehending them, control them. Against this, we may retort that the production of art is subject to market rules and exterior conditions, and that whilst people may indeed use art in this way, the art that they are using is advertising art, pictures bought for their subjects, "B" movies and *True Romances*, whose dialogue is with the subconscious. Berger and Luckmann's model is too deliberate; is not religion in Western societies, now less attached to institutions, becoming more like religion in simple societies? Something which *is* the order of life, which, as Leinhardt says of the Dinka people, enables us to "transcend and dominate" suffering, rather than to explain it? Many people seem to treat values like intuitive functionalists, accepting doctrines and acting as they require not because they believe in them, but because ultimately they have good effects. Religion is thought to be somehow good in moderation.

We accept that a belief in flying saucers or in the Anti-Christ needs explanation; this view entails that we should also look at the subsuming structure of all our basic beliefs—our sets of antitheses about what is natural and unnatural, our conception of children and grown-ups, for instance. But the most imperialist sociologists of religion do not argue that we should try to explain *all* the beliefs of a society. We still make distinctions between beliefs which seem unrealistic, irrational and, therefore, in need of explanation, and others—scientific or political—which seem natural, and therefore not to need explaining. Are secular belief-systems no more than alternative cosmologies and sets of values? If we accept that some beliefs are "rational", does this mean that *no* explanation is needed as to why they are held, or that a different *kind* of explanation is needed? Some authors, while accepting that "scientific" cosmologies are correct, argue that they must also be explained (Peel, 1969). Two points can be made about the general argument.

In discussing communism, positivism, nationalism, psychiatry and so on as functional alternatives to religious beliefs, it is usually conceded that they are equally adequate as explanations of the world. They explain as much of life, in as much detail, as convincingly. The main difference is thought to lie in the control of the after-life, which gives religion superior sanctions for its demands and an obvious personal goal—the entry to heaven, paradise, or a superior reincarnation. For this reason, conventional religion was thought to be more powerful and more permanent than other sorts of ideology. But the qualities of religious and secular ideologies do not remain fixed and permanent. Christianity itself is changing in that the after-life is emphasized less and less. In particular, *negative* sanctions such as hell and damnation are no longer held except by the most fundamentalist, and even they show signs of reinterpreting punishments as mental, not physical, and becoming reserved for the generally immoral, not those who merely challenge the control of the sect by dying unshriven, or by not believing. Among liberal theologians, and increasingly among Christian laymen, definite belief in an after-life is becoming rarer. This point will be returned to as part of the declining power of religious institutions to define the social situation.

The difference between believing in a religion and believing in science has been discussed in terms of the relative adequacy of two sets of beliefs. But beliefs occur in a social context.

We do not adopt more "rational" beliefs simply because they are such; we must perceive that they are. Many studies have asked the question how, in a secular culture, men adopt and maintain religious beliefs. But perhaps we could learn something about the interplay between holding beliefs, and the social contexts in which beliefs are located and confirmed or disconfirmed, if we looked at the process of coming to hold scientific or non-religious perspectives.

Studies (Budd, 1967 and forthcoming) of small groups of working-class and middle-class atheists in England show that the shift away from religious belief was bound up with the social situation, with the general meaning of believing in religion. To believe meant being part of a pattern of associates, worship and opinions with which the religious institution was bound up. In Western societies, religions have become overwhelmingly associated with "respectability" and political conservatism or privatism. The attempts of radical priests and theologians to break out of the narrow range of concerns to which religion has been restricted have revealed the resistance of both religious and non-religious institutions to religion becoming involved in "controversial" areas of life. Similarly, when men described how they abandoned a religious cosmology for a scientific one, it was rare for them to comprehend the two sets of beliefs and choose between them; rather, some social situations led them to find religious beliefs decreasingly appropriate. In Scandinavia, where religious belief and practice is rare, the religious are in the same position as the atheist in nineteenth-century England —cut off from other activities and likely to find themselves confined to a small circle of interests and acquaintances (Allardt *et al.*, 1958).

One cause of "choosing" science as against religion is the works of those eminent thinkers and moralists who have made a case for a morality and a metaphysic which is based on science but supports classical humanist ideals. Many of those who are converted to a "scientific" ideology have read these authors rather than discovering an ethic in science itself. In the same way, Solzhenitsyn describes Russian intellectuals, no longer sure of the content of socialist ethics, basing their moral convictions on the ideals for which the early revolutionists suffered *because*, perhaps, they suffered for them.

## 2 STRANGE GODS

We know virtually nothing of secular belief-systems. How do people come to hold them? Do they resort to religious beliefs at any point? In particular, many such ideologies are unable to offer the believer any sense of personal importance or uniqueness. Are pseudo-sciences such as astrology, spiritualism and scientology used to shore up this and other points where scientific positivism threatens to be inadequate?

We also know little about religious beliefs and actions which are not institutionalized. In particular, careful historical studies are needed of the points at which "religious" values are referred to in order to justify action. It is widely acknowledged that much behaviour concerned with politics and social movements is expressive and reinforces group solidarity, but recently, protest movements among young adults in many Western societies have become more radically "religious". In a position of political impotence, there has been a rapid proliferation of routines and occasions of symbolic protest and magical victories: the exorcism of the Pentagon, the demonstration, with its temporary "occupation" of certain areas, the public burnings of draft-cards. Some of the more radical campus-ministries in America bend the liturgical resources of the church to these ends, as when the ashes of draft-cards are laid on altars. Such activities, together with the attempts of a few Americans to devise their own marriage or community ceremonies, offer an interesting example of a counter-culture feeling itself excluded from both contemporary mores and the religions which support them, trying to create symbols which will embody the feelings of the "Woodstock nation".

Theological writing and controversy has little general interest or prestige compared to its position in the nineteenth century. Even the controversy with eminent biologists led at first to an increased interest in religion, so that by the late nineteenth century theology was still the most popular reading-matter in England. By the mid twentieth century, despite occasional flurries of interest, theology had lost its audience. The dominant modes of thought about man's nature and his place in the world are scientific and social-scientific. (See R. Robertson, 1970, for an exploration of the way in which sociological perspectives are coming to affect theology.) Many authors have stressed the immense power of psychiatry to redefine men's goals and behaviour; the studies of the contact of psychiatrists and clergymen show that the belief-system and techniques of the former are now seen as superior and are generally victorious.

The social sciences employ two methods of thinking about man which are alien to traditional religious conceptions. The first is that of "plastic man", *Homo sociologus*, man whose essence is created by society. He is not only morally but existentially relative to his social group. (For a critique of the *truth* of this perspective, see Wrong [1961]; and for a critique of its *desirability*, see Dahrendorf [1968].) For such a being, without free will and morally relative, sin and redemption are inappropriate. The second attribute of the social scientist's man is that he is powerful; by the use of knowledge, he can control and direct himself and his society. "We are as gods, and may as well get good at it." Etzioni's *The Active Society* is a good exposition of this view. It was in attacking this model of man that the neo-orthodox theologians challenged and largely defeated the liberal Protestant theology of the pre-war period. Contemporary moralists are divided between the mythology of the ultimately impotent man who endures, and the optimistic one who seeks for further powers; the majority of theologians take the powerless side, but some popular religious authors hold that religion helps man to control his life and his fate.

## 3 THE LOSS OF CONTROL

One of the most interesting effects of secularization, which has still not fully worked itself out, is the loss of power of religious institutions to *define the situation*. They no longer have the power to present social issues or conflicts entirely within their own frames of reference. The fascination of sects for outsiders lies in the fact that they do try to constrain their members to a bizarre and novel view of reality; *When Prophecy Fails* was a study of an extreme case of this.

The loss of the power to define has come about in several ways. Perhaps the most important is the loss of control over activities which are now ruled by secular knowledge and values. If religious leaders try to do more than legitimate what is done, they may be told that this is "not their sphere", an unthinkable comment in a sacred society. In societies with more than one religion, secular forces, such as those of economic change, make it increasingly difficult for all men not to be treated alike; the "special relationship" between established church and the state is on the retreat, and with it, the links between the political and the sacred realms. In the third world, cultural nationalism has the same effect; Christianity loses its pre-eminence as the Westernized élites lose theirs; local religions may be too inappropriate to the new society for them to succeed. For fear of alienating now-voluntary support, religious bodies can make neither inclusivist nor exclusivist claims to truth for their doctrines, but must simultaneously attract new members yet avoid attack on non-members. This affords theologians little room for manœuvre (Berger, 1967 and 1969).

A consequence of such changes is that public discussion of social and moral dilemmas now often refers to "the religious arguments" as a category to be taken into consideration by believers, but not one that is preeminent. Moral arguments come to be treated as a different and more important category. For example (Berger, 1967), the First World War was ex-tensively discussed in England in terms of theodicy and its Christian merits, whereas the Second World War was not. English adolescents are concerned about the moral aspects of life, but see religion as something separate (Eppel and Eppel, 1968). (Like many others, they condemn the religious for not living up to the "religious" standards which they accept them-selves.) Religion is unlike political life, where the dogma is well established that compromise and expediency are an inescapable part of achieving anything, and do not destroy political ideals. The view that religious institutions and functionaries may be corrupt and worldly without affecting what they represent may be accepted by members of churches, but by no one else.

Christian apologists have been repeatedly forced to change their minds by new knowledge originating outside the religious sphere, and the more they have attempted to "bring religion up to date", the more they find themselves in a crisis of plaus-ibility. In open societies religious ideas are unique, in that changes in dogma are hard for the laity to accept, whereas changes in scientific and other ideas they find easy—almost expected—though scientists themselves may find them harder.

These changes, and the decrease in direct contact between most of the population and religious institutions via church services or a religious education, are part of a major shift in patterns of ideas and sources of authority. The most dramatic and interesting effect of secularization is not that fewer people go to church, but that a certain way of thinking, a range of issues, has been radically altered. This can be studied in two ways: the changes in theology and the social circumstances and intellectual arguments which brought them about (*The Hidden God* [Goldmann, 1969] is one of the few examples); and large-scale studies of the way that people, including non-churchgoers, now think about topics such as death and the after-life, the morality of day-to-day behaviour, and the control that we have over our futures. Research into the way in which people's beliefs fall into a series of patterns, and more analysis of the contents of popular religious literature, would make this area clearer. The problem is that which Merton discerned for the sociology of knowledge, of which this is a part; how to unite a tradition of large-scale theorizing about ideas and their role in society with the empirical study of attitudes and values in concrete situations.

In many ways, anthropological studies of religion have been more successful and interesting than those carried out by sociologists, because, viewing the society from outside, they have simultaneously considered all its values, ideas and social patterns, and thus found it natural to relate them to one another. They have described the operation of religious ideas in non-religious contexts, such as in determining the right relationship between cattle and men, or men and the weather. Sociologists studying religion, partly because of the complex, segmented and specialized nature of life and thought in industrial and literate societies, and partly because they fear that only behaviour can be studied objectively enough, have confined the subject too rigidly to institutionalized religion, which is decreasingly common and thus decreasingly important. The sense of a subject matter slipping between their fingers led sociologists of religion to look for alternatives to religious *institutions*. Now that more attention is being paid generally to myth and symbol, social identity, and the role of values in action, sociologists of religion will perhaps be encouraged to embark on these uncharted waters.

# Annotated Bibliography

Joint books and articles have been listed by name of first author. Items have been selected from the several thousand works on the sociology of religion because they are either mentioned in the text, or relevant to the issues discussed in the text, or works of high quality in the field. No attempt has been made to cover works in anthropology or psychology, or historical studies of religion in any society except those of Britain and the United States.

ABERCROMBIE, N.; BAKER, J.; BRETT, S.; FOSTER, J. (1970). "Superstition and Religion: the God of the Gaps", in *A Sociological Yearbook of Religion in Britain*, 3, ed. D. A. MARTIN and M. HILL. London: S.C.M. Press. Superstitious beliefs in Islington.

ABERLE, D. (1962). "A Note on Relative Deprivation as Applied to Millennial and other Cult Movements", in THRUPP (1962). Critique of the concept as it is used in the explanation of religious movements.

ABRAMSON, H. J.; NOLL, C. E. (1966). "Religion, Ethnicity and Social Change". *Review of Religious Research*, 8 (1): 11–26. The variations within American Catholicism in terms of the social class and ethnic group of the congregation. Some social and political differences are due to ethnic group alone.

ABRECHT, P. (1961). *The Churches and Rapid Social Change*. Garden City: Doubleday. Useful source of references to the ways in which changing political and social structures affect missionary activities.

ADORNO, T. W.; FRENKEL-BRUNSWIK, E.; LEVINSON, D. J.; SANFORD, R. N. (1950). *The Authoritarian Personality*. 2 volumes, New York: Harper. Discussion of the relationship of religious or non-religious beliefs to other opinions and personality-dimensions. One of the first works to show evidence of a difference between "conventional" and "personal" religious beliefs.

ALLARDT, E.; JARTTI, P.; JYRKILA, F.; LITTUNEN, Y. (1958). "On the Cumulative Nature of Leisure Activities". *Acta Sociologica*, 3 (4): 165–172. Finnish survey, showing that where the religious are a minority, their activities are "intensified", i.e. they belong to few other organizations and associate mainly with each other.

ALLEN, R. O.; SPILKA, B. (1967). "Committed and Consensual Religion: a Specification of Religious-Prejudice Relationships". *Journal for the Scientific Study of Religion*, 6 (2): 191–206. "True" and "Conventional" religion.

ALLPORT, G. W. (1950). *The Individual and His Religion*. New York: Macmillan. Summary of psychological data on religious believers.

157

ALLPORT, G. W. (1954). *The Nature of Prejudice*. Cambridge, Mass.: Addison-Wesley.

ALLPORT, G. W. (1966). "The Religious Context of Prejudice". *Journal for the Scientific Study of Religion*, 5 (3): 447–458. Studies of association between extrinsic religious beliefs and prejudice.

ALPERT, H. (1938). "Durkheim's Functional Theory of Ritual". *Sociology and Social Research*, 23: 103–108. Also in R. A. NISBET, *Emile Durkheim* (1965). Englewood Cliffs, New Jersey: Prentice-Hall.

ANDERSON, C. H. (1968). "Religious Communality among White Protestants, Catholics and Mormons". *Social Forces*, 46 (4): 501–508. How does religious belief affect community adhesiveness?

APTER, D. E. (1963). "Political Religions in the New Nations", in GEERTZ (1963). Argues that political religions are functional alternatives to supernatural religion on some dimensions but not others.

ARGYLE, M. (1959). *Religious Behaviour*. London: Routledge. Good summary of social and psychological characteristics of religious believers.

ARIES, P. (1967). "La Mort Inversée. Le Changement des Attitudes devant la Mort dans les Sociétés Occidentales". *Archives Européenes de Sociologie*, 8 (2): 169–195. Discussion and review of Gorer's work on contemporary treatments of death and mourning.

BALTZELL, E. D. (1964). *The Protestant Establishment—Aristocracy and Caste in America*. New York: Random House. Certain Protestant denominations in America are structurally important as meeting grounds for and reinforcements of the values of members of the power élite.

BANTON, M. (ed.) (1966). *Anthropological Approaches to the Study of Religion*. A.S.A. Monograph, No. 3, London: Tavistock. Several articles on the definitions of religion and their implications for the study of religion.

BARBER, B. (1941). "Acculturation and Messianic Movements". *American Sociological Review*. 6 (5): 663–669. Under what sets of conditions does deprivation among American Indians result in a messianic response?

LA BARRE, W. (1969). *They Shall Take Up Serpents—Psychology of the Southern Snake-Handling Cult*. New York: Schocken. Psychoanalytic interpretation of a fundamentalist cult among poor white Southerners in the United States.

BARTLEY, W. W. (1964). *The Retreat to Commitment*. London: Chatto and Windus. Analysis of recent intellectual trends in theology, which argues that the "leap-of-faith" school is an invalid defence of religious truth produced by erosion of the ontological status of theological explanations.

BECKER, C. L. (1932). *The Heavenly City of the Eighteenth-Century Philosophers*. New Haven: Yale University Press. An attack on the *philosophes* for having retained theocratic assumptions surreptitiously inside a supposedly secular world-view.

BELLAH, R. N. (1957). *Tokugawa Religion*. Glencoe, Illinois: Free Press.

Was the religion of the Tokugawa class of Japan related to their role in modernization and can it be fitted into Weber's concept of the Protestant ethic?

BELLAH, R. N. (1958). "Religious Aspects of Modernization in Turkey and Japan". *American Journal of Sociology*, 64 (1)· 1–5. Discusses the deliberate use made of movements claiming religious ultimacy to reorder values in two traditional societies.

BELLAH, R. N. (1964). "Religious Evolution". *American Sociological Review*, 29 (3): 358–374. Attempt to re-establish an evolutionary schema for religion.

BELLAH, R. N. (ed.) (1965). *Religion and Progress in Modern Asia*. New York: Free Press. Thirteen articles on the relationship between religion, value-change and modernization in Asia. The epilogue makes very large claims for the role of religion in societal change.

BELLAH, R. N. (1967). "Civic Religion in America". *Daedalus*, 96 (1): 1–21. An important article setting out the thesis that certain general ideological themes in America compose a civic religion which the three major religions all support, and to which quasi-religious social ceremony is related.

BELSHAW, C. S. (1950). "The Significance of Modern Cults in Melanesian Development". *The Australian Outlook*, 4: 116–125, reprinted in BIRNBAUM and LENZER (1969). Argues that widely separated cult-movements were produced by structural conditions, i.e. the exclusion of natives from effective ways of gaining access to European ways of life. Cults, by using symbols of this, achieve magical control over it.

BENDIX, R. (1959). *Max Weber—an Intellectual Portrait*. New York: Doubleday. Summary and discussion of Max Weber's work, with particular emphasis on his sociology of religion.

BENZ, E. (1959). "On Understanding Non-Christian Religions", in ELIADE and KITAGAWA (1959). Reprinted in BIRNBAUM and LENZER (1969).

BERGER, P. L. (1954). "The Sociological Study of Sectarianism". *Social Research*, 21 (4): 467–485. Suggests a three-fold typology of sects according to the nature of their contact with the Spirit.

BERGER, P. L. (1958). "Sectarianism and Religious Sociation". *American Journal of Sociology*, 64 (1): 41–44. Sectarianism should be understood as a type of religious sociation not necessarily leading to a body outside the church.

BERGER, P. L. (1961). *The Noise of Solemn Assemblies—Christian Commitment and the Religious Establishment in America*. New York: Doubleday. One of many books in which he discusses the popularity of religion in America despite its real powerlessness. Conclusion is that "the social irrelevance of religion is its functionality".

BERGER, P. L. (1967). *The Sacred Canopy—Elements of a Sociological Theory of Religion*. New York: Doubleday. Religion is primarily an ontological framework which shores us up against the paralysing consciousness of chaos. Competition between religious groups has a profound and adverse effect on the ability of religion to do this.

BERGER, P. L. (1969). *A Rumor of Angels—Modern Society and the Rediscovery of the Supernatural*. New York: Doubleday. *The Sacred Canopy* rewritten for theologians.

BERGER, P. L.; LUCKMANN, T. (1963). "The Sociology of Religion and the Sociology of Knowledge". *Sociology and Social Research*, 47 (4); 417–427. An imperialist claim for the sociology of religion based on an idealist and ethical conception of the structuring of reality.

BERGER, P. L.; LUCKMANN, T. (1966). *The Social Construction of Reality: A Treatise in the Sociology of Knowledge*. New York: Doubleday. Immensely influential exposition of phenomenological view that social life is centrally concerned with constructed meanings.

BERGER, P. L.; NASH, D. (1962). "Church Commitment in an American Suburb—An Analysis of the Decision to Join". *Archives de Sociologie des Religions*, 13: 105–120. Important study based on recent joiners of three Congregationalist suburban congregations—joining was mainly due to familialism. That is, churches were chosen for proximity and social flavour by young couples with children of Sunday-school age.

BERGSON, H. (1935). *The Two Sources of Morality and Religion*. London: Macmillan. (First published, 1932.) Early attack on the Durkheimian view of religion as being too external, static, and behavioural.

BERKES, N. (1963). "Religious and Secular Institutions in Comparative Perspective". *Archives de Sociologie des Religions*, 16: 65–72. Much of religious behaviour which we interpret as ritualist, etc., may merely refer to the past forms of social organization within which the religion was evolved. Examples given from Muslim Turkey.

BERKOWITZ, M. I.; JOHNSON, E. J. (1967). *Social Scientific Studies of Religion: A Bibliography*. Pittsburgh: University of Pittsburgh Press. Over 6,000 titles; useful, though some inaccuracies and many omissions, especially of books.

BESTOR, A. E. (1950). *Backwoods Utopias; the Sectarian and Owenite Phases of Communitarian Socialism in America, 1663–1829*. Philadelphia: University of Pennsylvania Press. Good historical account of a series of quasi-religious movements produced during periods and areas of expansion and social uncertainty.

BETTANY, F. G. (1926). *Stewart Headlam*. London: John Murray.

BETTELHEIM, B. (1954). *Symbolic Wounds—Puberty Rites and the Envious Male*. Glencoe, Illinois: Free Press. Considers initiation rites as socially instituted symbolic mechanisms for establishing sexual identity.

BIRCH, A. H. (1959). *Small Town Politics*. London: Oxford University Press. Community study of Glossop, small Derbyshire mill town.

BIRNBAUM, N. (1955). "Monarchs and Sociologists: a Reply to Professor Shils and Mr Young". *Sociological Review*, 3 (1): 5–23.

BIRNBAUM, N.; LENZER, G. (1969). *Sociology and Religion: A Book of Readings*. Englewood Cliffs, New Jersey: Prentice-Hall. Focuses on historical development of the study of religion as a general force, rather than the study of specific religious collectivities.

BITTNER, E. (1963). "Radicalism and the Organization of Radical Movements". *American Sociological Review*, 28 (6): 928–940. Beliefs which differ from the ordinary contemporary world-view are permanently threatened; the article discusses the various organizational solutions to this dilemma.

BLAUNER, R. (1966). "Death and the Social Structure". *Psychiatry*, 29 (4): 378–394. Death poses a problem for societal stability which is responded to and contained by kinship, fertility and religious factors. But neither the nature of mortality nor its social impact is the same in all societies.

BOAS, F. (1911). *The Mind of Primitive Man.* New York: Macmillan.

BOCOCK, R. J. (1970). "Ritual: Civic and Religious". *British Journal of Sociology*, 21 (3): 285–297. Argues that Protestant societies overlook the immense amount of civic ritual connected with particular institutions—cities, schools, law courts, regiments, political parties. Demarcates this from religious ritual, and argues that the Anglican church, as promoter of much civic ritual, is internally divided over its nature and value.

BOHANNAN, P. (1966). *Social Anthropology.* New York: Holt. The chapter on religion is a good short discussion of recent anthropological interpretations.

BOULARD, F. (1960). *An Introduction to Religious Sociology.* London: Darton, Longman and Todd. An introduction reporting the research by LeBras and others in the sociographic tradition in France.

BOWMAN, L. (1959). *The American Funeral: A Study in Guilt, Extravagance, and Sublimity.* Washington: Public Affairs Press. Takes up the Gorer studies of the process by which mourning in modern societies has become subject to individual definitions rather than sacred prescriptions.

BRADEN, C. S. (1963). *Spirits in Rebellion: The Rise and Development of New Thought.* Dallas: Southern Methodist University Press. A group of religions based on transcendental and other meliorist social thinkers of the nineteenth century. Important as showing a highly secularized and world-accepting theology which appeals to their predominantly middle-class supporters.

BRENNAN, T.; COONEY, E. W.; POLLINS, H. (1954). *Social Change in South West Wales.* London: Watts. Includes a study of the links between church membership and political and occupational membership.

BRESSLER, M.; WESTOFF, C. J. (1963). "Catholic Education, Economic Values, and Achievement". *American Journal of Sociology*, 69 (3): 225–233, reprinted in SCHNEIDER (1964). Finds no evidence that parochial education lowers achievement motivation among Catholics.

BREWER, E. D. C. (1952). "Sect and Church in Methodism". *Social Forces*, 30 (4): 400–408. Documents the transition.

BROTHERS, J. B. (1964). "Religion in the British Universities: The Findings of some recent Surveys". *Archives de Sociologie des Religions*, 18: 71–82. Student culture is secular, but still ties between Anglicanism and upper-middle class.

BRYSON, G. E. (1945). *Man and Society. The Scottish Inquiry of the Eighteenth*

*Century*. Princeton: Princeton University Press. Modernization of Scottish society stems from the philosophy of the Enlightenment.

BUCKNER, H. T. (1965). "The Flying Saucerians—A Lingering Cult". *New Society*, 154, 14–17. Cult of arcane knowledge, which is not sufficiently elaborate or central to sustain a membership.

BUDD, S. (1967). "The Loss of Faith: Reasons for Unbelief among Members of the Secular Movement in England, 1850–1950". *Past and Present*, 36: 106–125. Loss of faith among members of a working-class anti-clerical organization was related to moral, not intellectual, rejection of Christianity and a relative freedom from traditional bonds.

BUDD, S. (1973). *Varieties of Unbelief: a Sociological Account of the Humanist Movement in Britain*. London: Heinemann. Historical and sociological study of the various anti-clerical movements, secular religions, and religions of science and ethics in Britain.

BURCHARD, W. W. (1954). "Role Conflicts of Military Chaplains". *American Sociological Review*, 19 (5): 528–535. Role-conflict had largely ended in rationalization or compartmentalization.

BURNEY, P. (1970). "Evolution sociale et conscience Chrétienne: 1. Le conflit de deux attitudes devant la douleur et la damnation". *Archives de Sociologie des Religions*, 30: 71–86. "2. Les nouvelles conceptions Chrétiennes de la douleur et de la damnation". *Archives de Sociologie des Religions*, 31: 51–68. Study of theological shifts in relation to changing social experience and technology.

BURRIDGE, K. O. L. (1960). *Mambu—A Melanesian Millennium*. London: Methuen. A study of Cargo Cults.

BURRIDGE, K. O. L. (1969). *New Heaven, New Earth—A Study of Millenarian Activities*. Oxford: Blackwell. General theory of millenarianism.

CALLEY, M. J. C. (1965). *God's People—West Indian Pentecostalist Sects in England*. London: Oxford University Press. The West Indian congregations in Birmingham are more fervent and sectarian than their English counterparts.

CAMPBELL, E. Q.; PETTIGREW, T. F. (1959). "Racial and Moral Crisis: the Role of Little Rock Ministers". *American Journal of Sociology*, 64 (5): 509–516. Analysis of factors affecting ministers of Little Rock, whose personal beliefs were pro-integration, but few of whom either made or maintained any public stand because of the pressures exerted on the position of the minister by both church hierarchies and congregations.

CARTER, P. A. (1954). *The Decline and Revival of the Social Gospel—Social and Political Liberalism in American Protestant Churches, 1920–40*. New York: Cornell University Press.

CATTON, W. R. (1957). "What Kind of People does a Religious Cult Attract?" *American Sociological Review*, 22 (5): 561–566.

CHAMBERLAYNE, J. H. (1964). "From 'Sect' to 'Church' in British Methodism". *British Journal of Sociology*, 15 (2): 139–149. The transition from conversionist sect to church was accompanied by the slowly rising social status of members.

CHARLTON, D. G. (1963). *Secular Religions in France, 1815–1870*. London: Oxford University Press for Hull University. The formation and decline of these "constructed" religions are an interesting commentary on Durkheim's theory that values of modern secular societies could be enshrined in collective worship.

CLARK, B. R. (1956). "Organizational Adaptation and Precarious Values". *American Sociological Review*, 21 (3): 327–336. Describes some of the survival mechanisms used by bodies who are uncertain of their goals and find them challenged; very applicable to many religious organizations.

CLARK, E. T. (1949). *The Small Sects in America*. Abingdon, Tennessee: Cokesbury Press. Useful source of factual information.

CLARK, S. D. (1948). *Church and Sect in Canada*. Toronto: University of Toronto Press. Church/sect conflict here complicated by frontier/settled area and nationalist/colonialist social and political issues.

COHN, N. (1957). *The Pursuit of the Millennium*. London: Secker and Warburg. Vivid descriptions of millennial and apocalyptic movements in the Middle Ages, which he sees as precursors of National Socialism.

COLE, C. C. (1954). *The Social Ideas of the Northern Evangelists*. New York: Columbia University Press. Bears out Weber's views on the tendency for evangelical Protestantism to support pro-industrial sentiments.

CONVERSE, P. E. (1964). "Belief Systems in Mass Publics", in D. E. APTER, *Ideology and Discontent*, Glencoe, Illinois: Free Press. Important article, which demonstrates that very few people have coherent, explicit ideologies, so that sampling specific beliefs and attitudes gives misleading results. Belief-systems of individuals must be understood as wholes.

COURLANDER, H.; BASTIEN, R. (1966). *Religion and Politics in Haiti*. Washington, D.C.: Institute for Cross-Cultural Research. Shifting political role and intellectual assessments of voodoo.

COXON, A. P. M. (1965). *A Sociological Study of the Social Recruitment, Selection, and Professional Socialization of Anglican Ordinands*. Unpublished Ph.D. thesis, University of Leeds.

COXON, A. P. M. (1967). "Patterns of Occupational Recruitment: the Anglican Ministry". *Sociology*, 1 (1): 73–80. Prospective ordinands are now older, more lower-middle or working class, and less conventionally educated than they were: their definition of their role is also changing from a theological to a pastoral image.

CRUSE, H. (1967). *The Crisis of the Negro Intellectual*. New York: William Morrow.

CUMMING, E.; HARRINGTON, C. (1963). "Clergyman as Counselor". *American Journal of Sociology*, 69 (3): 234–243, reprinted in SCHNEIDER (1966). Clergy occupy a major position as counsellors, but their normative involvement leads to conflict with other counselling agencies, which are minimal for educated clergy of middle-class congregations, and maximal for clergy of working-class congregations.

CURRIE, R. (1968). *Methodism Divided: a Study in the Sociology of Ecumenicalism*.

London: Oxford University Press. Account of the economic and social, as well as the personal and theological, factors behind Methodist schism and reunion. Concludes that ecumenicalism is produced by organizational weakness, but fails to result in the desired larger membership.

DAHRENDORF, R. (1968). "Homo Sociologus: On the History, Significance and Limits of the Category of Social Role", and "Sociology and Human Nature". *Essays in the Theory of Society*. London: Routledge.

DANIEL, V. E. (1942). "Ritual and Stratification in Chicago Negro Churches". *American Sociological Review*, 7 (3): 353–361. Study of forty Negro churches which finds the same correlations as for American whites between churches with a middle-class membership whose lives are not centred on religion, and a proletariat who are either committed members of ecstatic sects or irreligious.

DAVIES, J. K. (1962). "The Mormon Church: Its Middle-Class Propensities". *Review of Religious Research*, 4 (2): 84–95. The effect of the increasing numbers of middle-class church leaders has been to alter the social message of the church; attacks are now directed at labour unions and the "rough" aspects of working-class life, rather than at the wealthy.

DAVIS, K. (1949). *Human Society*. New York: Macmillan. The chapter on religion, like those on other institutions, provides an excellent simple exposition of the functionalist viewpoint.

DEMERATH, N. J., III (1965). *Social Class in American Protestantism*. Chicago: Rand McNally. Discusses the surveys, by the author and others, which analyse the effect of social class on religious belief and practice, and of both on other opinions.

DEMERATH, N. J., III; HAMMOND, P. E. (1969). *Religion in Social Context*. New York: Random House. Elementary textbook on Weberian themes.

DESROCHES, H. (1955). *Les Shakers Américains—d'un neo-Christianisme à un présocialisme?* Paris: Editions Minuit. An analysis of the communal ideas of the Shakers as showing tension between being expressed in religious or political form. Very relevant to the issue of functional alternatives.

DESROCHES, H. (1956), "Socialisme et sociologie du Christianisme". *Cahiers Internationaux de Sociologie*, New Series, Third Year, 21: 149–167. (Translation in BIRNBAUM and LENZER, 1969.) Argues that socialism is in no sense comparable to a religion.

DOHRMAN, H. T. (1958). *California Cult—the Story of "Mankind United"*. Boston: Beacon Press. Account of a modern cult, appealing mainly to "seekers" and claiming to use science to combat hidden forces of evil.

DOUGLAS, M. (1966). *Purity and Danger*. London: Routledge.

DOUGLAS, M. (1970). *Natural Symbols—Explorations in Cosmology*. London: Barrie and Rockliff. Both of Douglas's books are fascinating attempts to explore the sets of symbols which lie beneath systems for ordering experience and give them their power.

DURKHEIM, E. (1898). "L'Individualisme et les intellectuels". *Revue Bleue*, 4ᵉ série, 10: 7–13. Important article analysing different forms of individualism: claims that it is the intellectual's religion on which he bases his actions in just the same way as men use supernatural religions in a less complex society.

DURKHEIM, E. (1899). "De la Définition des phénomènes religieux", *L'Année Sociologique*, 2: 1–28. Early stage of his theory of religion. Defined here as socially compulsory beliefs.

DURKHEIM, E. (1947). *The Elementary Forms of the Religious Life*. New York: Free Press. (First published in 1912.)

DYNES, R. R. (1955). "Church-Sect Typology and Socio-Economic Status". *American Sociological Review*, 20 (5): 555–560.

EISENSTADT, S. N. (ed.) (1968). *The Protestant Ethic and Modernization*. New York: Basic Books. Important collection of articles on "Protestant ethic" thesis, dealing with methodology, historical accuracy, and applicability outside Europe. A good bibliography and article by Eisenstadt on the stages in the controversy.

EISTER, A. W. (1950). *Drawing Room Conversion—a Sociological Account of the Oxford Group Movement*, Durham, North Carolina: Duke University Press. Emotional needs of middle-class membership cast a movement with conventional revivalist ideas into cult form.

EISTER, A. W. (1957). "Religious Institutions in Complex Societies: Difficulties in the Theoretic Specification of Functions". *American Sociological Review*, 22 (4): 387–391.

ELIADE, M.; KITAGAWA, J. M. (1959). *History of Religions: Essays in Methodology*. Illinois: University of Chicago Press.

ELLEGARD, A. (1958). *Darwin and the General Reader—the Reception of Darwin's Theory of Evolution in the British Periodical Press, 1859–1872*. Göteborg: Göteborgs Universitets Arsskrift, 64 (7). Pioneering study of different levels of interpretation of Darwin's work according to readership of journal in which review appeared.

EMMET, I. (1964). *A North Wales Village*. London: Routledge.

EPPEL, F. M.; EPPEL, M. (1966). *The Age of Uncertainty*. London: Routledge. Survey of opinions of English adolescents on moral and political issues.

ERIKSON, E. H. (1962). *Young Man Luther: A Study in Psycho-analysis and History*. New York: Norton. A (indeed, *the*) psychoanalytic biography—based principally on the metaphors of Luther's sermons.

ERIKSON, K. T. (1966). *Wayward Puritans; a Study in the Sociology of Deviance*. New York: Wiley. A study of the early New England colony which establishes statistically that it was a theocracy in which dissidence took the form of heresy, but that as government became more secular, deviance assumed a more normal channel.

ESSIEN-UDOM, E. U. (1962). *Black Nationalism*. Illinois: Chicago University Press. The best account of the Black Muslims. Analysis presents it as offering symbolic gains to poor Negroes, who cannot hope for many concrete ones.

EVANS-PRITCHARD, E. E. (1937). *Witchcraft, Oracles and Magic among the*

*Azande.* Oxford: Clarendon Press. Raises clearly the practical as well as the intellectual difficulties in understanding and explaining beliefs which one does not accept.

EVANS-PRITCHARD, E. E. (1956). *Nuer Religion.* Oxford: Clarendon Press. Account of the religious beliefs of a people with no developed religious cult, dogma or mythology.

EVANS-PRITCHARD, E. E. (1965). *Theories of Primitive Religion.* London: Oxford University Press. A cogent attack on the majority tradition within anthropology, which, disbelieving in religion, analyses the religious world-view by inference; "If I were a horse . . ."

FANFANI, A. (1935). *Catholicism, Protestantism and Capitalism.* London: Sheed and Ward.

FARQUHAR, J. H. (1929). *Modern Religious Movements in India.* London: Macmillan. These early nationalist, reform, deistic and other liberal religions were reflections of intellectual trends in Britain, and were grafted on to a religious tradition which absorbed them in a way very different from and far more easily than Christianity.

FAUSET, A. H. (1944). *Black Gods of the Metropolis: Negro Religious Cults of the Urban North.* Philadelphia: University of Pennsylvania Press. Studies of five Negro religious cults.

FENN, R. K. (1969). "The Secularization of Values—An Analytical Framework for the Study of Secularization". *Journal for the Scientific Study of Religion,* 8 (1): 112–124. "Secularization" means different things to structural-functionalists and to action theorists.

FENN, R. K. (1970). "The Process of Secularization: A Post-Parsonian View". *Journal for the Scientific Study of Religion,* 9 (2): 117–136. It follows from Parsons's definitions that all action is ultimately moral and oriented to ultimate values. Fenn argues that American society is becoming secular in a way that Parsons overlooks, because there are several value-systems, no hierarchies of values for individuals, and considerable differentiation between levels of the social system.

FERNANDEZ, J. W. (1964). "African Religious Movements—Types and Dynamics". *Journal of Modern African Studies,* 2: 531–549; reprinted in ROBERTSON (1969). Attempt to locate syncretist movements in the transition to the more secular and nationalist movements of the modern African state.

FESTINGER, L.; RIECKEN, H. W.; SCHACHTER, S. (1956). *When Prophecy Fails.* New York: Harper. How do the members of a millennial group react when the end of the world fails to come?

FEUER, L. S.; PERRINE, M. W. (1966), "Religion in a Northern Vermont Town: A Cross-Century Comparative Study". *Journal for the Scientific Study of Religion,* 5 (3): 367–382. Proportions of the population at worship are relatively unchanged.

FICHTER, J. H. (1950). "Urban Mobility and Religious Observance". *American Catholic Sociological Review,* 9 (3): 130–139.

FICHTER, J. H. (1954). *Social Relations in the Urban Parish*. Chicago: University of Chicago Press. Decrees of commitment among Catholic parishioners.

FICHTER, J. H. (1961). *Religion as an Occupation—a Study in the Sociology of Professions*. Indiana: University of Notre Dame Press. A good summary, in the sociographic tradition, of material on the characteristics and training of Catholic priests.

FICHTER, J. H. (1965). "American Religion and the Negro". *Daedalus*, 94 (4): 1085–1106. Useful historical summary.

FIRTH, R. (ed.) (1957). *Man and Culture: An Evaluation of the Work of Bronislaw Malinowski*. London: Routledge.

FISCHOFF, E. (1944). "The Protestant Ethic and the Spirit of Capitalism—the History of a Controversy". *Social Research*, 2 (1): 53–77. A good survey.

FORD, T. R. (1960). "Status, Residence, and Fundamentalist Religious Beliefs in the Southern Appalachians". *Social Forces*, 39 (1): 41–49. Finds that the educated and middle class in this area are *not* less fundamentalist on many indices.

FORDE, D. (1958). *The Context of Belief*. Liverpool: Liverpool University Press. Critique of the Durkheimian view that rituals are symbolic expressions of social relationships, and argues that rituals must be seen in terms of psychological, sociological and biological systems.

FRAZER, J. G. (1890). *The Golden Bough*. London: Macmillan. Compendium of religious and magical rituals from an evolutionary perspective; immensely influential outside anthropology, and expanded in the third edition (1907–1915) to twelve volumes.

FRAZIER, E. F. (1964). *The Negro Church in America*. New York: Schocken Books.

FREUD, S. (1930). *Civilization and its Discontents*. London: Hogarth Press.

FREUD, S. (1934). *The Future of an Illusion*. London: Hogarth Press. (First published 1928.)
In these books, Freud explains both the origins of religious sentiments and their connections with neurosis. From them stems much of the hostility of psychoanalysis, and hence of the culture of educated liberalism, to religion.

FUKUYAMA, Y. (1961). "The Major Dimensions of Church Membership". *Review of Religious Research*, 2 (3): 154–161. Pioneering study of variations in religious belief and commitment within congregations, related to social class.

GATEWOOD, W. B. (1966). *Preachers, Pedagogues and Politicians: the Evolution Controversy in North Carolina, 1920–1927*. Chapel Hill: University of North Carolina Press.

GAUSTAD, E. S. (1962). *Historical Atlas of Religion in America*. New York: Harper and Row. Account and maps of the growth and regional distributions of the various religious bodies in the United States from 1650.

GEERTZ, C. (ed.) (1963). *Old Societies and New States*. New York: Free Press.

GEERTZ, C. (1966). "Religion as a Cultural System", in BANTON (1966).

GEERTZ, C. (1968). "Religion—Anthropological Study", in *Encyclopaedia of the Social Sciences*, ed. D. SILLS. New York: Macmillan.

GELLNER, E. (1962). "Concepts and Society". *Transactions of the Fifth World Congress of Sociology*, reprinted in B. R. WILSON (1970). Discusses the problems involved in the interpretation of beliefs in their social context.

GEORGE, C. H.; GEORGE, K. (1961). *The Protestant Mind of the English Reformation*. Princeton, New Jersey: Princeton University Press. Examination of theology of Christianity before the formation of capitalist economic groups casts doubt on Weber's thesis.

GLENN, N. D.; HYLAND, R. (1967). "Religious Preference and Worldly Success—Some Evidence from National Surveys". *American Sociological Review*, 32 (1): 73–85. Re-analysis of survey data 1943–1965 shows Catholics to be superior in status to American Protestants, but to be under-represented in the wealthiest group. However, they are concentrated in the non-South and large cities where mobility is highest.

GLOCK, C. Y. (1960). "Religion and the Integration of Society". *Review of Religious Research*, 2 (2): 49–60. The way in which and whether religion acts to integrate society. Discusses why churches in America are so amenable to secular values.

GLOCK, C. Y. (1964). "The Role of Deprivation in the Origin and Evolution of Religious Groups", in LEE and MARTY (1964). Accounts for the origins of religious groups in terms of five types of relative deprivation which may result in a religious response.

GLOCK, C. Y.; RINGER, B. B. (1956). "Church Policy and the Attitudes of Ministers and Parishioners on Social Issues". *American Sociological Review*, 21 (2): 148–156. Clergy are more liberal than laity, but explicit only where laity are divided, i.e. on issues of morality and not of secular power.

GLOCK, C. Y.; STARK, R. (1965). *Religion and Society in Tension*. Chicago: Rand McNally. Empirical studies of the connections between religious and other beliefs.

GLOCK, C. Y.; RINGER, B.B.; BABBIE, E. R. (1967). *To Comfort and to Challenge: A Dilemma of the Contemporary Church*. Berkeley and Los Angeles: University of California Press. Survey of Episcopalian clergy and parishioners, which illustrates the dilemma for religious organizations in both changing and solacing their members.

GODDIJN, W. (1960). "The Sociology of Religion and Socio-religious Research in the Netherlands". *Social Compass*, 7 (4): 360–369. Good outline of religious change and secularization in Holland.

GOLDENWEISER, A. A. (1917). "Religion and Society: A Critique of Émile Durkheim's Theory of the Origin and Nature of Religion". *Journal of Philosophy, Psychology and Scientific Methods*, 14. Reprinted in LESSA and VOGT (1965).

GOLDMANN, L. (1964). *The Hidden God*. London: Routledge. Brilliant and pioneering study of relationships between theology and experience in seventeenth- and eighteenth-century France.

GOLDMANN, L. (1969). *The Human Sciences and Philosophy*. London: Cape.

GOLDSCHMIDT, W. R. (1947). *As You Sow*. New York: Harcourt, Brace and World. Study of a Californian farming community, and the part religion plays in determining social status.

GOLDSEN, R. K.; ROSENBERG, M.; WILLIAMS, R. M.; SUCHMAN, E. A. (1960). *What College Students Think*. Princeton, New Jersey: Van Nostrand. See especially the chapters on secular religion, and religious beliefs and the social fabric.

GOLDSTEIN, B.; EICHHORN, R. L. (1961). "The Changing Protestant Ethic: Rural Patterns in Health, Work and Leisure". *American Sociological Review*, 26 (4): 557–565. The puritanical beliefs of farmers in the Middle West, whose dislike of debt and willingness to ignore fatigue and sickness makes them irrational in economic terms.

GOLLIN, G. L. (1967). *Moravians in Two Worlds: a Study of Changing Communities*. New York: Columbia University Press. A study of the factors determining why a Moravian community in America became industrialized and secularized, and one remaining in Saxony did not. Theological beliefs did not determine the priority given to economic activity.

GOODE, E. (1967). "Some Critical Observations on the Church-Sect Dimension—Church-Sect Reappraised". *Journal for the Scientific Study of Religion*, 6 (1): 69–76.

GOODE, W. J. (1951). *Religion Among the Primitives*. New York: Free Press. Survey of religion in five primitive societies finds it generally fulfilling an integrative role. In an excellent introduction, Kingsley Davis outlines some of the dilemmas of method in studying religion.

GOODY, J. (1961). "Religion and Ritual—the Definitional Problem". *British Journal of Sociology*, 12 (2): 142–164.

GORER, G. (1955). *Exploring English Character*. London: Cresset Press. A mine of information on English attitudes and values based on a questionnaire sent in by five thousand volunteers. Invaluable in that it documents the values and opinions on religious matters of the irreligious or inactive.

GORER, G. (1965). *Death, Grief and Mourning*. London: Cresset Press. Puts forward evidence for the view that our distaste for death, uncertainty about an after-life, and truncation of mourning rituals, have led to suffering among the bereaved. Death is our society's pornography.

GREELEY, A. M. (1963). *Religion and Career—A Study of College Graduates*. New York: Sheed and Ward. Findings show that American Catholics are equally as likely to be educated, and to be ambitious for business success, as Protestants.

GREELEY, A. M.; ROSSI, P. H. (1966). *The Education of Catholic Americans*. Chicago: Aldine. An examination of the effects of Catholic and secular education on the achievements and aspirations of children, used to argue that the "Protestant ethic" thesis no longer holds.

M

GREEN, R. W. (ed.) (1959). *Protestantism and Capitalism—the Weber Thesis and its Critics*. Boston: Heath. Summary of Weber's views, and articles by some of his supporters and detractors.

GRISWOLD, A. W. (1934). "New Thought—a Cult of Success". *American Journal of Sociology*, 60 (3): 309–318. New Thought movements emphasize the rightness of worldly success, and appeal to those who have it.

GUSFIELD, J. R. (1966). *Symbolic Crusade*. Urbana, Illinois: University of Illinois Press. Study of the temperance movement and of the moral structure of American politics.

GUSTAFFSON, B. (1950). *Kyrkolivøch Samhällsklass i Sverigoemkring 1800 (Church Life and Social Life in Sweden around 1880*—English Summary). Stockholm: S. K. D. Bokförlag. Artisans, the city born and urban workers were more hostile to the church than those born or living in the country, or industrial workers.

GUSTAFFSON, B. (1953). *Socialdemokratien och Kyrkan 1881–1890 (Social Democracy and the Church*—English Summary). Stockholm: S. K. D. Bokförlag. The socialist movement gained its first members mainly from those who were opposed to religion, especially members of class-conscious workers' associations, and the poor quarry- and mine-workers. The churches were highly class-conscious and emphasized the lowly position of the workers.

GUSTAFFSON, B. (1966). "People's View of the Minister and the Lack of Ministers in Sweden". *Archives de Sociologie des Religions*, 22: 135–144. Theological students see their main role as confessional and pastoral; the laity expect them to be leaders and administrators.

GUSTAFSON, P. (1967). ' UO-US-PS-PO: A Restatement of Troeltsch's Church-Sect Typology". *Journal for the Scientific Study of Religion*, 6 (1): 64–68.

HAMMOND, P. E.; MITCHELL, R. E. (1965). "The Segmentation of Radicalism—the Case of the Protestant Campus Minister". *American Journal of Sociology*, 71 (2): 133–143. Radicals can be contained within the organization by segmentation. Campus ministries serve this purpose.

HARRISON, P. M. (1959). *Authority and Power in the Free Church Tradition: A Social Case Study of the American Baptist Convention*. Princeton, New Jersey: Princeton University Press. Outstanding study of impact of organization of church on theology. Shows bureaucratization of a *religious* institution which is theologically opposed to formal authority.

HEBERLE, R. (1949). "Observations on the Sociology of Social Movements". *American Sociological Review*, 14 (3): 346–357. Discusses tendency of social movements to develop total ideologies and congregational overtones.

HEISE, D. R. (1967). "Prefatory Findings in the Sociology of Missions". *Journal for the Scientific Study of Religion*, 6 (1): 49–58. The study of missionary activities throws up rich material on the way different world-views collide and the effects of this.

HENRIQUES, N. (1961). *Religious Toleration in England, 1787–1833*. London: Routledge.

HERBERG, W. (1955). *Protestant, Catholic, Jew*. New York: Doubleday. Influential argument that religion in United States has become part of secular value-structure, so that the three religions are seen as alternative, and pressed into a similar shape.

HERBERG, W. (1962). "Religion in a Secularized Society". *Review of Religious Research*, 3 (4): 145–158 and 4 (1): 33–45. Religion and secularization—clear discussion of issues.

HICKEY, J. (1967). *Urban Catholics*. London: Chapman. A study of Catholics as a minority group in Cardiff.

HIGHET, J. (1960). *The Scottish Churches—a Review of their State Four Hundred Years after the Reformation*. London: Skeffington. Church membership in Scotland, at 59 per cent of the population, is about two and a half times the England and Wales level; the vast majority are Protestant and Presbyterian.

HILL, J. E. C. (1958). *Puritanism and Revolution: Studies in the Interpretation of the English Revolution of the Seventeenth Century*. London: Secker and Warburg.

HILL, J. E. C. (1964). *Society and Puritanism in Pre-Revolutionary England*. London: Secker and Warburg. Chapter on the extent to which society had already become secularized.

HILL, J. E. C. (1969). " 'Reason' and 'Reasonableness' in seventeenth-century England". *British Journal of Sociology*, 20 (3): 235–250.

HIMMELSTRAND, U. (1960). *Social Pressures, Attitudes and Democratic Processes*. Stockholm: Almqvist och Wiksell. Attitudes and their components, and the way in which they are affected by social processes. The empirical studies are not about religion, but methodology is very relevant.

HOBSBAWM, E. J. (1959). *Primitive Rebels: Studies in Archaic Forms of Social Movements in the Nineteenth and Twentieth Centuries*. Manchester: Manchester University Press. Studies of various movements, some of them quasi-religious, which the author considers as pre-political.

HOLT, J. B. (1940). "Holiness Religion—Cultural Shock and Social Reorganization". *American Sociological Review*, 5 (5): 740–747. The rapid growth of Holiness and Pentecostalist sects in the United States is due to social disorganization among recent rural migrants to large cities.

HOMANS, G. C. (1941). "Anxiety and Ritual: the Theories of Malinowski and Radcliffe-Brown". *American Anthropologist*, 43 (2): 164–172. Do we naturally feel an anxiety which magical rituals will soothe, or are they symbolic expressions of the concern which society expects us to feel at certain points?

HOPKINS, R. (1966). "Christianity and Socio-political Change in Sub-Saharan Africa". *Social Forces*, 44 (4): 555–562. The general effect of Christianity on the social structure has been disruptive and has led to modernization as defined by a number of indices, which in turn has led to a rejection of orthodox Christianity.

HORTON, R. (1960). "A Definition of Religion and its Uses". *Journal of the Royal Anthropological Institute*, 90 (2): 201–226. Religious behaviour varies along a continuum between manipulation (often termed magic) and communion.

HSU, F. L. K. (1952). *Religion, Science and Human Crisis—A Study of China in Transition and its Implications for the West.* London: Routledge. A study of an epidemic in a Chinese town, and who resorted to magic, who to religion and who to inoculation, and why.

HUME, D. (1757). *The Natural History of Religion.* London: A Millar.

INGLIS, K. S. (1963). *Churches and the Working Classes in Victorian England.* London: Routledge. Historical survey of political, social and theological changes as they affected membership of the churches.

JACKSON, A. K. (1961). "Religious Beliefs and Expressions of the Southern Highlander". *Review of Religious Research*, 3 (1): 21–39. In the Appalachian mountains, denominationalism of fundamentalist Protestant sects is proceeding, especially among the wealthier and better educated.

JACKSON, J. A. (1963). *The Irish in Britain.* London: Routledge. Weakening social control has resulted in growing unorthodoxy and transformed relations between priest and laity.

JAHODA, G. (1969). *The Psychology of Superstition.* London: Allen Lane. Review of the scanty literature on superstition in modern Britain.

JAMES, W. (1902). *The Varieties of Religious Experience.* New York: Longmans. Pioneering study which attempted to re-establish the reality of religious belief as a psychological fact.

JARVIE, I. C. (1966). "On the Explanation of Cargo Cults". *Archives Européennes de Sociologie*, 7 (2): 299–312. Claims the explanation creates a challenge to structural-functionalism.

JARVIE, I. C.; AGASSI, J. (1967). "The Problem of the Rationality of Magic". *British Journal of Sociology*, 13 (1): 55–74. Reprinted in B. R. WILSON (1970). Attack on the explanation of magic as rational behaviour, which does not take the beliefs of its participants into account.

JOHNSON, B. (1957). "A Critical Appraisal of the Church-Sect Typology". *American Sociological Review*, 22 (1): 88–92.

JOHNSON, B. (1961). "Do Holiness Sects Socialize in Dominant Values?" *Social Forces*, 39 (4): 309–316. Even though sectarian values are opposed to "the world", they help their members to succeed within it nonetheless.

JOHNSON, B. (1962). "Ascetic Protestantism and Political Preference". *Public Opinion Quarterly*, 26 (1): 38–44. Oregon survey of members of liberal and conservative denominations; theology of denomination affected voting behaviour independently of social class.

JOHNSON, B. (1966). "Theology and Party Preference among Protestant Clergymen". *American Sociological Review*, 31 (2): 200–208. Surveys of Baptist and Methodist clergy in Oregon found that, independent of the social status of their parishioners, the theologically conservative were more often Republican than were the theologically liberal or neo-orthodox.

JONASSON, C. T. (1947). "The Protestant Ethic and the Spirit of Capitalism in Norway". *American Sociological Review*, 12 (6): 676–686. Protestantism of the type Weber described was introduced with the nineteenth-century Haugean revivals and led to capitalist behaviour.

JONES, P. d'A. (1968). *The Christian Socialist Revival*. London: Oxford University Press. Historical account of the personalities and movements both inside and outside the English churches which were affected by socialism, and the reasons for the movement's lack of success.

JUDAH, J. S. (1967). *The History and Philosophy of the Metaphysical Movements in America*. Philadelphia: Westminster Press. Account of the intellectual origins of Spiritualism, New Thought, Theosophy, Christian Science, etc.

DE KADT, E. J. (1970). *Catholic Radicals in Brazil*. London: Oxford University Press. Study of a radical group within the Catholic church and its relationships with peasants and power structure.

KAUTSKY, K. J. (1925). *Foundations of Christianity: A Study in Christian Origins*. London: Allen & Unwin. (First published in 1908.) Interprets Christianity as a movement of world-denial on the part of an oppressed class in a decaying society.

KEPHART, W. M. (1950). "Status After Death". *American Sociological Review*, 15 (5): 635–643. Class factors affecting behaviour at funerals.

KIEV, A. (1964). "Psychotherapeutic Aspects of Pentecostal Sects among West Indian Immigrants to England". *British Journal of Sociology*, 15 (2): 129–138. Cathartic ritual, religious healing and community, and stress on the after-life as a response to social strain.

KING, M. (1967). "Measuring the Religious Variable". *Journal for the Scientific Study of Religion*, 4 (2): 173–185.

KLAUSNER, S. Z. (1964). *Psychiatry and Religion*. New York: Free Press. And see "The Religio-Psychiatric Movement", in *International Encyclopaedia of the Social Sciences*, ed. D. L. SILLS, 1968. The movement has been growing rapidly since the 1950s, mainly in the United States and Germany among Protestant clergy.

KLUCKHOLM, C. (1944). *Navaho Witchcraft*. Cambridge: Papers of the Peabody Museum, Harvard University. Emphasizes the psychological factors, and social and cultural aspects of primitive religion.

KNOX, R. A. (1950). *Enthusiasm*. London: Oxford University Press. Historical sketch of what the author sees as heretical movements in Christianity.

KNUDTEN, R. D. (1967). *The Sociology of Religion—an Anthology*. New York: Appleton-Century-Crofts. Reprints of forty-nine journal articles, all concerned with religion in modern America, and mainly reporting empirical findings.

KOCH, G. A. (1933). *Republican Religion—the American Revolution and the Cult of Reason*. New York: Holt. Historical account of religious fall-out from the Enlightenment in America.

KOLB, W. L. (1953). "Values, Positivism, and the Functional Theory of Religion—Growth of a Moral Dilemma". *Social Forces*, 31 (4): 305–310.

The functionalist sociologist cannot disillusion men about untrue but necessary beliefs.

KOSA, J.; RACHIELLE, L. D. (1963). "The Spirit of Capitalism, Traditionalism and Religiousness—A Re-examination of Weber's Concepts". *Sociological Quarterly*, 4 (3): 243–260. Ethnicity in America is a major variable affecting attitudes to work.

KROEF, J. M. VAN DER (1957). "Patterns of Cultural Change in Three Primitive Societies". *Social Research*, 24 (4): 427–456. The reaction of three societies in Western New Guinea to the impact of the West.

KRUJIT, J. P. (1959). "The Influence of Denominationalism on Social Life and Organizational Patterns". *Archives de Sociologie des Religions*, 8: 105–112. Account of the *columnization* of Dutch society, where secular institutions have become segregated on a religious basis.

LAHALLE, D. (1962). "Opinions religieuses et attitudes syndicales des ouvriers du textile au France Nord". *Archives de Sociologie des Religions*, 13: 73–86. Atheists and practising Catholics both more likely to be trade unionists than indifferents; *engagement* matters more than specific beliefs.

LANG, K.; LANG, G. E. (1960). "Decisions for Christ—Billy Graham in New York City", in M. R. STEIN; A. J. VIDICH; D. MANNING WHITE, *Identity and Anxiety—Survival of the Person in Mass Society*. Glencoe, Illinois: Free Press. Type of appeal of and respondent to mass evangelism.

LANTERNARI, V. (1963). *The Religions of the Oppressed: A Study of Modern Messianic Cults*. New York: Knopf. Excellent source of references to wide variety of sects and cults arising among the disprivileged. Good bibliography.

LASLETT, P. (1965). *The World we have Lost*. London: Methuen. New demographic material on the social structure of pre-industrial England suggests a low and seasonal pattern of religious activity.

LATOURETTE, K. S. (1938–1945). *A History of the Expansion of Christianity*. London: Eyre and Spottiswoode. 7 volumes. Definitive account.

LAWRENCE, P. (1964). *Road Belong Cargo*. Manchester: Manchester University Press. Millennial movements as pre-political.

LEACH, E. R. (1964). *The Political Systems of Highland Burma: A Study of Kachin Social Structure*. London: Bell.

LEACH, E. R. (ed.) (1967). *The Structural Study of Myth and Totemism*. London: Tavistock.

LEACH, E. R. (ed.) (1968). *Dialectic in Practical Religion*. Cambridge: Cambridge University Press. Collection of essays which stress the connections and distinctions between Buddhism as a philosophy and as a practical religion answering to the needs of peasants.

LEE, R. (1960). *The Social Sources of Church Unity*. New York: Abingdon Press. Sociological account of the ecumenical movement.

LEE, R.; MARTY, M. E. (1964). *Religion and Social Conflict*. New York: Oxford University Press.

LENSKI, G. E. (1953). "Social Correlates of Religious Interest". *American Sociological Review.* 18 (5): 533–544. Survey of the intensity of religious interest among white Protestants in Indianapolis—inversely related to upward social mobility.

LENSKI, G. E. (1961). *The Religious Factor—A Sociologist Looks at Religion.* New York: Doubleday. *The* outstanding empirical study of the effect of religion on attitudes and behaviour. Supports the Weberian link between Protestant attitudes to work and worldly success; but Negro Protestants share the attitudes but not the success.

LENSKI, G. (1962). "Religion's impact on Secular Institutions". *Review of Religious Research,* 4 (1): 1–16. Religion does affect behaviour, but this is because religious groups are subcultures which are affected by the churches round which they are organized.

LESSA, W. A.; VOGT, E. Z. (1965). *Reader in Comparative Religion: an Anthropological Approach.* New York: Harper and Row. Excellent reader on comparative religion.

LEVI-STRAUSS, C. (1961). *A World on the Wane.* London: Hutchinson. (Translation of most of *Tristes tropiques,* 1956.)

LEVI-STRAUSS, C. (1968). *Structural Anthropology.* London: Allen Lane. (Translation of *Anthropologie Structurale,* 1958.)

LEVI-STRAUSS, C. (1969). *Totemism.* Harmondsworth: Penguin Books. (Translation of *Le Totemisme aujourd'hui,* 1962.)

LEWIS, I. M. (1971). *Ecstatic Religion—an Anthropological Study of Spirit Possession and Shamanism.* Harmondsworth: Penguin Books. Ecstasy has here been treated as a social phenomenon: Lewis's explanation hinges on the possession of the peripheral and subjugated (mainly women) by amoral spirits versus the inspiration of the socially secure by ancestors or deities.

LEWIS, L. S.; LOPREATO, J. (1962). "Arationality, Ignorance, and Perceived Danger in Medical Practices". *American Sociological Review,* 27 (4): 508–514. The mothers of sick children are more likely to resort to arational behaviour (prayer and magic) if the progress of the disease is uncertain or medical science seems inadequate.

LIENHARDT, G. (1961). *Divinity and Experience—the Religion of the Dinka.* Oxford: Clarendon Press. Sensitive exploration of the religious cosmology of a pastoral people.

LINCOLN, L. E. (1961). *The Black Muslims in America.* Boston: Beacon Press.

LINTON, R. (1943). "Nativistic Movements". *American Anthropologist,* 45 (2): 230–240. Argues that many new religious movements are *redemptionist,* that is, they are efforts to restore the culture to a previous state.

LOFLAND, H. (1966). *Doomsday Cult.* New Jersey: Prentice-Hall. Study of a millennial group which is valuable because it pays careful attention to the process of joining, and to the interior rationality of the group's perspective and experience.

LOFLAND, H.; STARK, R. (1965). "Becoming a World-Saver: A Theory of Conversion to a Deviant Perspective". *American Sociological Review,* 30 (6):

862–875. Application of Smelser's seven-stage theory of social change to joining religious groups.

LONG, E. L. (1964). *The Religious Beliefs of American Scientists*. Philadelphia: Westminster Press. They are liberal, or likely to become so.

LOUDON, J. (1966). "Religious Order and Mental Disorder", in *Social Anthropology of Complex Societies*, ed. M. BANTON. London: Tavistock. Popular explanations of catastrophes.

LOVEJOY, A. O. (1961). *The Great Chain of Being*. Cambridge, Mass.; Harvard University Press. Pioneering study of a metaphor, and of the value of examining "unit-ideas" in intellectual history.

LOWIE, R. H. (1924). *Primitive Religion*. New York: Liveright. (Enlarged edition, 1948.) Good account and critique of the various theories of primitive religion.

LUCKMANN, T. (1959). "Four Protestant Parishes in Germany—A Study in the Sociology of Religion". *Social Research*, 26 (4): 432–448. Early study of dimensions of religiosity.

LUCKMANN, T. (1967). *The Invisible Religion—The Problem of Religion in Modern Society*. London: Collier-Macmillan. Leading work in the revival of the study of religion as very general and abstract thought structures, rather than those attached to institutions.

LÜETHY, H. (1964). "Once Again: Calvinism and Capitalism". *Encounter*, 22 (1): 26–38; reprinted in EISENSTADT (1968). Argues that Weber had originally been interested in rationality, the *Geist* of Western civilization: the challenge of Marx enclosed the debate, which should be widened to take the effect of religious ideas in history seriously.

LUKES, S. (1967). "Some Problems about Rationality". *Archives Européennes de Sociologie*, 8: 247–264. Reprinted in B. R. WILSON (1970). Summarizes the various positions taken by anthropologists to the rationality of the (mainly religious) beliefs of primitive peoples.

LUKES, S. (1968). *Émile Durkheim—an Intellectual Biography*. Oxford, unpublished D. Phil. thesis.

LURIE, A. (1967). *Imaginary Friends*. London: Heinemann. Horribly accurate exposure of the motives and defences of two sociologists studying a spiritualist cult—surely based on *When Prophecy Fails*?

MACINTYRE, A. (1967). *Secularization and Moral Change*. London: Oxford University Press. Secularization in Britain is ultimately due to the diverging moral worlds which developed with the formation of classes.

MACK, R. W.; MURPHY, R. J.; YELLIN, S. (1956). "The Protestant Ethic, Level of Aspiration and Social Mobility: An Empirical Test". *American Sociological Review*, 21 (3): 295–300. A large sample of lower-middle-class white males showed no apparent relationship between religion and either social mobility or different levels of aspiration.

MACPHERSON, C. B. (1962). *The Political Theory of Possessive Individualism*. Oxford: Clarendon Press. Political theory in relationship to an emergent capitalist order.

MALINOWSKI, B. (1925). *Magic, Science and Religion.* (First published in NEEDHAM (1925). Reprinted with other essays by Malinowski by Free Press, in 1948.) Classic statement of science as technical knowledge, religion and ritual as answers to psychological need.

MANDELBAUM, D. G. (1966). "Transcendental and Pragmatic Aspects of Religion". *American Anthropologist,* 68 (4): 1174–1191. Indian villagers separate the transcendental and pragmatic functions of religion, and assign different deities, rites and practitioners to each.

MANDIC, O. (1963). "Éléments païens dans la région révélée de type rural". *Archives de Sociologie de Religion,* 15: 59–62. Argues with illustrations from Yugoslav peasantry that they do not distinguish between "revealed", official religion and superstition—the two have always been intertwined.

MANN, W. E. (1955). *Sect, Cult and Church in Alberta.* Toronto: University of Toronto Press.

MARTIN, B. (1968). "Comments on some Gallup Poll Statistics". *A Sociological Yearbook of Religion in Britain* (1968), 1, ed. D. A. MARTIN. Concise discussion of evidence on religious beliefs of English population as a whole.

MARTIN, D. A. (1962). "The Denomination". *British Journal of Sociology.* 13 (1): 1–14. Argues that this should be considered as a separate and distinct type of religious organization.

MARTIN, D. A. (1968). *A Sociology of English Religion.* London: Heinemann. Useful source of information, and a pioneering attempt at describing the cultures of different churches.

MARTIN, D. A. (1968 on). *A Sociological Yearbook of Religion.* London: S.C.M. Press. (Volumes 1 and 2 edited by D. A. MARTIN; Volume 3 by D. A. MARTIN and M. HILL; Volume 4 by M. HILL.) Articles mostly concerned with empirical research on religious groups in Britain.

MARTIN, D. A. (1969). *The Religious and the Secular: Studies in Secularization.* London: Routledge. Cogent attack on inconsistencies in debates about secularization.

MARWICK, M. (1965). *Sorcery in its Social Setting: A Study of the Northern Rhodesia Cewa.* Manchester: Manchester University Press.

MARX, K.; ENGELS, F. (1957). *On Religion.* Moscow: Foreign Languages Publishing House. Collection of articles on religion, including Engels on Peasant War in Germany.

MARX, K. (1963). *Karl Marx: Early Writings.* London: Watts. Includes translations of two works concerned with religion, *On the Jewish Question'* and *Contribution to the Critique of Hegel's Philosophy of Right* (both first published in 1844).

MASS OBSERVATION (1948). *Puzzled People.* London: Gollancz. Impressions of religious belief in a London suburb.

MAY, H. F. (1949). *The Protestant Churches and Industrial America.* New York: Harper. Provides ample evidence for Weberian thesis, and demonstrates intellectual links between theology and social thought.

MAYER, A. J.; SHARP, H. (1962). "Religious Preference and Worldly Success". *American Sociological Review*, 27 (2): 218–227. Comparison of worldly success of religious groups in Detroit. Catholics were found to have by far the lowest.

MAYOR, S. (1967). *The Churches and the Labour Movement*. London: Independent Press. Historical material on the attitude of the churches in England to organized labour since 1850.

MEANS, R. L. (1966). "Protestantism and Economic Institutions: Auxiliary Theories to Weber's Protestant Ethic". *Social Forces*, 44 (3): 372–381. Suggests alternative causal routes between Protestantism and capitalism.

MEHDEN, F. R. von der (1968). *Religion and Nationalism in South-east Asia*. Madison, Wisconsin: University of Wisconsin Press. Nationalist feeling was first expressed within native religious movements, then formed sectarian political parties. In Burma and Indonesia, conflict resulted between religion and Marxism (which the nationalist movements had acquired as a legitimating structure).

MERTON, R. K. (1936). "Puritanism, Piety and Science". *Sociological Review*, 28 (1): 1–30. (Reprinted in R. K. MERTON, *Social Theory and Social Structure*, revised ed. 1957.)

MERTON, R. K. (1938). "Science and the Social Order". *Philosophy of Science*, 5 (3): 321–337. (Reprinted in R. K. MERTON, *Social Theory and Social Structure*, revised ed. 1957.)

MESSINGER, J. L. (1960). "Reinterpretations of Christian and Indigenous Belief in a Nigerian Nativist Church". *American Anthropologist*, 62 (2): 268–278. Good study of syncretism and its effects.

METZ, D. L. (1967). *New Congregations—Security and Mission in Conflict*. Philadelphia; Westminster Press. Study of six new congregations, where survival goals quickly triumphed over doctrinal objectives.

MEYER, D. B. (1960). *The Protestant Search for Political Realism, 1919–41*. California: University of California Press. The Protestant churches' developing awareness of political methods for pursuing their aims.

MOBERG, D. O. (1961). "Social Differentiation in the Netherlands". *Social Forces*, 39 (4): 333–337. The society has become *columnized*, i.e. all institutions are divided along religious lines. The non-religious become active humanists. Assessment of costs of this includes increased social control, and conservatism of Dutch churches and theology!

MOBERG, D. O. (1962). *The Church as a Social Institution*. Englewood Cliffs, New Jersey: Prentice-Hall. Comprehensive survey of literature on organizational aspects of religion.

MOBERG, D. O. (1967). "The Encounter of Scientific and Religious Values Pertinent to Man's Spiritual Nature". *Sociological Analysis*, 28 (1): 22–23. Most sociologists are biased against religion and so cannot assess it adequately, which leads to both moral and intellectual impoverishment.

MOONEY, J. (1965). *The Ghost Dance Religion, and the Sioux Outbreak of 1890*. A report to the Bureau of American Ethnology of 1892/3, reprinted by the

University of Chicago Press. Millennial cult as a response to stress of poverty and oppression.

MÜLLER, F. M. (1878). *Lectures on the Origin and Growth of Religion.* London: Longmans Green.

NADEL, S. F. (1954). *Nupe Religion.* London: Routledge. The invasion by Islam of an indigenous tribal religion. Very interesting account of the combinations of beliefs held, including systematic but unsuccessful attempt to derive general theory of conditions under which old religious rituals are retained, new ones substituted, or syncretic solution is reached.

NADEL, S. F. (1957). "Malinowski on Magic and Religion", in FIRTH (1957).

NEEDHAM, J. (1925). *Science, Religion and Reality.* London: Macmillan.

NIEBUHR, H. R. (1929). *The Social Sources of Denominationalism.* New York: Holt. The thesis that new denominations in America originated among the poor and changed as they became wealthier and the frontier moved on.

NISBET, R. A. (1967). *The Sociological Tradition.* London: Heinemann. The emergence of sociological thought from some common nineteenth-century themes—one being the moral and social effects of the decay of religion.

NUNN, C. Z.; KOSA, J.; ALPERT, J. J. (1968). "Causal Locus of Illness and Adaptation to Family Disruptions". *Journal for the Scientific Study of Religion*, 7 (2): 210–218. Religion no longer creates adaptive and stabilizing responses at stress-points unless *other* means of adaptation (e.g. science) have already failed or been exhausted.

OBENHAUS, V. (1963). *The Church and Faith in Mid-America.* Philadelphia: Westminster Press. The beliefs and opinions of clergy and laity in a Middle West county.

OBEYESEKERE, G. (1967). "Theodicy, Sin and Salvation in a Sociology of Buddhism", in LEACH (1967). Good critique of Weber's views on religion as world redemption.

O'DEA, T. F. (1957). *The Mormons.* Chicago: Chicago University Press. Excellent sociological account of social structure and origins.

O'DEA, T. F. (1961). "Catholic Sectarianism—A Sociological Analysis of the So-called Boston Heresy Case". *Review of Religious Research*, 3 (1): 49–63. A schismatic group at Harvard Theological Seminary, in fact trying to return to the original and sectarian form of the church. Useful as study of schismatic process in Catholicism.

O'DEA, T. F. (1966). *The Sociology of Religion.* New Jersey: Prentice-Hall. Good text which takes a unitary definition of religion-as-sacred and based on the experience of the breaking-point.

PARKER, E. C.; BARRY, D. W.; SMYTHE, D. W. (1955). *The Television-Radio Audience and Religion.* New York: Harper. Assessment of the New Haven audience for religious broadcasts, and the structure underlying the messages of some evangelists. One of the few American studies to look at the religious beliefs of the unchurched.

PARKIN, F. (1968). *Middle Class Radicalism—the Social Bases of the British Campaign for Nuclear Disarmament.* Manchester: Manchester University

Press. A discussion of the movement as a moral rather than a political protest—dominated by Nonconformists.

PARRATT, J. K. (1969). "Religious Change in Yoruba Society—A Test Case". *Journal of Religion in Africa*, 2 (2), 113–128. There has been no genuine "conversion" from traditional religion to Christianity—mission-educated are the socially élite groups.

PARSONS, A. (1965). "The Pentecostalist Immigrants: A Study of an Ethnic Central City Church". *Journal for the Scientific Study of Religion*, 4 (2): 183–197. The ritual and beliefs of these groups act for their poor Italian congregations simultaneously as magical solace and as stimulus to worldly success.

PARSONS, T. (1937). *The Structure of Social Action*. New York: McGraw-Hill.

PARSONS, T. (1954). "The Theoretical Development of the Sociology of Religion", in *Essays in Sociological Theory* (revised edition). Glencoe, Illinois: Free Press. Shift from analysis of religion in positivist terms was due to the application of evolution in study of human society, and stress on arational elements.

PARSONS, T. (1960). *Structure and Process in Modern Societies*. New York: Free Press. Parsons's views on secularization are fully set out on pp. 295–321, in "Some Comments on the Pattern of Religious Organization in the United States".

PARSONS, T. (1963a). "Christianity and Modern Industrial Society", in *Sociological Theory, Values, and Sociocultural Change*, ed. E. A. TIRYAKIAN, New York: Free Press. A discussion of religious evolution and the role of religion in modern industrial society; argues that in America it is more dominant than before as the basis for general moral community in a society with unprecedentedly high moral standards.

PARSONS, T. (1963b). "Death in American Society—A Brief Working Paper". *American Behavioural Scientist*, 6 (9): 61–65. Nature of death has changed, so, therefore, has the crisis that it represents.

PARSONS, T. (1968). "On the Concept of Value-Commitments". *Sociological Inquiry*, 38 (2): 135–160. Possibly Parsons's clearest exposition of his views on value-systems and their role in society.

PAUL, L. (1964). *The Deployment and Payment of the Clergy*. London: Church Information Office.

PEEL, J. D. Y. (1968). *Aladura—A Religious Movement among the Yoruba*. London: Oxford University Press. A study of two churches founded by those on the margins of Western society, and so for whom tension is strongest. The religion shows both the shift from primitive to world religion and the adaptation to industrialization.

PEEL, J. D. Y. (1969). "Understanding Alien Belief-Systems". *British Journal of Sociology*, 20 (1): 69–84. A good article on the "irrational beliefs" problem, which argues that *all* beliefs need to be explained in much the same way, that is, how do we come to hold them?

PELLING, H. (1968). *Popular Politics and Society in Late Victorian Britain*. London: Macmillan.

PICKERING, W. S. F. (1961). "Religious Movements of Church Members in Two Working-class Towns in England". *Archives de Sociologie des Religions*, 11: 129–140.

PICKERING, W. S. F. (1967). "The 1851 Religious Census—A Useless Experiment?" *British Journal of Sociology*, 18 (4): 382–407. Discusses findings for only British census to ask questions about religious adherence.

PICKERING, W. S. F. (1968). "Religion—A Leisure-time Pursuit?", in *A Sociological Yearbook of Religion in Britain*, 1, ed. D. A. MARTIN. North-of-England active churchgoers see religion as leisure-time activity; 30 per cent of sample felt churchgoing had some unpleasant social consequences, especially sectarians who experienced ridicule and snubs.

PIN, E. (1956). *Pratique religieuse et classes sociales dans une paroisse urbaine, Saint-Pothin à Lyon*. Paris: Spes. Sensitive exploration of class worlds and religious experience.

POPE, L. (1942). *Millhands and Preachers*. New Haven: Yale University Press. Excellent study of the social structure of a cotton town in the Southern United States during a period of labour unrest; examines the political implications of theological views, the attempts of mill owners to use churches as means of social control, the reasons for the lack of success of the Communist party, and the bringing to bear of different theological rationales on the strike.

POULAT, E. (1959). "The Future of the Worker Priests". *The Modern Churchman*, June, 191–199, reprinted in BIRNBAUM and LENZER (1969).

RADCLIFFE-BROWN, A. R. (1922). *The Andaman Islanders*. Cambridge: Cambridge University Press. Classic functionalist study of religious ceremony.

RADCLIFFE-BROWN, A. R. (1939). *Taboo*. Cambridge: Cambridge University Press. Reprinted in LESSA and VOGT (1965).

RADCLIFFE-BROWN, A. R. (1952). *Structure and Function in Primitive Society*. New York: Free Press. The classic statement of social functionalism.

RADIN, P. (1937). *Primitive Religion*. New York: Viking Press. How anthropologists actually collect information about religious beliefs, and how religious experience varies within simple societies.

RAPOPORT, R. N. (1954). *Changing Navaho Religious Values: A Study of Christian Missions to the Rimrock Navahos*. Cambridge, Mass.: The Peabody Museum, Harvard University.

REDFIELD, R. (1960). *The Folk Culture of Yucatan*. Chicago: University of Chicago Press. The decline of traditional religious beliefs is partly due to supplanting by Christianity, and partly to the secularizing influences of urban life. But sacred nature of traditional society is probably exaggerated in memories of older Indians.

REX, J.; MOORE, R. (1967). *Race, Community and Conflict: A Study of Sparkbrook*. London: Oxford University Press.

RICHTER, M. (1964). *The Politics of Conscience: T. H. Green and his Age*. London: Weidenfeld and Nicolson. Excellent study of the connections between ethical, philosophical and political movements and ideas in late Liberalism in England.

RICHTER, M. (1966). "Intellectual and Class Alienation: Oxford Idealist Diagnoses and Prescriptions". *Archives Européennes de Sociologie*, 7: 1–26. Culture-crisis in late-nineteenth-century England among secular intellectuals.

RIEFF, P. (1959). *Freud: The Mind of the Moralist*. New York: Viking Press.

RIEFF, P. (1966). *The Triumph of the Therapeutic: Uses of Faith after Freud*. New York: Harper. Exploration of the shifts in moral values and objectives as a result of the psychoanalytic revolution.

RINGER, B. B.; GLOCK, C. Y. (1954). "The Political Role of the Church as Defined by its Parishioners". *Public Opinion Quarterly*, 18 (4): 337–347. Finds that the more committed a parishioner, the more hostile to the political and social involvement of the church.

ROBERTSON, D. R. (1968). "The Relationship of Church and Class in Scotland", in *A Sociological Yearbook of Religion in Britain*, 1, ed. D. A. MARTIN. Found much higher levels of practice than in England, but same pattern. 56 per cent of sample *never* discussed religion, though thought it a good thing. Diffuse dissatisfaction with churches, saw religion in moral terms.

ROBERTSON, H. M. (1933). *Aspects of the Rise of Economic Individualism: A Criticism of Max Weber and his School*. Cambridge: Cambridge University Press. Re-emphasis on economic factors.

ROBERTSON, R. (1969). *The Sociology of Religion: Selected Readings*. Harmondsworth: Penguin Books. Studies of religion in a range of societies, focused on systems of meaning.

ROBERTSON, R. (1970). *The Sociological Interpretation of Religion*. Oxford: Blackwell. High-level analysis of the field. Emphasis on systems of ethical and intellectual beliefs.

RODD, C. S. (1968). "Church Affiliation and Denominational Values". *Sociology*, 2 (1): 79–90. The influence of church affiliation on attitudes in a Birmingham suburb.

ROHEIM, G. (1950). *Psychoanalysis and Anthropology—Culture, Personality and the Unconscious*. New York: International University Press. Connections between Australian puberty rites and Freudian theories of personality development.

ROSS, N. (1958). "Psychoanalysis and Religion". *Journal of the American Psychoanalytic Association*, 6 (3): 519–539. Attack on attempts to reconcile religion with psychiatry and psychoanalysis.

RUNCIMAN, W. G. (1970). "The Sociological Explanation of Religious Beliefs". *Sociology in its Place*. Cambridge: Cambridge University Press. Survey of philosophical problems involved in (a) defining religious beliefs as a separate category; (b) explaining the holding of beliefs in sociological terms.

SAMUELSSON, K. (1961). *Religion and Economic Action*. London: Heinemann. Attempt at demolition of Weberian thesis and, more generally, attack on beliefs as causal agents.

SARGENT, L. W. (1962). "Occupational Status in a Religious Group". *Review of Religious Research*, 4 (3): 149–155. Strong internal pressures have shifted Seventh Day Adventists from manual work to middle-class occupations, despite the stringent rules of conduct which separate them from the world.

SCHMIDT, P. W. (1931). *The Origin and Growth of Religion: Facts and Theories*. London: Methuen. Exponent of evolutionary theories. Interesting section on way in which analysis of religion was affected by successive batches of new empirical material from different areas.

SCHNEIDER, H. W. (1952). *Religion in Twentieth Century America*. Cambridge, Mass.: Harvard University Press. Most useful factual source.

SCHNEIDER, L. (1965). *Religion, Culture and Society*. New York: Wiley. Good reader.

SCHNEIDER, L.; DORNBUSCH, S. M. (1958). *Popular Religion: Inspirational Books in America*. Chicago: University of Chicago Press. Important and pioneering study of the contents of forty-six religious best-sellers, 1875 to 1955; documents the shift to "integrative" religion.

SEELEY, J. R.; SIM, R.A.; LOOSLEY, E. W. (1956). *Crestwood Heights—A Study of the Culture of Suburban Life*. New York: Basic Books. Interesting study of a wealthy Canadian community whose values centre on the dominant cultural issue of good inter-personal relations, and theology reflects this rather than the relations between men and God.

SEGER, L. (1957). *Durkheim and his Critics on the Sociology of Religion*. New York: Columbia University Monograph Series. Discusses Durkheim's views, their effects and followers, and their critics.

SIMPSON, G. E. (1955). "The Ras Tafari movement in Jamaica—A Study of Race and Class Conflict". *Social Forces*, 34 (2): 167–170. A religious movement which blends Marxism and the Bible in its rejection of both wealth and white dominance.

SKINNER, E. (1958). "Christianity and Islam among the Mossi". *American Anthropologist*, 60: 1102–1119. Illustrates the disruptive effect of missions on small societies.

SKLARE, M. (1955). *Conservative Judaism: An American Religious Movement*. Glencoe, Illinois: Free Press. Interpretation of Conservative Judaism as a response to the pressures of American society to create a structural equivalent to middle-class Christianity.

SKLARE, M.; GREENBLUM, J. (1967). *Jewish Identity on the Suburban Frontier: A Study of Group Survival in the Open Society*. New York: Basic Books. A study of changing religious identity among affluent Jews, as emphasis shifts from sacramentalism and *mitzvot* to morality and the Sunday synagogue.

SLATER, P. E. (1966). *Microcosm: Structural, Psychological and Religious Evolution in Groups*. New York: Wiley. Illustrates quasi-religious phenomena emerging in small groups as a response to uncertainty; as this declines, the group becomes secularized.

SLOTKIN, J. S. (1956). *The Peyote Religion—A Study in Indian-White Relations*. Glencoe, Illinois: Free Press. Early study of a retreatist movement among American Indians. Shows that effect of mescalin varies according to the social context in which it is taken.

SMELSER, N. J. (1959). *Social Change in the Industrial Revolution. (An application of theory to the Lancashire cotton industry, 1770–1840.)* London: Routledge.

SMELSER, N. J. (1962). *The Theory of Collective Behaviour*. London: Routledge. The major theoretical work in this field; disappointingly little attempt made to include major religious traditions.

SMITH, M. G.; AUGIER, R.; NETTLEFOLD, R. (1960). *The Rastafari Movement in Kingston, Jamaica*. Jamaica: University College of the West Indies. A religious movement appealing to poor urban Negroes with strong political and redemptionist overtones.

SMITH, W. R. (1889). *Lectures on the Religion of the Semites*. Edinburgh: Black. Pioneering study of rituals connected with sacrifice and feasting as defining and unifying tribal groups in the Near East.

SPENCER, H (1898). *The Principles of Sociology*. New York: Appleton and Co. (First published in 1876.) See especially volume 3, part VI, on ecclesiastical institutions.

SPILKA, B.; REYNOLDS, J. F. (1965). "Religion and Prejudice: A Factor-Analytic Study". *Review of Religious Research*, 6 (3): 163–168. Whilst religion is correlated overall with authoritarianism, a small number of religious people with strong non-conventional commitment are less conventionally prejudiced.

SPIRO, M. E. (1964). "Religion and the Irrational", in *Symposium on New Approaches to the Study of Religion*. Seattle: American Ethnological Society.

SPIRO, M. E. (1966a). "Buddhism and Economic Action in Burma". *American Anthropologist*, 68 (4): 1163–1173. The Buddhist world-view makes religious spending a sounder and more profitable investment than this-worldly saving.

SPIRO, M. E. (1966b). "Religion: Problems of Definition and Explanation", in BANTON (1966). Both this and the 1964 paper deal with the definition of religion and its rationality.

STACEY, M. (1960). *Tradition and Change—A Study of Banbury*. London: Oxford University Press. Excellent community-study which demonstrates the links between church, politics and social life in a small Oxfordshire market town with new light-industrial development.

STARK, R. (1963). "On the Incompatibility of Religion and Science: A Survey of American Graduate Students". *Journal for the Scientific Study of Religion*, 3 (3): 3–20.

STARK, R. (1964). "Class, Radicalism, and Religious Involvement in Great Britain". *American Sociological Review*, 29 (5): 698–706. Argues on rather slender evidence that class, political and religious/non-religious dimensions are connected.

STARK, R. (1965). "Social Contexts and Religious Experience". *Review of Religious Research*, 7 (1): 17–28. Direct religious experience was connected with viewing the congregation or a subgroup of it as a moral community rather than as an audience.

STARK, R.; FOSTER, B. D.; GLOCK, C. Y.; QUINLEY, H. (1970). *Wayward Shepherds: Prejudice and the Protestant Clergy.* New York: Harper. Study of unorthodox Californian clergy.

STARK, R.; GLOCK, C. Y. (1968). *American Piety: The Nature of Religious Commitment.* Berkeley and Los Angeles, California: University of California Press. Excellent empirical study of dimensions of religious belief and their associations with social class.

STEINBERG, S. (1965). "Reform Judaism: The Origin and Evolution of a 'Church Movement'". *Journal for the Scientific Study of Religion*, 5 (1): 117–129. Not all new religious groups start with sect-like organizational characteristics.

STEPHENSON, J. B. (1968). *Shiloh—A Mountain City.* Lexington, Kentucky: University of Kentucky Press. Study of mountain village in the Appalachians, and the role religion plays in this little-known type of American community.

STOUFFER, S. A. (1955). *Communism, Conformity and Civil Liberties—A Cross-Section of the Nation Speaks its Mind.* New York: Doubleday. Main worry of Americans is their health; seen in the pragmatic context of how to pay for treatment, rather than expectations of death, suffering, etc.

SUNDKLER, B. G. M. (1961). *Bantu Prophets in South Africa*, revised edition. Oxford: Oxford University Press. (First edition 1948.) Lack of opportunity and political oppression have bred syncretist groups among the Christianized Bantu; sensitive study of the variations in theology and organization between them.

SWANSON, G. E. (1960). *The Birth of the Gods: The Origin of Primitive Beliefs.* Ann Arbor, Michigan: University of Michigan Press. Attempt to test, by comparative analysis of religious beliefs and social organization from a large sample of primitive societies, some of the hypotheses about the origins of primitive religion.

SWANSON, G. E. (1967). *Religion and Regime: A Sociological Account of the Reformation.* Ann Arbor, Michigan: University of Michigan Press. Relates characteristics of the government of societies to whether they were receptive to Protestantism.

SYKES, R. E. (1969). "An Appraisal of the Theory of Functional-Structural Differentiation of Religious Collectivities". *Journal for the Scientific Study of Religion*, 8 (2): 289–299. American religion is generally said to be becoming increasingly functionally separated from other institutions; the evidence suggests that this is not happening but that religion is becoming a secondary institution.

TALMON, Y. (1962). "The Pursuit of the Millennium—The Relation between Religion and Social Change". *Archives Européennes de Sociologie*, 3: 125–148, reprinted in LESSA and VOGT (1965). Important survey of the theories of millennial movements as indices of secular discontent.

TALMON, Y. (1970). "Millenarianism", in *International Encyclopaedia of the Social Sciences*, ed. D. A. SILLS.

TAYLOR, S. (1963). "Some Implications of the Contribution of Émile

N

Durkheim to Religious Thought". *Philosophical and Phenomenological Research*, 24 (1): 125–134. Durkheim's explanation of religion was above all an emphasis on its social as distinct from its individual nature, its real existence rather than its origins in the emotions where the positivists had located it.

TAWNEY, R. H. (1927). *Religion and the Rise of Capitalism: A Historical Study.* London: Murray. Capitalism in sixteenth- and seventeenth-century England selected from the various Puritan religious traditions those strands which ratified the emergent industrial and social order.

THOMAS, K. (1971). *Religion and the Decline of Magic—Studies in Popular Beliefs in Sixteenth- and Seventeenth-century England.* London: Weidenfeld and Nicolson. Monumental study of ground-level beliefs in astronomy, witchcraft, chance, religion of all kinds, related to changes in the system of formal knowledge, the social structure and material conditions as they impinged on the common people.

THOMPSON, E. P. (1963). *The Making of the English Working Class.* London: Gollancz. Methodism as a vehicle of moral and social protest.

THOMPSON, K. A. (1970). *Bureaucracy and Church Reform: the Organizational Response of the Church of England to Social Change.* London: Oxford University Press. Social and theological changes which led to the formation of the Church Assembly.

THOMPSON, R. H. T. (1952). *The Church's Understanding of Itself.* London: S.C.M. Press. How people viewed their membership of the church in four Birmingham parishes.

THRUPP, S. L. (1948). *The Merchant Class of Medieval London.* Chicago: University of Chicago Press. Independence of merchant and artisan from influence of clergy not ended until Reformation.

THRUPP, S. L. (ed.) (1962). *Millennial Dreams in Action: Essays in Comparative Study.* The Hague: Mouton. (Supplement Z to *Comparative Studies in Society and History*.) Several excellent articles on the explanation of millennial movements, and of religious groups in general.

TIMES LITERARY SUPPLEMENT (1968). "Freud and Anthropology", 21 March, pp. 281–282. Review of Freud's influence on anthropological studies of religion.

TOWLER, R. (1969). "The Social Status of the Anglican Minister". In ROBERTSON (1969). (Earlier version appeared in *Crucible*, 1968, pp. 73–78.) Ministry face shrinkage, loss of social status, and increasing role uncertainty.

TROELTSCH, E. (1931). *The Social Teachings of the Christian Churches.* New York: Macmillan. (First published 1912.) *Locus classicus* for the discussion of the distinction between church and sect in their relation to society.

TURNER, H. W. (1968). "A typology for African Religious Movements". *Journal of Religion in Africa*, 1 (1): 1–34. Attempt to typologize the variety of independent churches which have branched out from Christianity.

TURNER, H. W. (1969). "The Place of Independent Religious Movements in the Modernization of Africa". *Journal of Religion in Africa*, 2 (1): 43–63.

Religion tends to break down tribal barriers, but because the sacred and political are being separated, religion does not have such implications for political revolt as it does in South Africa, where religion and politics are still fused by suppression.

TURNER, R. (1964). *The Social Context of Ambition*. San Francisco: Chandler.

TURNER, V. W. (1967). *The Forest of Symbols—Aspects of Ndembu Ritual*. New York: Cornell University Press.

TURNER, V. W. (1969). *The Ritual Process—Structure and Anti-Structure*. Chicago: Aldine. Analysis of ritual among Ndembu shows how symbols constitute a method of seeing the world. Uses the antithesis between *communitas* and structured society to explain sense of holiness, rites of passage, etc.

TYLOR, E. B. (1871). *Primitive Culture—Research into the Development of Mythology, Philosophy, Religion, Language, Art and Custom*. London: Murray.

UNDERHILL, R. M. (1966). *Red Man's Religion: Beliefs and Practices of the Indians North of Mexico*. Chicago: University of Chicago Press. Religion of North American Indians, the impact of Christianity and the syncretic religions produced.

UNDERWOOD, K. W. (1957). *Protestant and Catholic: Religious and Social Interaction in an Industrial Community*. Boston: Beacon Press. Excellent and neglected study of the relationships between the churches and between church and community in a New England paper town, during crisis precipitated by Catholic hierarchy's intervention in campaign for birth-control.

VAUGHAN, T. R.; SJOBERG, G.; SMITH, D. H. (1966). "The Religious Orientations of American Natural Scientists". *Social Forces*, 44 (4): 519–526. Over-representation of atheists, liberal Protestants and Jews; under-representation of Catholics; shift to liberal and non-religion, especially among younger scientists. Church affiliation least likely among those scientists at major universities rather than in government, business or minor universities.

VERNON, G. M. (1961). "Measuring Religion: Two Methods Compared". *Review of Religious Research*, 3 (3): 159–165. There is a distinction between a public profession of belief in religion, or a favourable attitude to it, and an identification of the self as religious.

VEROFF, J.; FELD, S.; GURIN, G. (1962). "Achievement Motivation and Religious Background". *American Sociological Review*, 27 (2): 205–217. Different rates of achievement motivation by religious background. The high rate among middle-aged Catholic men may mean that for this group it is more related to economic deprivation than effective ambition.

VIDICH, A.; BENSMAN, J. (1958). *Small Town in Mass Society*. New Jersey: Princeton University Press. Part 4 deals with the role of religion in concealing the stresses for a small town which is being encroached on by the values and social structure of large-scale society.

VOGT, E. Z.; HYMAN, R. (1959). *Water-Witching U.S.A*. Chicago: University of Chicago Press. Role of water-divining in containing anxiety.

VOGT, E. Z.; O'DEA, T. F. (1953). "A Comparative Study of the Role of Values in Social Action in Two South-Western Cities". *American Sociological Review*, 18 (6): 645–654. Mormon and Texan marginal communities have entirely different values on cooperation and independence, which affect their prospects of economic survival.

WACH, J. (1944). *The Sociology of Religion*. Chicago: University of Chicago Press. Good sections on individual religious experience and organizations.

WAGNER, H. R.; DOYLE, K.; FISHER, V. (1959). "Religious Background and Higher Education". *American Sociological Review*, 24 (6): 852–856. Attributes under-representation of Catholic college students to fact that the parental generation is less educated.

WALKER, D. P. (1964). *The Decline of Hell—Seventeenth-Century Discussions of Eternal Torment*. London: Routledge. Theological changes concerning the after-life are related to both growing knowledge and changed conceptions of responsibility and humanity.

WALLACE, A. F. C. (1956). "Revitalization Movements". *American Anthropologist*, 58 (2): 264–281. Many new religious movements are attempts to reactivate what is believed to be a declining aspect of the social structure.

WALLACE, A. F. C. (1966). *Religion: An Anthropological View*. New York: Random House.

WALLIS, W. D. (1939). *Religion in Primitive Society*. New York: Appleton-Century-Crofts. Relationships between private religious experience and organized expression.

WARD, C. K. (1961). *Priests and People: A Study in the Sociology of Religion*. Liverpool: Liverpool University Press.

WARDWELL, W. I. (1965). "Christian Science Healing". *Journal for the Scientific Study of Religion*, 4 (2): 175–181. A middle-class religion, with an emphasis on this-worldly benefits and well-being.

WARNER, W. L. (1959). *The Living and the Dead*. New Haven: Yale University Press. Cultural symbolism, secular and religious rites and popular myth in Yankee City.

WAX, R.; WAX, M. (1962). "The Magical World View". *Journal for the Scientific Study of Religion*, 1 (3): 179–188.

WEBER, M. (1930). *The Protestant Ethic and the Spirit of Capitalism*. London: Allen and Unwin. (First published in 1904–5.)

WEBER, M. (1946). "The Protestant Sects and the Spirit of Capitalism". *From Max Weber: Essays in Sociology*, ed. H. GERTH and C. W. MILLS. London: Routledge. (First published 1906.) New England bourgeois baptized into Protestant sects for largely pragmatic and social reasons.

WEBER, M. (1947). *The Theory of Social and Economic Organization*. London: Oxford University Press. (Part I of *Wirtschaft und Gesellschaft*, first published 1922.) Typologies of organizations, types of leadership, etc., both secular and religious.

WEBER, M. (1965). *The Sociology of Religion*. London: Methuen. (Chapter 5, *Wirtschaft und Gesellschaft*, first published 1922.) Many of Weber's ideas on the comparative analysis of world religions are outlined here. Excellent introduction by T. Parsons.

WEIMA, J. (1965). "Authoritarianism, Religious Conservatism, and Socio-centric Attitudes in Roman Catholic Groups". *Human Relations*, 18 (3): 231–240. In Holland, where Protestants have highest social status but feel threatened by Catholics politically, Protestants are anti-Catholic, the more so if authoritarian, whereas Catholics are anti-Jewish.

WEISBERGER, B. A. (1958). *They Gathered at the River*. Boston: Little, Brown. Revivalism began in the disorganization of the American frontier, but rapidly became institutionalized and adapted to a mass society.

WHITLEY, O. R. (1955). "The Sect-to-Denomination Process in an American Religious Movement: The Disciples of Christ". *South West Social Science Quarterly*, 36 (3): 275–281. Shift from sect to denomination associated with rural-urban transition.

WICKHAM, E. R. (1957). *Church and People in an Industrial City*. London: Lutterworth. Pioneering study of Anglicanism in Sheffield, which established nature and timing of retreat from churches by different social groups.

WILLIAMS, C. R. (1952). "The Welsh Religious Revival, 1904–5". *British Journal of Sociology*, 3 (3): 242–259. Last grass-roots revival in Britain; sparked off by culture-crisis.

WILLIAMS, R. M. (1956). "Religion, Value-Orientations, and Intergroup Conflict". *Journal of Social Issues*, 12 (3): 12–20. Catalogues major sources of religious conflict in contemporary America.

WILLIAMS, W. M. (1956). *Gosforth—The Sociology of an English Village*. London: Routledge. Chapter 10 deals with the social cleavages between Anglican, Bible-Christian and unchurched in a Cumberland village.

WILSON, B. R. (1959a). "An Analysis of Sect Development". *American Sociological Review*, 24 (1): 3–15. Typology of sects, which gives them different propensities for organizational change.

WILSON, B. R. (1959b). "The Pentecostalist Minister: Role Conflicts and Status Contradictions". *American Journal of Sociology*, 64 (5): 494–504. The theology of the sect places the meeting open to the "call of the Spirit"; in practice, the minister must develop techniques for controlling the meeting.

WILSON, B. R. (1961). *Sects and Society*. London: Heinemann. Study of the Elim, Christadelphian and Christian Science Churches which established the sociological rationale and method for the study of sects.

WILSON, B. R. (1966). *Religion in Secular Society*. London: Watts. Good short introduction to the issues raised by secularization.

WILSON, B. R. (ed.) (1967). *Patterns of Sectarianism: Organization and Ideology in Social and Religious Movements*. London: Heinemann. Number of studies of small religious groups, mainly in England.

WILSON, B. R. (ed.) (1970). *Rationality*. Oxford: Blackwell. Collection of most of the contributions to the recent debate on how we are to understand or explain those beliefs (often religious) of other peoples which to us are non-rational.

WILSON, B. R. (1971). *Religious Sects*. London: Weidenfeld and Nicolson. Good brief introduction by leading authority in the field.

WILSON, J. (1968). "The Relation between Ideology and Organization in a Small Religious Group: The British Israelites". *Review of Religious Research*, 10 (1): 51–60. Like Moral Rearmament, the British Israelites are neither sect nor cult but see themselves as an essential additive to orthodox Protestantism; both consequently never acquire totally committed members, and are highly accepting of the existing social order.

WINCH, P. (1964). "Understanding a Primitive Society". *American Philosophical Quarterly*, 1 (4): 307–324, reprinted in B. R. WILSON (1970). Restatement of position in *The Idea of a Social Science*, with special reference to religion.

WINTER, G. (1961). *The Suburban Captivity of the Churches*. New York: Doubleday. The large family congregations of the American suburbs, and decline of the old, young and poor congregations of the city centres, have resulted in complacency and conservatism among many American churches.

WINTER, G. (1968). *Religious Identity—A Study of Religious Organization*. New York: Macmillan. A survey of studies of the organization of the Protestant, Catholic, and Jewish faiths in America.

WORSLEY, P. M. (1956). "Émile Durkheim's Theory of Knowledge". *Sociological Review*, new series (1), 4: 47–62. Criticizes Durkheim's theory of society as ignoring the material constraints by which men are surrounded and which interact with social categories.

WORSLEY, P. M. (1957). *The Trumpet Shall Sound: A Study of "Cargo" Cults in Melanesia*. London: MacGibbon and Kee. The Cargo cults of Melanesia studied as reactions to colonialism and experience of the white man, which welded together people with a common sense of oppression who might then move to political organization.

WRONG, D. (1961). "The Over-socialized Conception of Man in Modern Sociology". *American Sociological Review*, 26 (2): 184–193. Attack on *Homo sociologus*.

YINGER, J. M. (1946). *Religion in the Struggle for Power*. North Carolina: Duke University Press. Summary of material on relations between church and state.

YINGER, J. M. (1957). *Religion, Society and the Individual*. New York: Macmillan. Introduction, followed by good selection of articles on various aspects of religion.

YINGER, J. M. (1960). "Contraculture and Subculture". *American Sociological Review*, 25 (5): 625–635. Religious and other movements may see themselves as either variants on a cultural theme, or fighting a wholly illegitimate culture.

YINGER, J. M. (1967). "Pluralism, Religion and Secularism". *Journal for the Scientific Study of Religion*, 6 (1): 17–28. Argues that religious pluralism may result in integrative functions being transferred to secular institutions with varying success. High degree of secularization essential for religious pluralism to remain stable.

YINGER, J. M. (1969). "A Structural Examination of Religion". *Journal for the Scientific Study of Religion*, 8 (1): 88–99. What should we include in a definition of religion? If we call it a response to chaos, our concept of chaos and our belief that we can be delivered from it changes.

YINGER, J. M. (1970). *The Scientific Study of Religion.* London: Collier-Macmillan. Detailed textbook which examines a wide range of data concerned with religion and society from the standpoint of "field theory" —an effort to integrate a functionalist and conflict analysis.

YOUNG, F. W. (1960). "Adaptation and Pattern Integration of a California Sect". *Review of Religious Research*, 1 (3): 137–150. Move from sect to church required intensive reformulation of a group's beliefs and its service. There was a decline in emotion and empathy at services as the world became more acceptable and less contaminating.

YOUNG, M.; SHILS, E. (1953). "The Meaning of the Coronation". *Sociological Review*, 1 (2): 63–81. Interpretation of the monarchy as powerless, and therefore capable of embodying general social values.

ZWEIG, F. (1952). *The British Worker.* London: Gollancz. Small sample of working men talking to a gifted interviewer.

ZWEIG, F. (1961). *The Worker in an Affluent Society.* London: Heinemann. Affluent workers are predominantly hostile to the churches—"hypocrites"—whilst adhering to Christian values.

# Index

Aberle, D., 51, 65, 66
Abramson, H. J., 109, 110
Adorno, T. W., 32
Allardt, E., 152
Allen, R. O., 32, 91
Allport, G. W., 32, 91
Anthropological explanations of r., 13, 15, 20–30, 44
Apter, D. E., 10, 61
Argyle, M., 9

Baltzell, E. D., 110
Barber, B., 69
la Barre, W., 33
Belief, r. as, 2, 4, 14, 26, 53 *et seq.*, 84, 86–103, 148–54
Bellah, R. N., 27, 61, 96–7
Belshaw, C. S., 68
Benz, E., 45
Berger, P. L., 4, 77, 81, 92, 117, 121, 139, 143, 148–9, 155
Bergson, H., 39
Bestor, A. E., 93
Bettany, F. G., 89
Bettelheim, B., 31
Birnbaum, N., 55, 56
Bittner, E., 79, 94
Boas, F., 25
Boulard, F., 3
Braden, C. S., 116
Brennan, T., *et al.*, 114
Brewer, E. D. C., 76, 105
Bryson, G. E., 62, 127
Buckner, H. T., 94
Budd, S., 16, 67, 144, 152
Burridge, K. O. L., 57

Calley, M. J. C., 95
Campbell, E. Q., *et al.*, 140

Carter, P. A., 97, 137, 138
Catton, W. R., 51, 94
Chamberlayne, J. H., 76, 105
Clark, S. D., 76, 77, 140, 142
Class-related aspects of r., 50, 55, 63–4, 88, 98–101, 104–18, 138
Cohn, N., 57, 68
Context-dependent, values and beliefs as, 26–9, 32, 36, 45, 48, 62, 79, 86, 89, 94, 103, 105–6, 109, 118, 145
Converse, P. E., 18
Courlander, H., 70
Coxon. A. P. M., 138
Cruse, H., 96
Cumming, E., 140
Currie, R., 76, 114, 141

Dahrendorf, R., 154
Davies, J. K., 76, 105
Davis, K., 46
Death, r. in relation to, 9, 34, 43, 47, 117
Demerath, N. J., 50, 54, 91, 111
Deprivation, r. as response to, 35, 51, 64–7
Desroches, H., 93, 129
Douglas, M., 27, 142
Durkheim, E., 6, 27, 35–42, 45, 46, 51, 84, 135, 145; critiques of, 39, 40–1

Eisenstadt, S. N., 62
Eister, A. W., 40, 77, 78
Ellegard, A., 143
Eppel, F. M., 155
Essien-Udom, E. U., 65, 96
Evans-Pritchard, E. E., 13, 25–6
Evolutionary theories, 19–25, 27, 37; critiques of, 25–7, 28–9

Fernandez, J. W., 72
Festinger, L., 67, 78, 94
Fichter, J. H., 74, 108, 139
Fischoff, E., 59
Forde, D., 40
Frazer, J. G., 8, 24
Freud, S., 30–1
Fukuyama, Y., 91, 92
Functional alternatives or equivalents to r., 9, 10, 16–17, 33, 38–9, 40, 49, 67, 84, 101–3, 119, 151
Functionalist explanations, 7, 37, 39, 42–4, 46–52; difficulties of, 47–52

Gatewood, W. B., 137
Geertz, C., 7, 47–8
Gellner, E., 14
George, C. H., 127
Glock, C. Y., 8, 32, 65, 90–2, 112, 117, 138, 140
Goldenweiser, A. A., 40
Goldmann, L., 56, 81, 156
Goldschmidt, W. R., 105, 107
Goldsen, R. K., 17, 19, 112
Goldstein, B., 58
Goode, E., 77–8
Goode, W. J., 49
Goody, J., 10
Gorer, G., 9, 87–8
Greely, A. M., 108–9
Green, R. W., 59
Green, T. H., influence of, 133
Griswold, A. W., 116
Gusfield, J. R., 97, 100
Gustaffson, B., 131

Hammond, P. E., 54, 140
Harrison, P. M. 74, 105
Headlam, S., 89
Heberle, R., 12
Heise, D. R., 70
Henriques, N., 128
Herberg, W., 90, 97
Hickey, J., 95
Hill, J. E. C., 124, 126
Historical explanations of r., 7, 53
Hobsbawm, E. J., 65

Holt, J. B., 106
Horton, R., 14
Hsu, F. L. K., 63
Hume, D., 19–20

Ideas as agents, 56, 57, 60, 79–81, 104–8
Intellectualist definitions of r., 10, 23, 45, 57, 148–50

Jahoda, G., 9, 30
James, W., 30
Johnson, B., 77, 106, 136
Jones, D'A., 133

Kadt, E. J. De, 56, 130
Kautsky, K. J., 57
Kephart, W. M., 117
Kiev, A., 95
Klausner, S. Z., 140
Kluckholm, C., 31, 95
Knox, R. A., 11
Kosa, J., 109
Kroef, J. M., van der, 70

Lang, G., 51
Lanternari, V., 57, 68
Lawrence, P., 57, 65, 68
Laslett, P., 124
Leach, E. R., 15
Lenski, G. E., 9, 108
Lévi-Strauss, C., 18, 27, 33, 41
Lewis, I. M., 142
Lewis, L. S., 34
Lofland, H., 33, 66–7, 94
Loudon, J., 89
Lowie, R. H., 25, 40, 45
Luckmann, T., 4–5, 77, 81, 121, 148–9
Lüethy, H., 62
Lukes, S., 15
Lurie, A., 94

MacIntyre, A., 55, 129, 133

Mack, R. W., 109
MacPherson, C. B., 61, 148
Malinowski, B., 24, 31, 42–3, 79
Mann, W. E., 76
Martin, D. A., 9, 74, 77, 88, 119, 139
Marwick, M., 26, 142
Marx on r., 53–6
Marxist explanations of r., 11, 12–13, 50–1, 129–30
Mass Observation, 88
Mayer, A. J., 108
Means, R. L., 61
Mehden, F. R. von der, 62, 69, 130
Merton, R. K., 127, 156
Messinger, J. L., 71
Metz, D. L., 117, 140
Meyer, D. B., 138
Millennialism, 56–7, 68–70
Moberg, D. O., 75
Mooney, J., 95
Müller, F. M., 21

New religious groups—explanations of, 51, 56–7, 61, 65, 68–73
Niebuhr, H. R., 75
Nineteenth-century and naturalist explanations of r., 1–2, 20, 26

O'Dea, T. F., 93, 119
Opiate, r. as, 31, 51, 54–6, 57
Origin of religious impulse, 14, 30

Parker, E. C., 8
Parkin, F., 9, 134
Parsons, A., 106
Parsons, T., 34, 46–8, 57, 79–80, 121–4, 135, 154
Paul, L., 138
Peel, J. D. Y., 72, 151
Pelling, H., 114, 131
Personal religion, 87–92
Pickering, W. S. F., 67, 131, 139
Pin, E., 104
Politics and r., 56–7, 62, 65, 68–70, 70–1, 95, 97–101, 110, 112–14, 129–38

Pope, L., 55, 76, 106
Positivist explanations of r., 2, 4, 17
Poulat, E., 56, 130
Psychological explanations of r., 6–7, 12, 16–17, 20, 52

Radcliffe-Browne, A. R., 40, 43
Radin, P., 8, 25, 37
Rationality of r., 13–17, 42, 45, 58–9, 69, 151
Religion—its definition, 5–11; not a unitary thing, 41, 44, 49, 82–3, 102–3; as label, 94–6, 96–7; as meaning, 79–81; r. in relation to group characteristics, 64, 71, 88, 104–18; r. and social control, 24–5, 31, 36, 46, 49–50; as ritual, 37–9, 42, 43–4, 153; in relation to science, 15, 16–17, 23–4, 41–2, 46, 47, 55, 63, 89, 108, 115–16, 125–6, 137, 143–5, 152
Rex, J., 95
Richter, M., 133
Rieff, P., 31
Robertson, H. M., 61
Robertson, R., 41, 47, 57, 62, 75, 77, 78, 139, 153
Roheim, G., 31
Rudé, G., 80

Samuelsson, K., 14, 59, 61, 62, 127
Sargent, L. W., 76, 105
Schmidt, P. W., 20
Schneider, H. W., 117
Schneider, L., 88, 116
Sectarian religion, 93–6, 104–7, 111
Secularization, 49, 110–11, 119–46
Seeley, J. R., 116
Sklare, M., 76, 102, 103
Slater, P. E., 34
Slotkin, J. S., 95
Smelser, N. J., 132
Smith, W. R., 36
Spencer, H., 22, 24–5, 120
Spiro, M. E., 10, 15–16, 59
Stacey, M., 113

Stark, R., 8, 32, 90, 91–2, 112, 138
Steinberg, S., 76
Stephenson, J. B., 106
Stouffer, S. A., 35
Structuralist explanations of r., 5, 37–8
Suffering and illness, r. in relation to, 34, 35, 47, 57, 79
Sundkler, B. G. M., 69, 72
Superstition, 9, 20, 34, 89–90, 124–6
Swanson, G. E., 27, 50, 61
Sykes, R. E., 122
Syncretism, 70–3

Talmon, Y., 57, 65, 68
Tawney, R. H., 14, 61, 127
Thomas, K., 124–6, 133, 142
Thompson, E. P., 130
Thompson, K. A., 74
Thrupp, S. L., 127
Towler, R., 139
Troeltsch, E., 73–5
Truth—study of r. independent of its, 2, 5; implications of for study of r., 11–13, 36–7, 40, 54
Turner, R., 109
Turner, V. W., 27

Uncertainty, r. in relation to, 34–5, 60
Underwood, K. W., 110
Unimportance of r. as social phenomenon, 3, 17–18, 80, 90

Values as basis of social cohesion—critique of this, 48–9, 58–9, 80–1, 122–4; v. and ideas—r. as creating and maintaining, 36, 38–40, 46–7, 58, 79, 96, 121–2, 134–5
Vaughan, T. R., 108
Vidich, A., 97

Wach, J., 6
Walker, D. P., 128
Wallace, A. F. C., 29, 51
Ward, C. K., 75, 95
Wardwell, W. I., 116
Warner, W. L., 150
Weber on r., 11, 14, 53–4, 57–64, 73, 79–81, 105, 115, 123, 127, 146; On *Protestant Ethic*, 11, 14, 59–62
Wickham, E. R., 139
Wilson, B. R., 8, 68–9, 76–7, 117, 120, 139, 141
Wilson, J., 77, 79
Winch, P., 14
Winter, G., 75, 121
Worsley, P. M., 27, 65, 68
Wrong, D., 154

Yinger, J. M., 12, 54, 55, 77, 78, 119
Young, F. W., 107

Zweig, F., 88, 139